D1066033

The Making of Shakespeare's Dramatic Poetry

G.R. HIBBARD has taught at the universities of Southampton and Nottingham and is at present professor of English at the University of Waterloo. He has published editions of *Coriolanus, Taming of the Shrew, Timon of Athens, Merry Wives of Windsor,* and *Bartholomew Fair* as well as critical works on sixteenth- and seventeenth-century English literature.

The central concern of this book is the connection between what is said and what is done in the plays Shakespeare wrote between 1589 and 1598. Professor Hibbard begins by stressing the readiness and pleasure with which audiences in the late 1590s responded to Ancient Pistol. The popularity of this character is clear evidence that by 1598 Shakespeare had so altered the style of dramatic writing he inherited from his predecessors as to make it seem old-fashioned and absurd. The creation of Pistol shows that the playwright was fully conscious of what he had done. The revolutionary nature of this achievement is especially evident in *Hamlet* (1600–1), radically new yet heavily indebted to tradition, the product of Shakespeare's constructively critical attitude to his own art and that of others. To illustrate how he consistently builds on his own earlier work, Hibbard traces a group of associated ideas and images which recur often in the plays, from *2 Henry VI* to *Macbeth*. Hibbard then proceeds to a close critical examination of the various ways in which dialogue and verse are handled and made more flexible in the plays up to and including the Two Parts of *Henry IV*. Some, such as the earliest comedies, are dealt with in groups; but others, which can be looked on as growing points, are subjected to a more detailed analysis. Among the plays so treated are *Love's Labour's Lost, Romeo and Juliet, King John,* and, above all, the Two Parts of *Henry IV*.

The picture that emerges is of an artist who, at the start of his career, had trouble in reconciling the poet's love of 'taffeta phrases' and sensuous description with the dramatist's impulse to push an action forward. Gradually, however, Shakespeare succeeded in bringing the two sides of his art into harmony. By the time he wrote *Henry IV*, he was making dramatic poetry out of the seemingly 'unpoetical' and enriching dramatic prose with the figurative use of language normally found in verse.

G.R. Hibbard

The Making of Shakespeare's Dramatic Poetry

UNIVERSITY OF TORONTO PRESS
Toronto Buffalo London

Toronto Buffalo London
Printed in Canada

ISBN 0-8020-2400-9 (cloth)
ISBN 0-8020-6424-8 (paper)

Canadian Cataloguing in Publication Data

Hibbard, G.R., 1915–
The making of Shakespeare's dramatic poetry
Includes index.
ISBN 0-8020-2400-9 (bound) ISBN 0-8020-6424-8 (pbk.)
1. Shakespeare, William, 1564–1616 – Versification.
2. Shakespeare, William, 1564–1616 – Technique.
I. Title.
PR3085.H52 822.3'3 C81-094009-4

Acknowledgments

Parts of this book have appeared in print before. A preliminary sketch of its general argument was published in *Shakespeare 1971*, edited by Clifford Leech and J.M.R. Margeson (Toronto and Buffalo 1972), under the title '"The Forced Gait of a Shuffling Nag."' I am grateful to the University of Toronto Press for permission to reproduce most of the substance and much of the detail of that essay. I owe a similar debt to Cambridge University Press for allowing me to make extensive use of material which first came out in the pages of *Shakespeare Survey*. Much of chapter 2 saw the light of day in volume 23 as 'Words, Action, and Artistic Economy,' while both chapter 1 and chapter 11 draw on '*Henry IV* and *Hamlet*,' published in volume 30.

This book has been published with the help of a grant from the Canadian Federation for the Humanities, using funds provided by the Social Sciences and Humanities Research Council of Canada.

Contents

The Making of Shakespeare's Dramatic Poetry

Tradition and the Shakespearean Talent

A modern audience is likely to find Ancient Pistol somewhat tiresome. His rant may amuse for a time, but it soon begins to pall and grow tedious, because it is so consistently sustained at one unvarying hyperbolical level. The reactions of an Elizabethan audience to him appear to have been very different. If the title-pages of the earliest extant editions of the three plays in which he has a part are anything to go by, it would seem that they could not have too much of him. And title-pages are a useful guide. An Elizabethan printer bought the manuscript of a play in order to make money out of it. He therefore concocted a title-page for it that would serve as an advertisement, singling out for special mention on it the characters and actions that had made the strongest impression and appeal in performances. The first quarto of *2 Henry IV*, published in 1600, came out as 'The Second part of Henrie the fourth, continuing to his death, and coronation of Henrie the fift. With the humours of sir Iohn Falstaffe, and swaggering Pistoll.' The bad quarto of *Henry V*, published in the same year, announced itself as 'The Cronicle History of Henry the fift, With his battel fought at Agin Court in France. Togither with Auntient Pistoll.' Finally, in 1602, came the bad quarto of *The Merry Wives of Windsor*, with a lengthy and not altogether accurate title-page that runs as follows: 'A most pleasaunt and excellent conceited Comedie, of Syr Iohn Falstaffe, and the merrie Wiues of Windsor. Entermixed with sundrie variable and pleasing humors, of Syr Hugh the Welch Knight, Iustice Shallow, and his wise Cousin M. Slender. With the swaggering vaine of Auncient Pistoll, and Corporal Nym.' Pistol, it will be noticed, is the one constant item on all three title-pages, while Mistress Quickly, who has stood the test of time far better than he, is never so much as mentioned on any of them, though she has a role in each of the plays concerned.

There is another curious thing about Pistol: he is not killed off in *Henry v*. The Epilogue to *2 Henry iv* promises that 'our humble author will continue the story, with Sir John in it, and make you merry with fair Katherine of France.' But 'our humble author' changed his mind. Falstaff does not appear at all in *Henry v*, though we are made very much aware of him in its second act. The Boy enters, in II.i, with the news that his master is 'very sick'; Nym comments 'The King hath run bad humours on the knight'; and Pistol diagnoses Falstaff's malady in his characteristic manner by saying 'His heart is fracted and corroborate.' Then, in II.iii, Mistress Quickly gives her moving account of Falstaff's death. Three of the knight's followers soon go the same way. Bardolph, Pistol, Nym, and the Boy all cross the sea to France, making their last appearance as a group in III.i, before the walls of Harfleur. After that we see no more of Bardolph and Nym. We learn, in III.vi, that Bardolph is about to be hanged for stealing 'a pax'; and, in IV.iv, the Boy reports that this sentence has been carried out and that Nym also has been hanged. Between the end of IV.iv and the opening of IV.vii the Boy himself is killed. Pistol, however, escapes his maker's death-dealing hand. After swallowing Fluellen's leek, in V.i, he speaks his determination to return to England, and, we are left to assume, does return there. Why does he not go the way of Nym and Bardolph? The obvious reason is that the opposition which has developed between him and Fluellen has become a very important part of the play and has to be brought to a fitting conclusion; but it does look also as though Shakespeare knew his audience could easier forgo Nym and Bardolph than their swaggering mate.

Pistol, when he first appeared on the stage in the last two or three years of the sixteenth century, was popular with theatre-goers then because they, unlike their modern counterparts, knew what he was talking about, realized what he stood for, and recognized the lines which he so gloriously misquotes and garbles. The student of Elizabethan drama occasionally recaptures something of what those early audiences must have felt when he comes across such a piece of fustian as

Shall packhorses,
And hollow pamper'd jades of Asia,
Which cannot go but thirty mile a day,
Compare with Caesars, and with Cannibals,
And Troiant Greeks? Nay, rather damn them with
King Cerberus; and let the welkin roar. (*2 Henry iv* II.iv.154–9)*

* The text used for all references to and quotations from Shakespeare is *The Complete Works* ed Peter Alexander, London and Glasgow 1951.

But, much as he may enjoy Pistol's ruthless mangling of two of the most notorious lines Marlowe ever wrote, even the dedicated student does not know precisely what the last three lines of the passage are based on. He has to content himself with the conjecture that the 'Cannibals' were once 'Hannibals' in, probably, some ranting play of the late 1580s now lost, and with the recognition that 'Troiant Greeks' are a splendid contradiction in terms, that 'King Cerberus' could be a conflation of King Cambyses and the three-headed monster of hell, and that the style has much in common with that of, for example, *Locrine* (c 1591). If all the plays that were put on in London between 1585 and 1597 had come down to us – only a mere fifty per cent even of those we know about has survived – it seems likely that we should be able to find in them the source of practically everything Pistol says, for, as Dover Wilson remarks, '[his] head is stuffed with play-ends from the old-fashioned ranting drama of the early nineties, mostly misunderstood.'* Pistol is clearly an inveterate playgoer, with a pronounced taste for the heroic. Much addicted to the mighty line, and blessed with a memory that is both retentive and extremely inaccurate, he is a master in the art of garbling. Audiences warmed to him because he had a double appeal for them. On the one hand, he reminded them of many a play that had given them pleasure in the past; on the other, he offered them the added and more refined pleasure of perceiving how absurd and ridiculous much in those old plays now appeared in the light of what Shakespeare was doing in the Two Parts of *Henry IV*. There is also the fascinating possibility that Pistol, most of whose identifiable play scraps come from dramas that seem to have belonged to the repertory of the Admiral's Men, was played by an actor who parodied the manner of Edward Alleyn, the leading member of that company. If this were the case, the part would have acquired an extra and very special piquancy.

Behind Pistol stands his creator; and the character has this peculiar interest: that, to an extent unparalleled, perhaps, among Shakespeare's characters, he allows us and even invites us to look into the mind and also, possibly, some of the activities of the playwright who gave him life. Pistol's inaccurate memory and his talent for mixing things up are obviously dependent for their very existence on Shakespeare's exact memory and his talent for keeping things straight. It is true that by 1598, the likely date for the composition of *2 Henry IV*, Shakespeare could have referred to the printed text of *Tamburlaine*, since it had been published in 1590; true also that he could have read *The Battle of Alcazar*, which Pistol misquotes at II.iv.169, as this play of Peele's came out in 1594; but the references to Hiren at lines 150–1 and 165 in the same scene are another matter altogether. They almost certainly tilt at another play by Peele, *The*

* 2 *Henry IV* ed J. Dover Wilson, Cambridge 1946, p 162

Turkish Mahomet and Hiren the Fair Greek (c 1588), which never, so far as we know, got into print. Pistol's playgoing is a deliberately distorted reflection of Shakespeare's playgoing; his admiring incomprehension an oblique expression of Shakespeare's critical acumen and understanding. All good parody springs from a tension between adverse criticism of the thing parodied and affection for it. It is precisely this mixture of attitudes that one is conscious of when hearing Pistol's vaunts and curses. The Shakespeare of 1598 is looking back with tolerant amusement on the Shakespeare of ten years before, who had, it may be guessed, listened with close attention, much admiration, and some reservations to the 'high astounding terms' that filled the drama of that time. The seven years in his life between the baptism of the twins, Hamnet and Judith, on 2 February 1585 and the appearance of Robert Greene's attack on him as 'an upstart Crow' in *Greenes Groatsworth of Wit* (1592) are usually described as 'the lost years,' the period for which we have no documentary evidence as to where he was or what he was doing. The speeches of Ancient Pistol suggest that one thing Shakespeare did do at that time, and do very thoroughly, was to frequent the theatre. Indeed, one is left wondering whether he missed a single play of any significance at all, from the time when he arrived in London to the time, towards the close of his active career, when he began to spend more of his days at Stratford.

By 1597, or thereabouts, Shakespeare was ready to create Pistol, to set him strutting upon the stage and mouthing his lines, because he had, during the previous five years or so, single-handedly transformed the dramatic medium in such a way as to make much that had been written for the popular theatre before the disastrous plague which began in August 1592, and especially the more heroic roles in that body of drama, appear old-fashioned, stilted, and inflexible. In the process of feeling his own way forward to new modes of dramatic expression he had, imperceptibly yet effectively, educated his audience, leading them to bring new expectations and new standards of judgment with them when they came to the playhouse. Pistol embodies his conscious recognition of what he had achieved, for the assumption behind the figure is that the playgoing public will not be taken in by him, as Master Justice Shallow and Mistress Quickly are,* but will appreciate him for what he is – a walking parody of old techniques and outworn modes of expression.

Shakespeare had, in fact, revolutionized the theatre, but he had done it gradually and without fuss. The earlier revolution, initiated by Marlowe's *Tamburlaine* about ten years before the composition of *Henry IV*, had been rather different. In the Prologue to his play Marlowe had proudly announced his break with the past. Taking up a deliberately

* See Anne Righter *Shakespeare and the Idea of the Play* London 1962, p 141.

challenging stance, he had proclaimed his scornful rejection of the 'jigging veins of riming mother wits / And such conceits as clownage keeps in pay.' He was later to make some concessions to clownage of the traditional kind in *Doctor Faustus*, and to evolve a clever new variety of it when he wrote *The Jew of Malta*; but he never changed his attitude towards the verse forms of the older drama. Right down to his death in 1593, his dramatic medium remained blank verse, with some admixture of prose. This rigid adherence to a principle may, perhaps, help to explain one of the most curious features of his dramatic *œuvre*: its lack of continuous development. Each of his plays, with the single exception of *The Massacre at Paris*, is a considerable achievement in its own right. Each bears the stamp of its author's personality upon it; each echoes, to a greater or less degree, with a music that is unmistakably Marlovian. Moreover, each play is an experiment; Marlowe does not do the same thing twice, not even in the Second Part of *Tamburlaine*. His plays are richly varied among themselves. But they do not convey a sense of an art that is constantly building on itself, drawing strength from its failures as well as from its successes, and moving towards some kind of stability. In short, the whole seems smaller than the sum of its parts. It seems certain that Keats, had he lived, would have gone on to write even greater poetry than that which he has left us. It would be hard to say this about Marlowe and his plays with anything like the same confidence, and harder still to say it about any other of the University Wits, all of whom were either dead or had abandoned the stage by the time the plague of 1592–4 was over.

It is precisely this sense of continuity and of a deep underlying unity within its apparent diversity, lacking from Marlowe's work, that Shakespeare's so abundantly and confidently gives. T.S. Eliot puts the matter well in his essay on John Ford, first published in 1932, where he writes:

> The standard set by Shakespeare is that of a continuous development from first to last, a development in which the choice both of theme and of dramatic and verse technique in each play seems to be determined increasingly by Shakespeare's state of feeling, by the particular stage of his emotional maturity at the time. What is 'the whole man' is not simply his greatest or maturest achievement, but the whole pattern formed by the sequence of plays; so that we may say confidently that the full meaning of any one of his plays is not in itself alone, but in that play in the order in which it was written, in its relation to all of Shakespeare's other plays, earlier and later: we must know all of Shakespeare's work in order to know any of it. No other dramatist of the time approaches anywhere near to this perfection of pattern, of pattern superficial and profound; but the measure in which dramatists and poets approximate to this unity in

a lifetime's work, is one of the measures of major poetry and drama.*

Illuminating as this comment is, it requires, like so many of Eliot's brilliant *aperçus*, some expansion and some qualification to make it fully acceptable and thoroughly useful. The continuous development of Shakespeare's art does indeed demand that each of his plays should, ideally, be seen in its relation to all his other plays, and, it might reasonably be added, to his non-dramatic writings as well. But, more than this, as the author of 'Tradition and the Individual Talent' rather surprisingly fails to mention, it needs to be seen also in its relation to the whole body of English drama in existence at the time when it was written. The general notion set out in that essay about the way in which each truly new work of art modifies the existing order is peculiarly applicable to Shakespeare's plays, for he was, of all the dramatists of his time, the best informed about English drama of the past, the keenest and most discriminating student of it, and the most skilful in exploiting it for his own specific purposes. It was he who saw what the 'jigging veins of riming mother wits' were really suitable for, and was thus able to employ them to far greater effect than they had ever been used before by making them the vehicles for the Pageant of the Nine Worthies in *Love's Labour's Lost* and for the 'tedious brief scene of young Pyramus / And his love Thisby' in *A Midsummer Night's Dream*.

Then, Eliot's 'continuous' can be misleading if it is allowed to carry any connotation of 'steady' with it. There are plays in which Shakespeare seems to be more concerned with consolidating advances he has already made than with doing anything radically new; there are others – *Romeo and Juliet*, *Henry IV*, and *Hamlet* seem obvious examples – in which his art takes a sudden leap forward, plays that might not unfittingly be described as 'growing points.' Furthermore, 'emotional maturity' – a rather suspect term if one thinks of Eliot's essay on *Hamlet* – has to be interpreted in a particular way to make it of any real use. To argue the degree of Shakespeare's own personal emotional maturity at any given time from the evidence offered by the plays he wrote at that time is to engage in idle speculation. The maturity he seems to have had from a very early stage in his career is artistic maturity, the mysterious inner knowledge which either assures the artist that his technical resources are capable of meeting the challenge he is about to subject them to, or warns him against undertaking a task for which he is not yet properly equipped.

Hamlet stands at the very centre of Shakespeare's developing art. Writ-

* T.S. Eliot *Selected Essays* 3rd edition, London 1951, pp 193–4

ten some eleven or twelve years after the Three Parts of *Henry VI* and, in all likelihood, *Titus Andronicus*, it comes exactly twelve years before *Henry VIII*, the last to be composed of the plays included in the First Folio. But its centrality is something more than a mere matter of chronology. If dates were all that needed to be considered, then *Julius Caesar, Twelfth Night*, and *Troilus and Cressida* would all have as much claim to the central position as *Hamlet*. Clearly they have not. *Twelfth Night*, the last of the romantic comedies, marks an end, not a transition or a new beginning. There is an elegiac undertone to its gaiety. The final impression left by *Julius Caesar*, admirably controlled and intelligent though it is, is of something tentative, of new possibilities glimpsed rather than fully worked out and realized, of the creative imagination submitted to deliberate restraint. As for *Troilus and Cressida*, though it looks forward to much that was to follow, the play is so experimental, even, in some ways, so idiosyncratic, that its place and importance in the evolution of Shakespeare's art as a poetic dramatist are not easy to determine. *Hamlet*, on the other hand, leads straight into the world of the other tragedies that were yet to come and with which it so insistently asks to be compared. It is radically new. Once it had been written, the entire body, not merely of Shakespeare's own work but of Elizabethan drama as a whole, took on a fresh appearance: 'All changed, changed utterly: / A terrible beauty is born.' And Shakespeare himself seems to have been aware of its newness. More than any other play in the canon, it transmits a sense of discovery and of the excitement of discovery. The dramatist has opened up a whole fresh area of human experience that cries out for further exploration. There is more in this new found land than can be condensed into the brief two hours' traffic of the stage; but, for once, Shakespeare, normally so practical about these matters, subordinates the physical endurance of his audience to the urgings of his daemon. Yet, long though the play is, some of its puzzles remain unsolved at the end, and even the significance of some of its action – the play-within-the-play, for example – is not evident. *Hamlet* is not a tidy play. It does not belong with the well wrought urns of literature. Instead, it is dynamic and disturbing as no play written in English before it is.

This dynamic disturbing quality is present from the very outset. The opening of *Hamlet* is unlike the opening of any earlier play. The rapid give and take of question and answer, in which the rhythms of colloquial speech overlay and partially mask the beat of the blank verse, precipitates the audience into a strange and frightening world for which no expository matter has prepared them. The initial challenge comes from the wrong man: from the sentry about to take over duty, not from the soldier he is relieving. The time is midnight; it is 'bitter cold'; and

Francisco feels 'sick at heart.' Spare, muscular, bare of imagery, these exchanges culminate in Horatio's question: 'What, has this thing appear'd again to-night?', bringing the tension to its first climax. It is not until Marcellus launches into a more extended speech than any we have heard hitherto that we become fully aware that this play is to be a poetic drama. Indeed, for many the recognition of this fact may well be postponed until Bernardo, after they have all sat down, says:

> Last night of all,
> When yond same star that's westward from the pole
> Had made his course t'illume that part of heaven
> Where now it burns. ... (I.i.35–8)

Here the calm narrative manner, with its delicately wrought beauty, states unequivocally that we are indeed in the presence of poetry. But this poetry is not uttered for our contemplation and delight alone; it has a further function. As we listen to it, with our eyes firmly fixed on the three figures who occupy the stage, we relax, exactly as they have done, lulled into a false sense of security that is rudely shattered by the sudden appearance of the Ghost. The poetry has been working towards a dramatic end: to ensure that the entry of the Ghost produces the highest possible degree of shock and surprise.

The scene unfolds, as T.S. Eliot has well emphasized,* like a movement in a symphony. With the coming of the Ghost, Shakespeare reverts to the manner in which he began. There is a sharp flurry of commands, questions, and cries of wonder, rising in a crescendo to Horatio's demand:

> Stay! speak, speak! I charge thee, speak! (I.i.51)

Then, as the Ghost makes its exit, a carefully controlled diminuendo takes over, starting with more questions and exclamations, until eventually the three characters sit down once more, and, in answer to Marcellus's query, Horatio embarks on his narrative, which goes some way towards filling in the background for us, though it falls far short of being a full-scale exposition. But there is significant variation within the repetitive pattern. Unlike Bernardo, whose account was so abruptly interrupted, Horatio is allowed to finish his. Then, prompted by Bernardo's agreement with him, he goes on to give that general disquisition on the significance of omens and unnatural events, which serves as such a fitting prelude to the second entry of the Ghost. This time, however, he adjures it in a far more formal and ritualistic fashion than he did on the first occasion, prefacing each of his demands with the word 'If' and concluding it with 'Speak to me' or

* *Poetry and Drama* Cambridge, Mass. 1952, pp 15–21; rptd in *On Poetry and Poets* London 1957, pp 75–7

some slight variant of those words. As he ends his speech '*The cocke crowes*,' as the Second Quarto has it, and there is a sudden burst of action. Marcellus, on Horatio's order, strikes at the Ghost with his partisan, only to find that there is nothing there. Thereupon, instead of the excited comment that followed on the first disappearance of the apparition, we now hear something much graver and more thoughtful in tone. Marcellus remarks regretfully:

> We do it wrong, being so majestical,
> To offer it the show of violence. ... (I.i.143–4)

These words establish the key in which the rest of the scene is to be played. Solemnly, and with pronounced religious overtones, the verse gradually modulates into the lyrical grace of Horatio's picture of 'the morn, in russet mantle clad,' after which he makes his suggestion that they acquaint 'young Hamlet' with the events of the night. It is the first indication we have had of the Prince's existence. Calm has come after the terror and the excitement, but, along with it, more matter for the curiosity to feed on.

The opening of *Hamlet* is different from that of any previous play because, in this tragedy, Shakespeare was exploring a new kind of experience, which demanded and brought into being a new kind of dramatic expression. But it can equally well be said that the fact that this new form of dramatic expression was now within Shakespeare's reach made the formulation of this new experience possible. The two processes of exploration and formulation are, in fact, inseparable from each other. Their interdependence was memorably described by Michelangelo when he wrote:

> Non ha l'ottimo artista alcun concetto
> Ch'un marmo solo in sè non circoscriva
> Col suo soverchio; e solo a quello arriva
> La man che ubbidisce all'intelletto.*

The potential form of the work of art is already there in a specific piece of raw material, visible to the informed eye of the artist. But that form can only be released and given actuality by the trained hand working in obedience to the requirements of the creative intelligence; and the trained hand wields an instrument. The instrument that lay ready to Shakespeare's hand, round about the year 1601, was the dramatic medium he had forged in the course of writing all the plays that preceded *Hamlet*. It was an extraordinarily complex and versatile tool. Its chief component

* Sonnet xv, 1–4. 'The greatest of sculptors does not have a single intuition that is not already contained within some piece of unworked marble; and that potential form can only be released and realized by the hand that obeys the artist's judgement.'

parts – in so far as an art that is essentially one single activity will admit of any division into parts at all – were: first, his unparalleled and constantly increasing command of the rich resources of the English language; secondly, his mastery of blank verse and, with it, of any other verse form he might choose to employ; thirdly, his proficiency in the writing of prose; fourthly, his intimate knowledge of the acting company to which he belonged and for which he wrote; and, finally, his equally intimate knowledge of the theatre where his plays would be staged, and of those who frequented it.

The first scene of *Hamlet*, superb in its orchestration, demonstrates the flexibility and range of his verse, answering immediately and unerringly to every demand that is made on it. But it also demonstrates something else. The impact made by the Ghost stems in no small measure from the fact that it says nothing whatsoever. In the theatre, where speech is the norm, silence can be both piquant and significant. For the audiences that saw *Hamlet* in the early seventeenth century the Ghost's failure to speak must have been even more impressive that it is for us today. After all, the first theatrical ghost that most of us ever see is this ghost. Shakespeare's audience, on the other hand, were thoroughly familiar with stage ghosts. They knew the Ghost of Don Andrea, solemnly ushering in the action of *The Spanish Tragedy*, and then intervening at the end of each act, except the last, to comment lugubriously and disappointedly on its progress. They had seen and heard the Ghost of Albanact in *Locrine*, pursuing his conqueror Humber with threats of revenge, not to mention the Ghost in the *Ur-Hamlet*, who, according to Thomas Lodge, 'cried so miserably at the Theatre, like an oister-wife, Hamlet, revenge.'* All these, and many more like them, were loquacious ghosts. Their costume, their mode of utterance, and their standard sentiments are mockingly and amusingly described for us by the anonymous author of *A Warning for Faire Women* (1599). In the Induction to his play, he has Comedy twitting Tragedy for her recourse to stock figures, including

> a filthie whining ghost,
> Lapt in some fowle sheete, or a leather pelch,

who

> Comes skreaming like a pigge halfe stickt,
> And cries *Vindicta*, reuenge, reuenge.†

* Quoted from *Narrative and Dramatic Sources of Shakespeare* ed Geoffrey Bullough, vol VII, London and New York 1973, p 24

† *A Warning for Faire Women* (1599) A2v

To an audience accustomed to ghosts that behaved in this manner the Ghost in *Hamlet* must have been an innovation indeed.

Yet, mute though the Ghost is, he is not without his means of communication. His actions and gestures have their own histrionic eloquence. The resources of the dramatic poet, unlike those of other poets, are not confined to words alone. On the Ghost's first entry, the necessary stage directions are skilfully worked into the dialogue. Bernardo says: 'It would be spoke to'; and, when Horatio accuses it of usurping both 'the time of night' and

> that fair and warlike form
> In which the buried majesty of Denmark
> Did sometimes march,

Marcellus indicates the proper response for this victim of usurpation to make to such a charge by commenting 'It is offended' (I.i.45–50). It is, presumably, at this same moment that the Ghost gives the frown which Horatio remembers at line 62. Even its gait is carefully spelled out. Immediately before it makes its exit, Bernardo says: 'See, it stalks away,' and at line 66 Marcellus makes it plain that a 'martial stalk' is its normal manner of locomotion. On its second appearance, Shakespeare resorts to the stage direction '*It spreads his armes*' (Q2) when Horatio bids it stay; but, once again, most of the directions for its behaviour are worked into the speeches of the other characters. Moreover, a considerable amount of matter that has its bearing on the playing of the Ghost's part in this scene is held over until the latter part of I.ii. It is from the answers Horatio and the soldiers give to Hamlet's questions that the actor taking the role of the Ghost learns that he must wear 'his beaver up,' show 'A countenance more in sorrow than in anger,' and fix his eyes 'Most constantly' upon his interlocutors (I.ii.229–34).

Deploying an art that conceals art, Shakespeare the poet and Shakespeare the man of the theatre have worked together to create a scene in which that which is said becomes one with and indissoluble from that which is done. The opening of *Hamlet* is, among other things, a consummate demonstration of what poetic drama can be and can do, and of the complex skills that go into its making. It is also, in its originality, a most fitting prelude to a play that is full of new things. It will suffice to mention here only the most obvious and striking of them. The emotional intensity generated in the Prince's 'nunnery' scene with Ophelia (III.i) and then again, on a larger scale, in the closet scene with his mother (III.iv) far outdoes that created in any previous scene between two characters – the final speech of Marlowe's Doctor Faustus, though parts of it are addressed to God and other parts to Lucifer and Mephistophiles, is, in effect, a soliloquy, since it receives no answer – either in Shakespeare's own work or in that of his contemporaries or predecessors. Hamlet's assumption of 'an antic disposition' opens the way for riddling allusive speeches that oscillate rapidly and violently from personal insult to bitter searching comments on man and his world and back again, giving birth in the process to a satire that is truly 'tragical.' His use of the soliloquy adds a new dimension to that old device, endowing it with potentialities hitherto hardly glimpsed much less realized. Nearly every important character in the play, as well as some of the less important, has his own individual idiom, a mode of utterance which we come to recognize as uniquely his. Claudius even has two voices and languages: the public and the private. Never before had a play in English asked so many fundamental questions or framed them in such a disturbing and compelling manner. *Hamlet*, it is no exaggeration to say, radically extended and altered the very meaning of the word 'tragedy.'

Yet, despite the revolutionary and profoundly innovative nature of *Hamlet*, there is, paradoxically but rightly, no other play in the entire canon that is more deeply rooted in the dramatic past. Its dependence on all that its author had learned in the course of composing the plays that came before it will, it is hoped, emerge to some degree later in this study; but its close connections with earlier non-Shakespearean drama call for immediate attention. Behind *Hamlet* stands *The Spanish Tragedy* of Thomas Kyd, that massive dramatization of a father's revenge for his murdered son which seems to have remained popular with the ordinary playgoer right down to the closing of the theatres in 1642. The two features of it that appear to have made the deepest impression on the age, and especially on other dramatists, are the madness of the avenging hero, Hieronimo, and his use of a play-within-the-play to achieve his ends. Both, considerably modified but none the less perfectly recognizable, are present in *Hamlet*. But there are other links as well. Hieronimo, like Hamlet, tests the validity of the rather questionable information that, quite literally, falls into his hands, before he attempts to use it. Like Hamlet too, he begins by seeking for justice, publicly done and publicly acknowledged. It is not until he finds himself denied access to the King, who should be the ultimate source of justice on earth, that he resorts to plots. Consequently, there is a long period of delay between the first intimation he has of the identity of his son's murderers and his final execution of revenge on them.

Somewhere along the line that runs from *The Spanish Tragedy* to *Hamlet* lies the mysterious *Ur-Hamlet*, of which we know so little, first mentioned by Thomas Nashe in his preface to Robert Greene's

Menaphon (1589). According to what Nashe says of it, this play would seem to have been liberally studded with 'Tragicall speeches' drawn from '*English Seneca*';* to which Lodge adds the bit of information, quoted at page 12, describing the tone in which the Ghost cried for revenge. Nevertheless, these scraps of intelligence are not without their value. One thing Shakespeare would seem to have learned from the lost play – of which he could just conceivably be the author – was how not to present a ghost. The majestical commanding presence that haunts the battlements of Elsinore must have a voice that is in keeping both with its appearance and with the lines it is given; they are emphatically not lines that can be spoken with the shrill raucousness of an 'oister-wife.' Moreover, while *Hamlet* is rich in 'Tragicall speeches' and in 'good sentences,' as Nashe ironically calls them – no play more so – neither the speeches nor the 'sentences' are culled from Seneca. They come fresh from the mint of their author's imagination. Indeed, *Hamlet*, with its extraordinary wealth of highly quotable *adagia*, soon came to supersede, for English speakers, one of the functions that had made the writings of Seneca so popular with the men of the Renaissance.

Unfortunately, we do not know whether the *Ur-Hamlet* included a play-within-the-play or not. If it did, it could well have been helpful to Shakespeare in something more than the negative sense of showing him what to avoid; for it is in his two plays-within-the-play that his constructive use of earlier dramatic writing is particularly apparent. The great *exemplum* of this device at the time when he was writing *Hamlet* was, of course, 'The Tragedy of Soliman and Perseda' in act IV of *The Spanish Tragedy*, which is, at one and the same time, the catastrophe of the main action, a shocking reversal for the play audience on the stage, and a tremendous *coup de théâtre* in its effect on the audience in the theatre. Brilliant though it is, however, Kyd's play-within-the-play labours under a grave disadvantage: it is not clearly marked off, in terms of style, from the larger action within which it is set. At least it is not so marked off in the text as we have it. But Kyd does seem to have had some awareness of the desirability of differentiating it from the rest of his play, and, at one stage, to have had in mind a means of achieving this end. When Hieronimo puts his proposal for the play to Balthazar, Lorenzo, and Bel-imperia, he says:

> Each of us must act his part
> In unknown languages,
> That it may breed the more variety.
> As you, my lord, in Latin, I in Greek,

* *The Works of Thomas Nashe* ed R.B. McKerrow, Oxford 1958, III.315. 30–4

> You in Italian, and for because I know
> That Bel-imperia hath practised the French,
> In courtly French shall all her phrases be. (IV.i.172–8)*

It is an ingenious but desperate expedient, which seems to have been abandoned as unworkable before the play got into print.

Shakespeare, in order to keep his two inset plays separate in manner both from the rest of *Hamlet* and from one another, preferred to rely on his and his audience's knowledge of earlier English drama. 'Aeneas' tale to Dido ... where he speaks of Priam's slaughter' is consistently elevated in tone and remains on a hyperbolical level throughout. But it is not – and here I find myself in complete agreement with Clifford Leech† – meant as burlesque. Hamlet himself praises it, and the play from which it is supposed to come, highly. Furthermore, it has its bearing on the Prince's own situation. Pyrrhus, like Hamlet, is seeking revenge for the death of his father. That revenge takes the form of killing a king under the very eyes of his wife; and Hamlet stops the declamation at the point where it is about to take up Hecuba's lament. Behind the whole passage lies Marlowe's treatment of these same events in his *Dido, Queen of Carthage,* first published, as the joint work of Marlowe and Nashe, in 1594, but written at least three years, and possibly seven, before that date. There Marlowe had sought to create an English equivalent, in dramatic form, for Virgil's description of the fall of Troy, capable of arousing in his audience that sense of *admiratio* or wonder which the age regarded as the proper effect of heroic poetry. Shakespeare attempts to do something of the same kind by using a rather generalized Marlovian style as a sort of intermediary between himself and Virgil.

The deliberate cultivation of an epic manner in the Player's speech is evident, as it is again in the Prologue to the near-contemporary *Troilus and Cressida,* in the strikingly unusual nature of the vocabulary. Shakespeare employed more new words – 'new' in the sense that they do not occur in any of his previous writings – in *Hamlet* than in any other play he ever wrote.‡ And the fact that he did so affords further confirmation that in this play he was trying to find expression for a hitherto unexplored and uncharted form of experience. But, even for *Hamlet,* the incidence of new and rare words in 'Aeneas' tale to Dido' is exceptionally high. In the course of its seventy-six lines there are no fewer than ten words which he had never used before and was never to use

* *The Spanish Tragedy* ed Philip Edwards, London 1959

† Clifford Leech 'The Hesitation of Pyrrhus' in *The Morality of Art* ed D.W. Jefferson, London 1969, pp 41–9

‡ See Alfred Hart 'The Growth of Shakespeare's Vocabulary' *RES* 19 (1943) 242–54.

again.* Most of them appear to be designed to give the sense of elevation and dignity proper to heroic poetry, and two, 'o'er-sized' and 'o'er-teemed,' convey a feeling of excess and extremity. Equally epic is the recourse to formal and carefully worked out similes of the kind that is often labelled 'long-tailed.' When the crash of falling Troy 'Takes prisoner Pyrrhus' ear' and his uplifted sword seems to stick in the air, Shakespeare continues thus:

> So, as a painted tyrant, Pyrrhus stood
> And, like a neutral to his will and matter,
> Did nothing.

Then, after the long pause enforced by the metrical incompleteness of that last line, the two similes in the passage beget another considerably more elaborate than they are, and that, in turn, leads into yet another:

> But as we often see, against some storm,
> A silence in the heavens, the rack stand still,
> The bold winds speechless, and the orb below
> As hush as death, anon the dreadful thunder
> Doth rend the region; so, after Pyrrhus' pause,
> A roused vengeance sets him new a-work;
> And never did the Cyclops' hammers fall
> On Mars's armour, forg'd for proof eterne,
> With less remorse than Pyrrhus' bleeding sword
> Now falls on Priam. (II.ii.471–86)

The general reminiscence of Marlowe's manner colouring the Player's speech makes it sound somewhat archaic within the context of *Hamlet*, while its epic qualities give it a definite stiffness and, perhaps, even a touch of the cumbrous by contrast with the range and ease of the verse in the play proper. It stands out as something of a set piece and a forcible reminder of that earlier age when tragedy was more self-consciously heroic than it was by 1600, except in the hands of George Chapman.

The archaism of the second play-within-the-play is of a very different kind. The poetic cheese with which 'The Mouse-trap' is baited is decidedly and designedly mouldy. Like the style of acting called for, to which Hamlet draws attention when he calls out 'Begin, murderer; pox, leave thy damnable faces and begin,' it had been lying around unused for a long time. Its three main features are: first, its almost unremitting

* The words are: 'total' (451); 'impasted' (453); 'o'er-sized' (456); 'coagulate' (456); 'Repugnant' (465); 'whiff' (467); 'unnerved' (468); 'fellies' (489); 'mobled' (496); 'o'er-teemed' (502).

employment of closed couplets; secondly, its recourse to long-winded periphrases; and, thirdly, its wrenching of normal syntax for the sake of rhyme. Moreover, what it has to say is, for the most part, trite and platitudinous. The burlesque intent is plain from the opening of the first speech, where the Player King requires six full lines in order to tell the Player Queen 'We have been married thirty years' – a gratuitous piece of information which she might have been expected to know as well as he. But precisely which play or playwright is Shakespeare holding up to ridicule? We seem to have a pointer in the words with which Hamlet, having kept Lucianus waiting while he bandies bawdry with Ophelia, eventually exhorts the actor to get on with the play: 'Come; the croaking raven doth bellow for revenge.' This sentence is a conflation of two lines in *The True Tragedy of Richard the Third*, published in 1594, and written, it is thought, somewhere around 1590. The two lines run thus:

> The screeking Rauen sits croking for reuenge.
> Whole heads of beasts come bellowing for reuenge. (1892–3)*

The speech from which they come has been well described by M.C. Bradbrook as 'probably the most prodigious piece of epiphora in the English drama,'† and it positively invites parody; but there is nothing within 'The Mouse-trap' itself which smacks in any way of *The True Tragedy of Richard the Third.* Hamlet's garbled quotation may tell us something about the approximate date Shakespeare has in mind, but it does not help us to identify a play or plays.

Perhaps the Player King's use of the term 'Phoebus' cart' in his first line may provide a better lead to the object of the mockery? After all, Shakespeare had made fun of this 'poetic' circumlocution for the sun before. Set on exhibiting his histrionic virtuosity and his easy command of 'a part to tear a cat in,' Bottom has hardly been two minutes on the stage when he launches into that piece of bombast in which 'Phibbus' car,' a fittingly mechanical version of the same old mythological vehicle, occupies a prominent place. The commentators who trace Bottom's eight-line outburst (*A Midsummer Night's Dream* I.ii.25–32) back to a couple of passages‡ in John Studley's translation of Seneca's *Hercules Oetaeus* (1581), where 'Phoebus' car' also makes its appearance, are probably right to do so. But the metre of 'The Mouse-trap' is all wrong for Studley. His

* *The True Tragedy of Richard III* ed W.W. Greg for the Malone Society, Oxford 1929

† M.C. Bradbrook *Themes and Conventions of Elizabethan Tragedy* Cambridge (1935) 1960, p 99

‡ Cf *A Midsummer Night's Dream* ed Stanley Wells, Harmondsworth 1967, pp 129–30

medium is the 'fourteener,' not the heroic couplets of Shakespeare's inset play.

The conclusion to be drawn from these negative attempts at identification is that Shakespeare, in this part of *Hamlet*, is not parodying specific plays or even specific dramatists. 'The Mouse-trap' is, it seems to me, the complement to the speeches of Ancient Pistol. His part is made up of collectors' items; it is a compendium of absurdities. 'The Mouse-trap,' on the other hand, is the precipitate from a more analytical approach to some of the failings in some of the plays of the 1580s and early 1590s. Having identified these failings, Shakespeare exemplifies them in the style and conduct of his play-within-the-play, which are so ludicrously different from the style and conduct of the rest of the tragedy. Indeed, it is not beyond the bounds of possibility that in one respect at least he may well be poking fun at some of his own earlier writing. The closest parallel I can think of to the thudding couplets of the Player King is the soliloquy (II.iii.1–30) with which Friar Lawrence makes his entry into *Romeo and Juliet*, where they are also used for the expression of a string of moral platitudes.

Continuity, Contrarieties, and Self-Criticism

The continuity which so evidently exists between Shakespeare's plays and earlier drama is a direct consequence of his attitude towards the writings of his predecessors as well as of his wide and intimate acquaintance with them. He not only knew his dramatic heritage inside out, but he also studied it in a fashion that can best be described as constructively critical. Nor did he restrict the exercise of this constructively critical faculty to the work of others, he applied it rigorously and continuously to his own. Indeed, his capacity for self-criticism is, it seems to me, one of the main sources of and reasons for the continuity and the fundamental unity which make themselves so insistently felt within his work as a whole. One play grows out of another, sometimes as the natural sequel to it – the obvious instance is the two main historical cycles – sometimes as the dialectical issue of it. In *King Lear* the point of view from which the action is seen is that of the sufferers; in *Macbeth*, on the other hand, it is that of the characters who inflict the sufferings. *Coriolanus* deals with the Roman republic in the vigour of its youth; *Antony and Cleopatra* with that same republic in its final stage of decay. Coriolanus and Volumnia are the antitheses to Antony and Cleopatra. It is as though the exploration of one situation demands and calls into being the exploration of its opposite.

The most extended example we have of this constructively critical faculty operating at the level of demonstrable revision is provided by the two versions – the first draft and the finished product – of some lines in *Love's Labour's Lost* (IV.iii.292–361), happily preserved for us by the carelessness of the printers of the Quarto of 1598, who, presumably, failed to notice a cancellation in the manuscript they were working from. The first version runs thus:

And where that you have vow'd to study, lords,
In that each of you have forsworn his book,
Can you still dream, and pore, and thereon look?
For when would you, my lord, or you, or you, 295
Have found the ground of study's excellence
Without the beauty of a woman's face?
From women's eyes this doctrine I derive:
They are the grounds, the books, the academes,
From whence doth spring the true Promethean fire. 300
Why, universal plodding poisons up
The nimble spirits in the arteries,
As motion and long-during action tires
The sinewy vigour of the traveller.
Now, for not looking on a woman's face, 305
You have in that forsworn the use of eyes,
And study too, the causer of your vow;
For where is any author in the world
Teaches such beauty as a woman's eye?
Learning is but an adjunct to ourself, 310
And where we are our learning likewise is;
Then when ourselves we see in ladies' eyes,
With ourselves,
Do we not likewise see our learning there?

These lines have all the appearance of something that has failed to come out, of a potentially good idea that has proved recalcitrant to the handling. They begin rather prosily; 'where that' and 'In that' sound like lawyers' jargon. Urgency, which should be the key-note of the speech, only starts to make itself heard with the rush of verbs that comes in the third line. The word 'ground' at line 296 is clumsily repeated at line 299. Then, at line 301, the speech momentarily catches fire as Shakespeare works in an effective simile, which, incidentally, picks up and develops an earlier comment by Berowne: 'Small have continual plodders ever won / Save base authority from others' books' (I.i.86–7). But the fire immediately dies down. The argument becomes repetitive and involved, and, in the incomplete penultimate line, degenerates into something that looks suspiciously like verbal doodling. The speech should make a logical progression, and does so up to line 304. At that point, however, there is an abrupt transition from one line of thought to another, and the speech never recovers its sense of direction. Instead of mounting to a triumphant conclusion, it founders in its own involutions.

Obviously dissatisfied with this essay, Shakespeare now makes an entirely fresh start, with the following results:

O, we have made a vow to study, lords,
And in that vow we have forsworn our books. 315
For when would you, my liege, or you, or you,
In leaden contemplation have found out
Such fiery numbers as the prompting eyes
Of beauty's tutors have enrich'd you with?
Other slow arts entirely keep the brain; 320
And therefore, finding barren practisers,
Scarce show a harvest of their heavy toil;
But love, first learned in a lady's eyes,
Lives not alone immured in the brain,
But with the motion of all elements 325
Courses as swift as thought in every power,
And gives to every power a double power,
Above their functions and their offices.
It adds a precious seeing to the eye:
A lover's eyes will gaze an eagle blind. 330
A lover's ear will hear the lowest sound,
When the suspicious head of theft is stopp'd.
Love's feeling is more soft and sensible
Than are the tender horns of cockled snails;
Love's tongue proves dainty Bacchus gross in taste. 335
For valour, is not Love a Hercules,
Still climbing trees in the Hesperides?
Subtle as Sphinx; as sweet and musical
As bright Apollo's lute, strung with his hair.
And when Love speaks, the voice of all the gods 340
Makes heaven drowsy with the harmony.
Never durst poet touch a pen to write
Until his ink were temp'red with Love's sighs;
O, then his lines would ravish savage ears,
And plant in tyrants mild humility. 345
From women's eyes this doctrine I derive.
They sparkle still the right Promethean fire;
They are the books, the arts, the academes,
That show, contain, and nourish, all the world,
Else none at all in aught proves excellent. 350
Then fools you were these women to forswear;
Or, keeping what is sworn, you will prove fools.
For wisdom's sake, a word that all men love;
Or for Love's sake, a word that loves all men;
Or for men's sake, the authors of these women; 355

> Or women's sake, by whom we men are men –
> Let us once lose our oaths to find ourselves,
> Or else we lose ourselves to keep our oaths.
> It is religion to be thus forsworn;
> For charity itself fulfils the law, 360
> And who can sever love from charity?

It is an astonishing piece of rewriting. The intial changes, designed to produce greater clarity and directness, are of a kind that can be paralleled in the revisions of other poets. They are, however, crucial. The substitution of the exclamatory 'O, we have made a vow' for the somewhat cumbrous 'And where that you have vow'd' gives precisely that touch of urgency which is so conspicuously missing from the first draft. Moreover, the fact that Berowne now says 'we,' not 'you,' involves him in what is to follow in a way that he was not involved originally. In keeping with this beginning, the second line is simplified, and the third, good though it was, ruthlessly excised. The fourth line of the earlier version (295), exciting and compelling in its reiterations, is retained with the one alteration of 'lord' to 'liege,' in order to avoid echoing the 'lords' of the first line. So far there is no difficulty in seeing why the changes have been made. But now something totally unexpected happens. At line 317 the speech suddenly takes off, so to speak, and for the next thirty lines shows scarcely any dependence at all on the initial draft. It is as though the critical impulse and effort prompting the alterations I have just described have left the way clear for a great burst of creative energy. The new phrase 'leaden contemplation' opens the flood-gates, and a controlled torrent of richly evocative images comes pouring through them. It is not until line 346 that Shakespeare goes back once more to his first draft and repeats the line 'From women's eyes this doctrine I derive.' But, although he retains this line unaltered, his critical attitude towards that first draft persists. The two lines that followed it there are kept, more or less, but their order is reversed, and they undergo significant changes in wording. 'They sparkle still the right Promethean fire' has a scintillating immediacy that is not to be found in 'From whence doth spring the true Promethean fire.' As for the last eleven lines of the revised version, they move irresistibly, step by step, to their spendidly paradoxical conclusion, instead of stumbling to an inconclusive halt, as the final lines of the first draft did.

At first sight, it is the lyrical flow and the imaginative richness of the second version that catch the eye and delight the ear. But a close inspection of the structure of the speech suggests that the essential basis of its superiority lies in its firm logical progression. By the time Berowne says 'From women's eyes this doctrine I derive' that doctrine has been fully expounded, as it has not been expounded in the first draft. The images, compelling though they are, exist within a coherent and skilfully articulated argument.

Conflict, in some shape or form, is basic to drama. Shakespeare had, it seems to me, to a quite unusual degree the common human tendency to see life in terms of great fundamental oppositions, of those contraries without which there can, according to William Blake, be no progression: of good and evil, of innocence and guilt, or reason and passion, of order and chaos, and so one could continue. It may well be one of the main reasons for his universal appeal that he does tend to see things in this way. But, unlike most of us, he was also intensely aware of the close relationship between the positives and the negatives, of their dependence on each other for their very being, and, above all, of the readiness with which they can change places with one another, so that 'Lilies that fester smell far worse than weeds' (Sonnet 94), or, with the converse image transferred from a lyrical to a dramatic context, so that Othello can call Desdemona 'thou weed / Who art so lovely fair and smell'st so sweet / That the sense aches at thee' (IV.ii.67–9).

Among these great oppositions, one, which he used time after time with an ever increasing relevance and dramatic impact, is that between light and darkness, day and night. His handling of it evinces on a large scale and over a long period of time the working of that same constructively critical approach to his own work which led him to rewrite those unsatisfactory lines in *Love's Labour's Lost*. Its first impressive appearance is in *2 Henry VI* IV.i, a scene that is generally accepted as Shakespeare's even by those who do not regard him as the sole author of the play. In this scene the Duke of Suffolk is murdered by Walter Whitmore. The setting is the coast of Kent, immediately after the conclusion of a sea-fight in which Suffolk has been taken prisoner; and the scene opens with the following words, spoken by the Lieutenant who commands the Duke's captors:

> The gaudy, blabbing, and remorseful day
> Is crept into the bosom of the sea;
> And now loud-howling wolves arouse the jades
> That drag the tragic melancholy night;
> Who with their drowsy, slow, and flagging wings
> Clip dead men's graves, and from their misty jaws
> Breath foul contagious darkness in the air.
> Therefore bring forth the soldiers of our prize;
> For, whilst our pinnace anchors in the Downs,

Here shall they make their ransom on the sand,
Or with their blood stain this discoloured shore.
Master, this prisoner freely give I thee;
And thou that art his mate make boot of this;
The other [Suffolk], Walter Whitmore, is thy share. (IV.i.1–14)

Some sixteen or seventeen years later, about 1606, Shakespeare wrote *Macbeth*. In III.ii of that play Macbeth tells his wife of the arrangements he has made, completely unknown to her, for the murder of Banquo and his son Fleance. The dialogue in which he conveys the information to her runs as follows:

MACBETH O full of scorpions is my mind, dear wife!
Thou know'st that Banquo, and his Fleance, lives.
LADY MACBETH But in them nature's copy's not eterne.
MACBETH There's comfort yet; they are assailable.
Then be thou jocund. Ere the bat hath flown
His cloister'd flight; ere to black Hecate's summons
The shard-borne beetle with his drowsy hums
Hath rung night's yawning peal, there shall be done
A deed of dreadful note.
LADY MACBETH What's to be done?
MACBETH Be innocent of the knowledge, dearest chuck,
Till thou applaud the deed. Come, seeling night,
Scarf up the tender eye of pitiful day,
And with thy bloody and invisible hand
Cancel and tear to pieces that great bond
Which keeps me pale. Light thickens, and the crow
Makes wing to th' rooky wood;
Good things of day begin to droop and drowse,
Whiles night's black agents to their preys do rouse.
Thou marvell'st at my words; but hold thee still:
Things bad begun make strong themselves by ill.
So, prithee go with me. (III.ii.36–56)

The first seven lines of the Lieutenant's speech in *2 Henry VI* and the speeches of Macbeth, especially the eight lines that begin with the words 'Come, seeling night,' are obviously based on the same association of ideas and images. In each case the coming-on of night is equated with imminent crime, and more specifically with murder. The contrast between day and night is, in both passages, also a contrast between good and evil. Day is pitiful and kind; night is pitiless and cruel. Day reveals crime; night hides it. Even the figure of Hecate, queen of the night and goddess of witchcraft, is present in both passages, for, though she is not mentioned by name in the Lieutenant's lines, the 'jades' he refers to are the dragons which were supposed to draw her chariot – 'night's swift dragons,' as Puck calls them in *A Midsummer Night's Dream* (III.ii.379). Moreover, in both passages day and night are endowed with human attributes. The lines from *Macbeth* are plainly a reworking, probably at an unconscious level, of the opening of the Lieutenant's speech. But they are anything but a repetition of it. Despite their strongly marked similarities of idea and image, the two passages are poles apart in their dramatic impact; and the differences between them in this respect are an index of the extent of which Shakespeare's mastery of dramatic poetry had grown in the period that separates them from each other.

The seven lines with which the Lieutenant begins serve a double function. First, they indicate the time of day to the audience: it is late evening, and night is about to fall. But, secondly, they have a further and more important purpose: they are there to create atmosphere, to fill the spectators with a sense of gloom and foreboding, to raise their fears and expectations, and so prepare them for the murder that is to follow. To achieve this effect, Shakespeare resorts to what were almost standard items of the tragic poet's stock-in-trade round about the year 1590: figures and images drawn from classical mythology, and particularly from his beloved Ovid. Hecate with her dragons would seem to come from book VII of the *Metamorphoses*, where Medea cries at the end of her great invocation to the triform goddess and the forces of nature associated with her:

> *Nec frustra volucrum tractus cervice draconum*
> *Currus adest.* (218–19)

There are also parallels with the work of Marlowe. A.S. Cairncross, in a note to his New Arden edition of *2 Henry VI*, cites Barabas's lines at the beginning of act II of *The Jew of Malta*:

> Thus like the sad presaging Rauen that tolls
> The sicke mans passeport in her hollow beake,
> And in the shadow of the silent night,
> Doth shake contagion from her sable wings. ... (640–3)

Even closer are these lines from the final speech of Bajazeth in *1 Tamburlaine*:

> O highest Lamp of euerliuing *Ioue*,
> Accursed day infected with my griefs,
> Hide now thy stained face in endles night,

And shut the windowes of the lightsome heauens.
Let vgly darknesse with her rusty coach,
Engyrt with tempests wrapt in pitchy clouds,
Smother the earth with neuer fading mistes:
And let her horses from their nostrels breathe
Rebellious winds and dreadfull thunderclaps. ... (2071–9)*

The Lieutenant's lines are a piece of atmospheric writing which many have found impressive in a vague general sort of way, but not, I would suggest, a passage of true dramatic poetry. Ostensibly addressed to the men under his command, the Lieutenant's words are, throughout the course of those first seven lines, meant not for them but for the audience. They are not part of the action. And, if one goes on the ask how a brutal soldier comes to express himself in these high-flown terms, no satisfactory answer can be found, because this is a matter, not of the Lieutenant talking to his men, but of the playwright using him as a mouthpiece in order to speak directly to the spectators in the theatre. When the Lieutenant is freed from this puppet role and becomes a character in his own right, rapping out orders as to what is to be done,the tone and manner of his speech undergo a radical change. What he says now is factual and practical, not atmospheric and 'poetical,' apart from the one flourish provided by the proleptic use of 'discoloured.' There is, in fact, a marked and inescapable discontinuity between the first seven lines and the rest of the speech – a discontinuity that is emphasized, not disguised, by Shakespeare's patent attempt to cover up the crack with 'Therefore.' As a statement of logical consequence the word is painfully spurious, unless it can be taken as a kind of dramatic shorthand, standing for something such as 'So, before it grows quite dark.'

In the last seven lines the Lieutenant comes to life. He is now a man of action speaking to other men on the stage with him. His words cover the ground quickly, especially in the last three lines, each of which contains a verb:

Master, this prisoner freely give I thee;
And thou that art his mate make boot of this;
The other, Walter Whitmore, is thy share.

And, though the word order is not that of prose, the lines do have the prose virtues of lucidity and conciseness. The first seven lines, on the other hand, are consciously and deliberately 'poetical.' The most striking feature of them is their piling-up of adjectives in twos and even threes.

* The text used for references to and quotations from Marlowe is *The Works of Christopher Marlowe* ed C.F. Tucker Brooke, Oxford 1910.

The day is 'gaudy, blabbing, and remorseful'; the night 'tragic melancholy'; darkness 'foul contagious'; and the dragons' wings 'drowsy, slow, and flagging.' The whole thing is static and pictorial; and the total impression it creates is of a striving for effect, rather than of an effect achieved. It is felt as something applied to the scene, not as something that leads into the scene and is an essential part of it. Here Shakespeare's eye and his imagination are not fixed on the characters he has brought on to the stage and on the action those characters are involved in, but on the audience whose feelings and reactions he seeks to stimulate and manipulate.

The same sense of discontinuity and divided aims keeps on making itself felt throughout the rest of the scene. Whenever the Lieutenant gives orders or advice, he employs the direct utterance of the last seven lines of his initial speech. This style is not only the dramatist's medium for keeping the action moving, but also a manner that fits the Lieutenant's nature. But Shakepeare also saddles this character with the task of stating the moral significance of the scene, of putting into words the attitude to, and the judgment on, Suffolk and his deeds that the play expresses, and of explaining to the spectators why his death is fitting and fully deserved. When he has to fill this other role, the Lieutenant reverts to the manner of his opening lines. He quotes a Latin tag, refers to Sylla, and resorts to elaborate and carefully worked out figures, saying, for example, to Suffolk:

> And thou that smil'dst at good Duke Humphrey's death
> Against the senseless winds shalt grin in vain,
> Who in contempt shall hiss at thee again;
> And wedded be thou to the hags of hell
> For daring to affy a mighty lord
> Unto the daughter of a worthless king,
> Having neither subject, wealth, nor diadem.
> By devilish policy art thou grown great,
> And, like ambitious Sylla, overgorg'd
> With gobbets of thy bleeding mother's heart. (76–85)

Considered as a piece of dramatic poetry, and judged against Shakespeare's later achievement, this scene is a jumble. The Lieutenant has three functions in it: to evoke atmosphere, to act in his own character, and to serve as the voice of history. But these three functions remain three separate things that have not been fused into one thing, capable of making a single complex yet unified impression. The dramatist rendering the action, the rhetorician moving his audience and guiding its responses, and the poet exercising his invention and ranging over his topics, are all present and active here. But they do not co-operate; they clash, because each goes his own way.

In the dialogue between Macbeth and his wife there is no discontinuity, no confusion of dramatic purpose. The invocation to night, though obviously rhetorical in form, is not a set piece that can be detached from the rest of the scene as the Lieutenant's first seven lines can, but an integral part of it, arising naturally and unforcedly out of the action and leading back into it. Shakespeare's primary concern now is not, it seems to me, with his audience and with what he can do to them, but with the two figures on the stage, with the situation they are involved in, and with what happens between them. The information Macbeth gives to Lady Macbeth is not there to forward the plot. The audience knows already, having witnessed the interview between Macbeth and the Murderers in the previous scene, III.i, that the murder of Banquo is to be carried out 'to-night.' Much of the scene's significance lies in the fact that it is only now, when all the arrangements have been made, that Macbeth acquaints his wife with them. The relationship between them has changed radically. It is now he who leads the way, while she follows with a weary acquiescence. Moreover, he is now at least as much interested in night and its attendant evils as he is in her. There is, surely, an element of sensual indulgence in the lines that begin 'Ere the bat hath flown her cloister'd flight,' a deliberate embracing of evil that reaches its climax in the invocation itself, where Macbeth appears to forget the presence of his wife altogether in his rapt contemplation of an action that absorbs his entire attention.

The invocation to night is far more precise, concrete, and terrifying than the Lieutenant's description of night's onset. It begins with an image that is implicit and active, not painstakingly wrought and static: that of night as a falconer and day as a falcon, which is contained in the technical word 'seeling.' This epithet, when its exact meaning is apprehended, produces an intense sense of pain and cruelty, which is heightened by the impact of the next line, 'Scarf up the tender eye of pitiful day.' The vividly evoked action from the daily life of Elizabethan England is far more shocking than the conventional paraphernalia of dragons' wings and dead men's graves. Night as the falconer, and day as the suffering falcon, have taken on the attributes of living things through a kind of verbal shorthand that concentrates on action, as distinct from pictorial description. The nouns 'falcon' and 'falconer' are not used at all, but we see why night's hand is 'bloody and invisible' – 'bloody' from its task and 'invisible' to the hawk – and we can then accept the sudden leap of the imagination from falconry to the law, perhaps suggested or reinforced by the hinted pun on 'seeling' and 'sealing,' that comes with the next lines:

Cancel and tear to pieces that great bond
Which keeps me pale.

And then, as though in answer to Macbeth's call, night does begin to fall. He describes it happening in lines that enact the scene they paint. 'Light thickens.' How exact and also how disturbing the word 'thickens' is to evoke a sense of the clear spaces of air filling with darkness! 'And the crow makes wing to th' rooky wood.' It is a familiar, almost a homely, image. We have all seen the crow doing it. It is a recognized part of the evening scene. But here, as so often in *Macbeth*, the familiar and the homely carry sinister overtones. 'Thickens' takes the mind back to that earlier invocation of act I, scene v, in which Lady Macbeth calls on 'thick night' to come down and hide the murder of Duncan, which she is planning, not only from the eye of the world but also from the very knife itself.

The contrast between day and night that has been so powerfully developed is finally condensed and clinched in the antithetical couplet:

Good things of day begin to droop and drowse,
Whiles night's black agents to their preys do rouse.

Here the contrasted rhythms reinforce the contrasted ideas. The first line is flagging and relaxed, with a heavy caesura after the word 'day.' The second is tense, keyed up, and mounts to its conclusion without a break. Goodness is ineffective; like the day, it is failing and in retreat. Evil is dynamic and on the attack. The antithesis between daylight, goodness, and pity, on the one hand, and darkness, evil, and ruthlessness, on the other, is now complete. To read these lines, or to hear them spoken, is to experience the contrast as something real and tangible. They have this effect because Shakespeare is now working from within the consciousness of a particular character at a particular moment. The words could be spoken by no one but Macbeth. They are part of his personal idiom, they are the product of his unique experience. The sense of horror in the face of cruelty, coupled with the fascinated attraction towards cruelty, and the hypnotized absorption in the effort to shape the future and make it present, all these are characteristic of Macbeth, evident in his speech and in his actions from the moment that he meets the Witches. Equally characteristic of him is the way in which he uses endearments and the familiar language of love to his wife as he reveals his sinister purpose, bidding her 'be jocund,' calling her 'dear wife,' and, most striking and shocking of all, making his plans a kind of love offering to her:

Be innocent of the knowledge, dearest chuck,
Till thou applaud the deed.

And, of course, the speech bears eloquent witness to the raw exposed nerves, so evident in everything Macbeth says and does at this stage in the action.

The lines can convey all this, because they are deeply embedded in, and an indissoluble part of, that total experience which is the play. They stir echoes in the mind; they look back, and they look forward. The contrast they embody is not something specially laid on for the occasion, as it is in the Lieutenant's first seven lines, but something structural. As many critics have pointed out, the greater part of the action of *Macbeth*, up to the coming of Malcolm and the English forces, takes place in mist or darkness. Time after time, the hero and his wife call on the dark to hide what they are about to do, not merely from the eyes of others, but from their own eyes as well.

> Stars, hide your fires;
> Let not light see my black and deep desires.
> The eye wink at the hand; yet let that be
> Which the eye fears, when it is done, to see. (I.iv.50–3)

So soliloquizes Macbeth, having heard Duncan proclaim Malcolm Prince of Cumberland. In the very next scene Lady Macbeth echoes these words while adding her own peculiar vehemence to them:

> Come, thick night,
> And pall thee in the dunnest smoke of hell,
> That my keen knife see not the wound it makes,
> Nor heaven peep through the blanket of the dark
> To cry 'Hold, hold.' (I.v.47–51)

The Lieutenant's lines are not rooted in *2 Henry VI* as Macbeth's lines are rooted in his play. The connecting links of image, association, and echo do not exist, because *2 Henry VI* as a whole, though its affiliations with *Macbeth* are many,* embodies no such precise yet complex experience as that which is to be found in the later play. Before Shakespeare wrote Macbeth's invocation to night even he, I venture to say, did not know how Macbeth should feel at this moment. In order to know, he had to find the words, had to make his hero vocal. And these words are linked with all that has gone before, because what Shakespeare finds and reveals now grows out of what he has made of Macbeth and his situation earlier in the play. Macbeth speaks as he does here, because he is the man who has seen 'pity, like a naked new-born babe' (I.vii.21), who

* See *Macbeth* ed Kenneth Muir, London 1951, appendix D.

has cried 'Stars, hide your fires' (I.iv.50), and who has voiced the moral confusion raised in his mind by the Witches' prophecy with the words:

> This supernatural soliciting
> Cannot be ill; cannot be good. (I.iii.130–1)

The dialogue in *Macbeth* fulfils a whole series of closely interrelated purposes. It sets the scene; it creates atmosphere; it prepares the way for the murder of Banquo; it even manages, through a concealed stage direction in the antepenultimate line, to indicate the amazement, bordering on incomprehension, with which Lady Macbeth receives her husband's statement. But simultaneously it dramatizes that isolation of husband and wife from one another, which is such an integral part of their tragedy; it renders the state of mind of each; and, by implication, rather than explicit statement, it endorses those values of goodness and pity on which the play ultimately rests in the very process of realizing in concrete terms the menace and the destructive energy of the forces ranged against those values. This is, in fact, supremely economical writing in which every word is doing a fantastic amount of work; and the difference in poetic quality and in dramatic impact between it and the passage from 2 *Henry VI* is an index of the extent to which Shakespeare's art as a poetic dramatist had developed during the sixteen or so years that lie between the two plays.

How, then, did this extraordinary growth in the capacity to knit words and action into a single indivisible entity take place? The best one can do in attempting an answer to the question is to look at some of the sign-posts on the way. The same set of ideas and associations that informs the first seven lines of the Lieutenant's speech is to be found again in *The Rape of Lucrece*, that 'graver labour' on which Shakespeare exercised such conscious art and artifice. In that poem, after the rape has taken place and Tarquin has slunk away, Lucrece launches into a sustained tirade against Night, part of which runs thus:

> O comfort-killing Night, image of hell!
> Dim register and notary of shame!
> Black stage for tragedies and murders fell!
> Vast sin-concealing chaos! nurse of blame!
> Blind muffled bawd! dark harbour for defame!
>   Grim cave of death! whisp'ring conspirator,
>   With close-tongu'd treason and the ravisher! ...
>
> O Night, thou furnace of foul reeking smoke,
> Let not the jealous Day behold that face
> Which underneath thy black all-hiding cloak

Immodestly lies martyr'd with disgrace!
Keep still possession of thy gloomy place,
That all the faults which in thy reign are made
May likewise be sepulcher'd in thy shade.

Make me not object to the tell-tale Day.
The light will show, character'd in my brow,
The story of sweet chastity's decay,
The impious breach of holy wedlock vow;
Yea, the illiterate, that know not how
To cipher what is writ in learned books,
Will quote my loathsome trespass in my looks. (764–812)

The resemblances between this speech and the Lieutenant's opening lines are clear enough. Again night is associated with hell, murder, sin, and concealment, while the day is described as 'tell-tale,' the equivalent of 'blabbing' in the play. There are also marked similarities of manner. Shakespeare still relies heavily on adjectives, especially compound adjectives, and on a heaping-up of illustrative images. Once more the mode is highly rhetorical, particularly in the first stanza where there are nine exclamations. There is no missing the calculated study and artifice that have gone into the making of this passage; they ask for notice and admiration. Nevertheless, these lines are, I think, a great advance on those from *2 Henry VI*. In the first place, they occur, not in a dramatic context, but within the framework of an ornate Ovidian narrative poem, where the centre of interest is not the story, but the arguments, the laments, the tirades, and the decoration for which the story provides the opportunity; and they do not slow up the movement of the narrative, because the poem is slow-moving by design. Secondly, the tirade against Night is firmly keyed to the structure of which it is part. It does not, like the Lieutenant's lines, erupt out of nowhere; it has been carefully prepared for, and it comes as the culmination of a sort of wave movement which has been gathering impetus for the previous seven hundred and fifty lines. In the first stanza of the poem Tarquin's lust is described as a 'lightless [hidden or smouldering] fire.' In the second Lucrece is equated with light when her face is referred to as

that sky of his [her husband's] delight,
Where mortal stars, as bright as heaven's beauties,
With pure aspects did him peculiar duties. (12–14)

Reaching Lucrece's house, Tarquin hides his purpose in coming there from her, praises her husband's exploits in the war, and appears as the perfect guest

Till sable Night, mother of Dread and Fear,
   Upon the world dim darkness doth display,
   And in her vaulty prison stows the Day. (117–19)

It is at this point that the main action of the poem begins; and from here onwards these initial references to light and dark are caught up and developed like a theme in a musical composition. Five lines later comes this:

Now leaden slumber with life's strength doth fight;
   And every one to rest themselves betake,
   Save thieves, and cares, and troubled minds that wake. (124–6)

And then, after forty lines of moral reflection, Tarquin's first move is heralded by the following stanza:

Now stole upon the time the dead of night,
When heavy sleep hath clos'd up mortal eyes;
No comfortable star did lend his light,
No noise but owls' and wolves' death-boding cries;
Now serves the season that they may surprise
   The silly lambs. Pure thoughts are dead and still,
   Whiles lust and murder wake to stain and kill. (162–8)

The wolves have appeared already in *2 Henry VI*, but here they are something more than a conventional atmospheric item, for soon Tarquin will be called a wolf and Lucrece a lamb. The images are being set to work; their connotations are being extended and interwoven with one another. Night has become the time for lust, theft, and pangs of conscience, as well as the time for murder. The 'universal wolf' of *Troilus and Cressida* is more than hinted at in the wolf of *The Rape of Lucrece*, for, when Tarquin finally puts an end to Lucrece's pleas, Shakespeare writes:

This said, he sets his foot upon the light,
For light and lust are deadly enemies;
Shame folded up in blind concealing night,
When most unseen, then most doth tyrannize.
The wolf hath seiz'd his prey; the poor lamb cries. ... (673–7)

As a result of these recurrent waves of imagery, in which darkness and the crimes that accompany it are associated with Tarquin, while light and its suggestions of purity and innocence are attached to Lucrece, the tirade against Night comes as a fitting climax to what has gone before it. Working within a well-established narrative convention that calls for studied artifice, Shakespeare finds it much easier to exploit the possibilities of the opposition between light and darkness than he does, at this stage in his career, within the more complicated framework of a play, where 'the two hours' traffic' of the stage allows little room for the elaboration of a figure, and where the poetry must be geared to the action in such a manner as to intensify it and to be intensified by it, instead of clogging and impeding it.

Perhaps the major artistic problem that confronted Shakespeare in the middle of the last decade of the sixteenth century was that of bringing his exuberant delight in words and figures of speech into harmony with the dependence of drama on action and character. In two plays, *Love's Labour's Lost* and *Richard II*, he even managed to make artistic capital out of this conflict between the 'poet' and the playwright in him, to have his cake as well as to eat it. The first is, among other things, a play about words and figures, exploring both their potentialities and their limitations. The second has for its protagonist a man of words, who, from the time that he returns from Ireland in III.ii, finds himself powerless. In this situation the only freedom left him is that of uttering his thoughts and feelings. It is when Richard is about to discover his own impotence that he, too, resorts, with an unconscious irony that deepens as the action develops, to the opposition of day and night. Having landed in Wales, he greets the earth of England with affection and bids it take his part against his enemies. The fanciful nature of his speech leads the Bishop of Carlisle to remind him that incisive action is required; and Carlisle's admonition is seconded by Aumerle. Thereupon Richard replies:

> Discomfortable cousin! know'st thou not
> That when the searching eye of heaven is hid,
> Behind the globe, that lights the lower world,
> Then thieves and robbers range abroad unseen
> In murders and in outrage boldly here;
> But when from under this terrestrial ball
> He fires the proud tops of the eastern pines
> And darts his light through every guilty hole,
> Then murders, treasons, and detested sins,
> The cloak of night being pluck'd from off their backs,
> Stand bare and naked, trembling at themselves?
> So when this thief, this traitor, Bolingbroke,
> Who all this while hath revell'd in the night,
> Whilst we were wand'ring with the Antipodes,
> Shall see us rising in our throne, the east,
> His treasons will sit blushing in his face,
> Not able to endure the sight of day,
> But self-affrighted tremble at his sin. (III.ii.36–53)

It is impossible not to admire the formal beauty of the detailed and elaborate simile that Shakespeare has placed in Richard's mouth, but, at the same time, as it unfolds itself in this leisurely manner, one also begins to share in the irritation and the exasperation that Carlisle and Aumerle have already voiced. Verse which would normally be felt as undramatic, an impediment in the way of the action, here fulfils a truly dramatic function. We listen to the King with a growing realization that in the crisis he is faced with he simply has not the time to indulge in this kind of thing. The picture he paints remains a beautiful one, but what impresses us in the end is its pitiful and painful unreality. There is a sense, I think, in which *Richard II* might fairly be regarded as Shakespeare's exploitation for dramatic purposes of his own growing awareness that the overtly 'poetical' and the dramatic are not altogether compatible with one another. In so far as the problem he was facing is concerned, *Richard II* seems to me to be a brilliant but temporary answer to it.

The way towards a more satisfactory and durable solution begins to appear in, among many other places, a passage in *King John* which takes up yet again the now familiar contrariety of day and night. In the third scene of act III John is at the height of his power. He has just defeated the French forces and taken his nephew Arthur prisoner. As the scene opens John hands the boy over to the care of Queen Elinor, telling him:

Thy grandam loves thee, and thy uncle will
As dear be to thee as thy father was.

Then, after giving the Bastard orders to return to England, John turns to Hubert de Burgh, and, with Arthur present, though occupied, in the background, engages Hubert in dialogue. The King begins by expressing his appreciation of Hubert's services to him, speaking in the most ingratiating terms he can think of. Eventually he draws from Hubert the admission he is angling for: 'I am much bounden to your Majesty.' Taking full advantage of this reponse, John continues:

Good friend, thou hast no cause to say so yet,
But thou shalt have; and creep time ne'er so slow,
Yet it shall come for me to do thee good.
I had a thing to say – but let it go:
The sun is in the heaven, and the proud day,
Attended with the pleasures of the world,
Is all too wanton and too full of gawds
To give me audience. If the midnight bell
Did with his iron tongue and brazen mouth
Sound on into the drowsy ear of night;
If this same were a churchyard where we stand,
And thou possessed with a thousand wrongs;

Or if that surly spirit, melancholy,
Had bak'd thy blood and made it heavy-thick,
Which else runs tickling up and down the veins,
Making that idiot, laughter, keep men's eyes
And strain their cheeks to idle merriment,
A passion hateful to my purposes;
Or if that thou couldst see me without eyes,
Hear me without thine ears, and make reply
Without a tongue, using conceit alone,
Without eyes, ears, and harmful sound of words –
Then, in despite of broad-eyed watchful day,
I would into thy bosom pour my thoughts.
But, ah, I will not! Yet I love thee well;
And, by my troth, I think thou lov'st me well. (30–55)*

In this speech there are near-reminiscences of the Lieutenant's lines in *2 Henry VI*. Instead of being 'gaudy, blabbing, and remorseful,' the day is 'all too wanton and too full of gawds'; later it is called 'broad-eyed' and 'watchful.' The 'dead men's graves' are replaced by 'a churchyard.' But, in spite of these resemblances, the total effect achieved is much closer to that of the invocation to night in *Macbeth*. The whole dialogue is obviously dramatic in the sense that John is talking to Hubert, not to the audience in the theatre. It is still more dramatic in the sense that John is thinking aloud, allowing a purpose to grow within his mind. And that purpose is one that he hardly dares to look at himself, much less reveal to Hubert who is to be the agent of it. John is testing and tempting himself, as well as the man he seeks to make his instrument. Night, the midnight bell, the churchyard, and the whole atmosphere of conspiratorial secrecy are evoked, not primarily to affect the feelings of the audience, though they do, of course, have this effect as well, but as a kind of imaginative stimulus with which John attempts to encourage himself while working Hubert to his purpose. Compared with the detailed and formalized contrasts of *2 Henry VI*, *The Rape of Lucrece*, and *Richard II*, the images here are barer and simpler. They derive much of their suggestiveness from their context, to which the presence of Arthur in the background contributes much, from the ingratiating tone of John's address to Hubert, using his name time after time, and, above all, from the tentative probings of the speech, moving towards the decisive command 'Death,' and then backing away from it before it is reached:

I had a thing to say – but let it go.

* I have, for obvious reasons, adopted Dover Wilson's readings of 'ear' for 'race' at line 39, and 'broad-eyed' for 'brooded' at line 52.

The manner is altogether subtler and more flexible than that of *2 Henry VI* or of *Richard II*. The rhythm is varied by functional changes of pace that correspond to the to-and-fro movement of the mind. The speech will run rapidly ahead for a time, and then come to an abrupt stop as John hesitates or changes direction. There is an interplay of the conversational and the formal, of the familiar and the 'poetical.' The contrast between day and night is not being developed for its own sake; it is being used and worked into the total situation. The sinister secrecy of the night, as it is conveyed through the verse, adds weight to, and is itself reinforced by, John's desire to communicate his purpose to Hubert without clothing it in words at all, or, indeed, without resorting to any of the senses for its transmission:

> Or if that thou couldst see me without eyes,
> Hear me without thine ears, and make reply
> Without a tongue, using conceit alone. ...

The sight of Arthur in his power plants the seeds of murder in John's mind; and we experience their growth as he experiences it. We are made aware both of his revulsion from murder and of his attraction towards it, and we feel the attraction gaining over the revulsion. Verse and action have fused together here and become one. The wealth of imagery is not a piece of self-indulgence on the part of Shakespeare the 'poet,' it is a necessary part of the dramatic situation, establishing the atmosphere conducive to John's final order that Arthur be put to death, working on the emotions of Hubert in a manner that is designed to detach him from the daylight world of clear moral judgment and lead him into the dark world of John's imaginings, and, at the same time, revealing the devious nature of the King himself.

The Shakespeare who was to write *Macbeth* is already clearly recognizable in this passage from *King John*, but a bridge leading from the one play to the other can be found in *Julius Caesar*. There, in II.i, the boy Lucius announces to Brutus that Cassius and several others are at the door. Brutus asks the boy whether he knows them, and is told that it is impossible to identify them, because their hats are pulled down to their ears and their cloaks cover the lower parts of their faces. While the boy is admitting them, Brutus soliloquizes:

> They are the faction. O conspiracy,
> Sham'st thou to show thy dang'rous brow by night,
> When evils are most free? O, then by day
> Where wilt thou find a cavern dark enough
> To mask thy monstrous visage? Seek none, conspiracy;
> Hide it in smiles and affability!
> For if thou path, thy native semblance on,

Not Erebus itself were dim enough
To hide thee from prevention. (II.i.77–85)

The association of conspiracy with a cavern and with night seems to have been caught up from the corresponding passage in *The Rape of Lucrece*, where night is called

Grim cave of death! whisp'ring conspirator,
With close-tongu'd treason and the ravisher! (769–70)

But Brutus's soliloquy, in its reliance on rhetorical questions, is a forcible reminder that Shakespeare's mature manner was not achieved through an abandonment of such devices. What does seem to have happened is that the contrast between day and night is now being handled in a much more rapid and allusive fashion. It contributes to Brutus's realization of the true nature of the activities he has become involved in, but it does not dominate the speech, which is primarily about conspiracy. Moreover, heightened though the language is, it acquires a degree of naturalness and spontaneity from the informal structure and rhythm of the verse. The result is metaphorical writing – conspiracy is not compared to a monstrous criminal, but presented as a monstrous criminal – that is also flexible, and that can follow and render the curve of a passionate emotion or thought.

It is no accident that the main signposts along the road that leads from *2 Henry VI* to *Macbeth* are to be found in *The Rape of Lucrece*, *King John*, and *Julius Caesar*, for the poem and the two plays all contributed to the making of *Macbeth*. Tarquin is in many ways a first draft of Macbeth himself; John is the first of Shakespeare's tragic criminals, the man of power who gives way to the temptation that the successful exercise of power brings with it; and Brutus, though power is not his aim, is none the less another victim of temptation who, as Wilson Knight has shown,* has much in common with Macbeth. Consciously or unconsciously, Shakespeare was aware when he came to write *Macbeth* of what he had achieved in, and learnt from, his own earlier works. Night, Hecate, murder, the wolf, Tarquin, John's self-stimulating thoughts, coupled with his desire for a secrecy beyond the reach of sense, are all brought together in one tremendous synthesis in the second half of Macbeth's air-borne dagger speech immediately before the murder of Duncan, when he says:

Now o'er the one half-world
Nature seems dead, and wicked dreams abuse
The curtain'd sleep; now witchcraft celebrates

* G. Wilson Knight *The Wheel of Fire* London 1930, pp 132–53

Pale Hecate's offerings; and wither'd murder,
Alarum'd by his sentinel, the wolf,
Whose howl's his watch, thus with his stealthy pace,
With Tarquin's ravishing strides, towards his design
Moves like a ghost. Thou sure and firm-set earth,
Hear not my steps which way they walk, for fear
Thy very stones prate of my whereabout
And take the present horror from the time,
Which now suits with it. (II.i.49–60)

Macbeth is, to quite an extraordinary degree, the final distillation from much that Shakespeare had writen before it. Perhaps this is one of the reasons for that intensity of utterance and urgency of movement which seem to me to be its distinctive characteristics.

Words, Action, and *Titus Andronicus*

I observed, when dealing with the first scene in *Hamlet*, that the Ghost, though silent, has his own means of communicating with the other characters on the stage and with the audience. The dramatic poet has at his command resources that are not available to other poets. Poems are written to be recited, perhaps to be sung, but mostly, today, to be read by the solitary individual. They are not written to be enacted by men and women impersonating imaginary figures and taking part in an action which almost invariably involves actual physical movement about a stage, and which usually leads to some kind of physical contact, if not conflict, with others. When we read a poem our attention is focused exclusively on the words; but this is rarely the case when we first see a play. We listen to the words; we are rightly annoyed if they are so badly spoken, or spoken in such unsatisfactory surroundings, that we do not hear them properly; but we listen to them primarily for the sake of what they tell us about the action and about the relationships of the characters with one another. Only in plays where wit is the dominant quality are the words the first thing that comes to mind when the performance is over. Asked for his opinion of a new play he has recently seen, the ordinary playgoer will usually respond by saying something about the plot and rather more about the various characters and the way in which they were handled by the actors.

Nevertheless, it is primarily through the words that we know these other things; and in all drama that really matters the interrelationship between plot, character, and dialogue is so close and intimate that they cannot properly be separated from one another. There are occasions when a physical movement or a gesture can be more eloquent and more in character than words would be. There are other occasions when we are suddenly jolted into the recognition that speech itself is a form of action. Moreover, the character who speaks and the circumstances in which he speaks can sometimes do the most extraordinary things to words, transforming what might, in other conditions, be ordinary or even commonplace into poetry that is quite heartbreaking or breathtaking in its impact.

Three familiar examples will, perhaps, serve to illustrate the point I am making. *Coriolanus*, as befits a play dealing with the politics of ancient Rome, is insistently and resonantly rhetorical; yet the climax to it takes the form of a simple gesture. For nearly one hundred lines, in v.iii, Volumnia has been pleading with her obdurate son, asking him to abandon his design to take revenge on the Rome that has banished him by putting it to the sword and setting fire to it. Her oration, as North so aptly calls it, is interrupted on two occasions only: first, by a couple of lines from the hero addressed to Aufidius and the other Volscian leaders; then, by six lines shared by Virgilia, her little son, and Coriolanus himself who utters a short but pregnant aside, saying as he rises from his seat:

> Not of a woman's tenderness to be
> Requires nor child nor woman's face to see.
> I have sat too long. (v.iii.129–31)

The last fifty-two lines are one unbroken appeal by Volumnia. At the end of it there comes the magical stage direction for the actor playing Coriolanus: *Holds her by the hand, silent.* The wordless gesture says all that needs to be said, and says it consummately. Watching it, we know that Coriolanus has no answer to his mother's arguments, reinforced, as they have been, by the actions of the three women and his young son, who are all kneeling in supplication before him. The movement of the hand, reaching for and clasping Volumnia's hand, tells us that he has yielded, overcome by tender emotions which he is incapable of expressing in any other way; it would be foreign to his nature and wholly out of character for him to attempt it. The gesture is also a vivid visual endorsement of what, by this stage in the action, we have been brought to see as the root cause of the tragic situation in which the hero finds himself. It is the instinctive reaction of a little boy trying to regain the love of the mother who has been scolding him. For the greater part of the play's course Coriolanus, the great soldier, has himself been a battleground on which the implacable warrior and the boy in him have fought out their unequal struggle. Now the little boy has won, and the warrior must face and take the consequences of the victory.

In all Shakespeare's work there is, I think, no finer instance of the speech that is felt as an action, as something positively done as well as said, than is to be found in the scene of Gloucester's blinding, III. vii of *King Lear*. Here, the relentless, mounting pressure of the questioning that the bound, helpless old man is submitted to by Regan and Cornwall has all the force of a physical assault. One is intensely aware of their demands for an answer raining down on him as the storm has rained down on Lear, driving him to evasion, and culminating in these exchanges:

> CORNWALL Cunning.
> REGAN And false.
> CORNWALL Where has thou sent the King?
> GLOUCESTER To Dover.
> REGAN Wherefore to Dover? Wast thou not charg'd at peril –
> CORNWALL Wherefore to Dover? Let him first answer that.
> (III. vii. 49–52)

Submitted to this incessant verbal attack, Gloucester sees at last precisely what he is up against, takes his stand, and utters his impassioned protest, not against what is being done to him, but against what has been done to his old master, Lear. To the reiterated 'Wherefore to Dover?' he replies:

> Because I would not see thy cruel nails
> Pluck out his poor old eyes; nor thy fierce sister
> In his anointed flesh rash boarish fangs.
> The sea, with such a storm as his bare head
> In hell-black night endur'd, would have buoy'd up
> And quench'd the stelled fires.
> Yet, poor old heart, he holp the heavens to rain.
> If wolves had at thy gate howl'd that dern time,
> Thou shouldst have said 'Good porter, turn the key'.
> All cruels else subscribe, but I shall see
> The winged vengeance overtake such children. (III. vii. 55–65)

This speech is far more than a speech in any ordinary sense of that word. It comes over to us as a heroic action of supreme courage and integrity; and, because it is so emphatically a challenging action, it provokes immediate physical consequences. With the words 'See't shalt thou never,' Cornwall calls on his servants to hold the chair to which Gloucester is tied, and sets his foot on the old man's eye.

The transfiguring effect that context and situation can exert on the simplest and most ordinary of words finds its apotheosis in Lear's line made up of the one word 'never' said five times over. But the entire speech to which that line belongs shares the same quality:

> And my poor fool is hang'd. No, no, no life!
> Why should a dog, a horse, a rat have life,

And thou no breath at all? Thou'lt come no more,
Never, never, never, never, never.
Pray you undo this button. Thank you, sir.
Do you see this? Look on her. Look, her lips.
Look there, look there! (V.iii.305–11)

If one first met that speech in the form of an isolated extract printed as prose, there would be little, apart from the subdued blank verse rhythm and the repetitions, to suggest that it was poetry at all. There is not a single image in it, the only adjective it contains is 'poor,' and the words are almost entirely monosyllabic. It is made up of exclamations, questions, statements, and requests, cast in short emphatic sentences. But coming from this character in this situation, with the full force of the entire action, summed up in the spectacle of the old king bending over his dead daughter, behind it, this speech – only seven lines in length – is the most moving and intense piece of poetry in the language. The reality and warmth of human love, the ineluctable fact of death, and the unintelligible nature of the universe in which they coexist are fused together here into an utterance that is quite overwhelming.

The three passages I have analysed, in order to illustrate the intimate nexus in great poetic drama between what is said and what is done, between what the audience hears and what it sees, are all taken from Shakespeare's mature work, because even he had to learn how to create that closely woven fabric in which the three essential elements of drama – action, characters, and dialogue – become inseparably intertwined with each other. My main concern in the rest of this book will be with that process of learning.

It is, I think, Shakespeare's failure in *Titus Andronicus* to effect the kind of integration I have described which is the most marked feature of that extraordinary play and the main reason for the strange and confusing impact which it makes. Up to 1925, when E.K. Chambers devoted a chapter in his *Shakespeare: A Survey* to a powerful defence of the drama's authenticity, it was customary among critics to explain its unusual qualities by invoking the name of Edward Ravenscroft, who published an adaptation of it in 1687. Seeking to justify his own apparent temerity, Ravenscroft says in his preface that he had 'been told by some anciently conversant with the Stage, that [*Titus Andronicus*] was not [Shakespeare's], but brought by a private Author to be Acted, and [Shakespeare] only gave some Master-touches to one or two of the Principal Parts or Characters.' For the next two and a half centuries most critics were only too happy to accept Ravenscroft's account of the play's origins and to agree with him that this tragedy 'seems rather a heap of Rubbish than a Structure.' Since 1925, however, things have changed radically. There is still, of course, no consensus about whether or not *Titus Andronicus* is a success in its own kind, nor is there likely to be; but the tendency to regard it as an authentic Shakespearean experiment has gained ground enormously. Like most critics today, I concur with Tillyard and others who see it as wholly Shakespeare's and think of it as very early, written in 1589 or thereabouts.* I also take the view adopted by many during the last forty years or so that it is a most ambitious piece of work.† Shakespeare's purpose in it is nothing less than to 'overgo' the two most popular plays of the time: Kyd's *The Spanish Tragedy* and Marlowe's *The Jew of Malta*. He seeks to surpass Kyd by presenting his audience with a carefully planned gradation of shocking actions, culminating in Tamora's eating the flesh, blood, and bones of her two sons, baked in a pie; and, as a rival in villainy to Barabas the Jew, he offers them Aaron the Moor. He also tries to outdo his two predecessors, and especially Kyd, in the art of making passion articulate and infectious. For this purpose he has recourse to the manner of Ovid, who meant so much to him throughout his career and who was the main influence on his two narrative poems, *Venus and Adonis* and *The Rape of Lucrece*. Indeed, the demonstrable links between *Titus Andronicus* and *The Rape of Lucrece* are one of the most important pieces of internal evidence for Shakespeare's authorship of the play.

At first sight, the choice of Ovid as a model for the manner of writing to be adopted would appear both natural and obvious. After all, it was he who had told the story of Tereus, Progne, and Philomel, which not only has its place in the action of *Titus Andronicus* but also deeply colours and affects Shakespeare's treatment of all that part of the material he was handling that deals with the rape of Lavinia and its consequences. Moreover, as Eugene M. Waith has so ably demonstrated,‡ one of Ovid's main concerns in the *Metamorphoses* is 'in the representation of the various passions and their extraordinary effects on various natures, human or divine,' which would seem to be very much what Shakespeare was after in composing his play. In addition to these motives for adopting the Ovidian manner, there was Shakespeare's own fondness for and admira-

* E.M.W. Tillyard *Shakespeare's History Plays* (1944), Peregrine edition, Harmondsworth 1962, pp 135–41

† See, for example, H.T. Price 'The Authorship of *Titus Andronicus*' *JEGP* 42 (1943); M.C. Bradbrook *Shakespeare and Elizabethan Poetry* London 1951, pp 104–10; E.M. Waith 'The Metamorphosis of Violence in *Titus Andronicus*' *Shakespeare Survey 10* (1957); A.C. Hamilton *The Early Shakespeare* San Marino 1967, pp 63–89; and Nicholas Brooke *Shakespeare's Early Tragedies* London 1968, pp 13–47.

‡ 'The Metamorphosis of Violence in *Titus Andronicus*'

tion of Ovid's cleverness, of his gift for 'smelling out,' as Holofernes puts it in *Love's Labour's Lost*, 'the odoriferous flowers of fancy, the jerks of invention' (IV.ii.119–20). The tale of Philomel is brutal and barbarous; but there is nothing brutal or barbarous about Ovid's telling of it. On the contrary, his way of handling it is cool, sophisticated, decorative, and detached. He describes horrors, but he does it in a tone that serves to keep those horrors at a distance from the reader. The technical virtuosity of the Roman poet was, I would suggest, both an attraction and a challenge to his Elizabethan imitator.

Seduced, perhaps, by the many appeals that the Ovidian manner held out to him, Shakespeare, when writing *Titus Andronicus*, failed to ask himself the all-important question of whether this manner could successfully be applied to a stage presentation in which the audience would actually see with their own eyes the kind of horrors that Ovid describes. The results of this failure make themselves abundantly and embarrassingly felt in II.iv, one of the central scenes in the play. The setting is a wood where a hunting party is being held. In the previous scene, Tamora's two sons, Chiron and Demetrius, have stabbed Lavinia's husband to death under her very eyes, and then, urged on by their mother, they have carried Lavinia off stage in order to violate her. Now, at the opening of II.iv, there comes a curt, devastating stage direction which spares the audience nothing: *Enter the Empresse Sonnes, with Lavinia, her hands cut off and her tongue cut out, and ravisht.* There is no question as to what the audience is meant to see; and it is not a pretty spectacle. The dialogue that ensues runs thus:

> DEMETRIUS So, now go tell, an if thy tongue can speak,
> Who 'twas that cut thy tongue and ravish'd thee.
> CHIRON Write down thy mind, bewray thy meaning so,
> An if thy stumps will let thee play the scribe.
> DEMETRIUS See how with signs and tokens she can scrowl.
> CHIRON Go home, call for sweet water, wash thy hands.
> DEMETRIUS She hath no tongue to call, nor hands to wash;
> And so let's leave her to her silent walks.
> CHIRON An 'twere my cause, I should go hang myself.
> DEMETRIUS If thou hadst hands to help thee knit the
> cord. (II.iv.1–10)

Thereupon they make their exit.

This is true dramatic poetry of a kind that could withstand the test of time. John Webster, who was particularly fond of this device, was, more than twenty years later, to put a most accurate description of it into the mouth of his Lodovico in the opening scene of *The White Devil*. Exposed to the reproaches and taunts of Antonelli and Gasparo, Lodovico makes the laconic comment:

> Very good,
> This Well goes with two buckets, I must tend
> The powring out of eather. (I.i.28–30)*

Ovid has no part in it. It is a variant on the old classical device of stichomythia, which Shakespeare could have learnt from Kyd, without needing to go back to Seneca or Euripides for it. And in this context it works admirably. The clever mannered writing, formal in its use of parallelisms, carefully calculated in its working up to the final heartless gibe, is perfectly suited to match and to embody the cold callousness and deliberate viciousness of the two young men. It is an expression of their characters as well as a means of directing the attention of the audience to the precise nature of the maiming Lavinia has been subjected to. The words fit the deed; what is heard coincides with, explains, and reinforces the impact of what is seen.

No sooner have Chiron and Demetrius made their exit than the sound of hunting horns is heard and Lavinia's uncle Marcus enters to see his niece attempting to flee from him. He promptly launches into one of the most extraordinary speeches that Shakespeare ever wrote:

> Who is this? – my niece, that flies away so fast?
> Cousin, a word: where is your husband?
> If I do dream, would all my wealth would wake me!
> If I do wake, some planet strike me down,
> That I may slumber an eternal sleep! 15
> Speak, gentle niece. What stern ungentle hands
> Hath lopp'd, and hew'd, and made thy body bare
> Of her two branches – those sweet ornaments
> Whose circling shadows kings have sought to sleep in,
> And might not gain so great a happiness 20
> As half thy love? Why dost not speak to me?
> Alas, a crimson river of warm blood,
> Like to a bubbling fountain stirr'd with wind,
> Doth rise and fall between thy rosed lips,
> Coming and going with thy honey breath. 25
> But sure some Tereus hath deflowered thee,
> And, lest thou shouldst detect him, cut thy tongue.
> Ah, now thou turn'st away thy face for shame!

* The text used for all quotations from and references to Webster's writings is *The Complete Works of John Webster* ed F.L. Lucas, London 1927.

And notwithstanding all this loss of blood –
As from a conduit with three issuing spouts – 30
Yet do thy cheeks look red as Titan's face
Blushing to be encount'red with a cloud.
Shall I speak for thee? Shall I say 'tis so?
O, that I knew thy heart, and knew the beast,
That I might rail at him to ease my mind! 35
Sorrow concealed, like an oven stopp'd,
Doth burn the heart to cinders where it is.
Fair Philomel, why she but lost her tongue,
And in a tedious sampler sew'd her mind;
But, lovely niece, that means is cut from thee. 40
A craftier Tereus, cousin, hast thou met,
And he hath cut those pretty fingers off
That could have better sew'd than Philomel.
O, had the monster seen those lily hands
Tremble like aspen leaves upon a lute 45
And make the silken strings delight to kiss them,
He would not then have touch'd them for his life!
Or had he heard the heavenly harmony
Which that sweet tongue hath made,
He would have dropp'd his knife, and fell asleep, 50
As Cerberus at the Thracian poet's feet.
Come, let us go, and make thy father blind,
For such a sight will blind a father's eye;
One hour's storm will drown the fragrant meads,
What will whole months of tears thy father's eyes? 55
Do not draw back, for we will mourn with thee;
O, could our mourning ease thy misery!

Confronted with this passage printed as prose, no one could doubt for a moment that it is, in fact, poetry. Quite apart from the insistent and regular rhythm, there is the heightened language one expects of poetry – clever alliterations, picturesque adjectives, and, above all, a wealth of figures, especially of similes. A luxuriant sensuous imagination is everywhere in evidence. So is the author's bent towards word-play. In line 16 'stern ungentle hands' are opposed to 'gentle niece'; and in line 40 there is an interplay between the figurative sense of 'cut from,' meaning 'precluded,' and the literal sense. Moreover, at least one of the images in this speech has already been used earlier in the play. When Marcus asks:

What stern ungentle hands
Hath lopp'd, and hew'd, and made thy body bare
Of her two branches ... ? (16–18)

one's mind goes back to the first scene, where Lucius says, as he drags Alarbus off to sacrificial execution:

> Let's hew his limbs till they be clean consum'd (I.i.129)

and then comments on his return:

> Alarbus' limbs are lopp'd. ... (I.i.143)

The recurrence of the words 'lopp'd' and 'hew'd' is a forcible reminder of the connection between what Lavinia's brothers did to Alarbus and what Alarbus's brothers have just done to her. The repetition serves a truly dramatic purpose; it is part of the play's significance.

But can this be said of the speech as a whole? To answer this question, it is necessary to ask what the function of the speech is meant to be, and how it comes to take the shape that it does. I would suggest that it is a conscious piece of imitation, deliberately designed to outdo the original on which it is modelled. Shakespeare is out to better the effect achieved by Kyd in the opening lines of scene v in act II of *The Spanish Tragedy*. This famous and, in its day, much admired scene begins with Hieronimo entering 'in his shirt' and saying:

> What outcries pluck me from my naked bed,
> And chill my throbbing heart with trembling fear,
> Which never danger yet could daunt before?
> Who calls Hieronimo? Speak, here I am.
> I did not slumber, therefore 'twas no dream, 5
> No, no, it was some woman cried for help,
> And here within this garden did she cry,
> And in this garden must I rescue her:
> But stay, what murd'rous spectacle is this?
> A man hang'd up and all the murderers gone, 10
> And in my bower, to lay the guilt on me:
> This place was made for pleasure not for death.
> *He cuts him down.*
> Those garments that he wears I oft have seen –
> Alas, it is Horatio my sweet son!
> O no, but he that whilom was my son. 15
> O was it thou that call'dst me from my bed?
> O speak, if any spark of life remain:
> I am thy father. Who hath slain my son?
> What savage monster, not of human kind,
> Hath here been glutted with thy harmless blood, 20
> And left thy bloody corpse dishonour'd here,
> For me amidst this dark and deathful shades
> To drown thee with an ocean of my tears?

The construction of the two speeches is the same. Each begins with a series of questions. Then comes the gradual realization of a shocking fact, leading on to the expression of the contrast between what the victim was and what the victim now is. In both cases the perpetrator of the deed is seen as an inhuman monster; and at the end of each passage there is a powerful statement of grief, cast in the form of a hyperbolical reference to floods of tears. However, while the one speech is – or so it seems to me – clearly based on the other, the difference between them, in terms of dramatic impact, is enormous. The first and inescapable distinction is in the matter of length: Marcus needs forty-seven lines to cover much the same ground that Hieronimo does in twenty-three. The discrepancy is particularly marked in the passages of gradual realization. Six lines suffice to convey Hieronimo's experience from the moment when he first sees the body to his recognition of it as Horatio's, even though he has the dark to contend with. Shakespeare, on the other hand, requires no fewer than seventeen lines to take Marcus, who has the advantage of broad daylight on his side, from his initial sight of Lavinia to a full understanding of what has happened to her. Moreover, unlike Hieronimo, who interrupts his flow of words to cut down Horatio's body, Marcus does nothing whatever but talk. The scene is completely static; the movement of the action has been slowed down to a crawl, with the result that the audience, instead of sharing Marcus's experience, is likely to see him as distinctly dim-witted and to find itself asking, 'When is he going to recognize the all too obvious and come to the point?' The attempt to 'overgo' Kyd has ended in a bad 'overdoing' of the effect he aimed at and achieved.

The same adverse criticism applies in an even greater measure to that part of Marcus's speech which is devoted to drawing the contrast between Lavinia as she was and Lavinia as she is. Kyd relies on a few deft touches: the 'sweet son' is now a 'bloody corpse.' Not so Shakespeare. Three elaborate figures, each developed in considerable detail, follow on one another's heels. In a narrative poem they would be in place, but on the stage they are unnecessary – the audience can see with its own eyes the contrast they depict – and they are also intrusive and distracting. They draw far too much attention to themselves, so that one becomes painfully aware of the ghastly incongruity between the frightful spectacle of Lavinia, with her bleeding stumps and mouth, and the 'favour and prettiness' that Marcus is making of it. Worse still, Shakespeare positively directs our attention to the incongruity by emphasizing the physical reality in the very process of converting it into verbal arabesques:

And notwithstanding all this loss of blood –
As from a conduit with three issuing spouts –

Yet do thy cheeks look red as Titan's face
Blushing to be encount'red with a cloud.

In addition, the lines are blatantly out of character. In this play, where almost every other participant in the action is so driven by passion as to appear near-lunatic, Marcus has stood out hitherto, and will stand out again, by virtue of the fact that he behaves in a manner which is, at least by comparison, rational, moderate, and, above all, practical. These, however, are scarcely the adjectives that his conduct in this scene calls for. He seems fully prepared to sacrifice his niece's life for a string of well turned similes.

The dramatist, working on the sensibilities of his audience through what he chooses to show them, and the poet, working on those same sensibilities through the words he offers to the ear, have failed to co-operate with and to complement each other. Instead, they have gone their separate ways and confounded each other's efforts. The spectacle on the stage in shocking in the extreme; but the poetry lavished on it is pretty, ornate, and fanciful. What we see cries out for something to be done, demands that action be taken at once, that Lavinia be cared for, helped, and comforted. But what we hear demands with equal force that we go on listening until the lament has been completed and brought to its proper close. The scene is, it seems to me, almost a paradigm of what is wrong with much of this play. The action of *Titus Andronicus* is violent to the last degree; but the dialogue is, for most of the tragedy's course, smooth and decorous. The world of the play is barbarous, 'a wilderness of tigers' as Titus so aptly puts it in III.i; but the speeches through which the human tigers who inhabit this jungle express their feelings and their intentions are, in general, studied and literary, suggestive of culture and civilization. Involved in deeds that belong to the nightmare or the madhouse, the characters speak as though they were taking part in a well-organized recitation. Having fallen into the pit where the murdered body of Bassianus has been flung, Martius seizes on this inopportune moment to give his brother Quintus a lyrical description of the scene that meets his eyes, saying of the dead man:

Upon his bloody finger he doth wear
A precious ring that lightens all this hole,
Which, like a taper in some monument,
Doth shine upon the dead man's earthy cheeks,
And shows the ragged entrails of this pit;
So pale did shine the moon on Pyramus
When he by night lay bath'd in maiden blood. (II.iii.226–32)

It is a beautiful, though again somewhat fanciful, set piece. But the circumstances in which it is spoken lend a singularly bizarre touch to it, leading one to ask how Martius can be unmindful of the practical exigencies of his own situation and of the urgent need for him to extricate himself from the hole.

The speech, though neatly enough organized in itself, lacks logic in the larger sense that it is quite inappropriate to the occasion. And this same lack of logic extends to the play as a whole. It is true that almost everything that happens in it is motivated by revenge of some kind; but, apart from this blanket notion, adequate and specific reasons to account for and justify the actions that are carried out are extremely hard to find. There is, however, a highly significant exception to this broad generalization. It occurs early in v.i. The banished Lucius, now inexplicably at the head of the army of the Goths, has just entered with his forces. To him comes a Goth bringing Aaron and his child as prisoners. Lucius threatens to hang the child first, and then the father. Thereupon, Aaron promises to talk, provided that his child is spared. Lucius agrees to the condition; but Aaron is not satisfied with his bare word and demands that he swear an oath. Not unreasonably, Lucius asks what value an oath can possibly have for Aaron, who is an atheist, saying:

> Who should I swear by? Thou believest no god;
> That granted, how canst thou believe an oath?

It is a logical question, and it receives a logical answer. Aaron replies:

> What if I do not? – as indeed I do not;
> Yet, for I know thou art religious
> And hast a thing within thee called conscience,
> With twenty popish tricks and ceremonies
> Which I have seen thee careful to observe,
> Therefore I urge thy oath. For that I know
> An idiot holds his bauble for a god,
> And keeps the oath which by that god he swears,
> To that I'll urge him. Therefore thou shalt vow
> By that same god – what god soe'er it be
> That thou adorest and hast in reverence –
> To save my boy, to nourish and bring him up;
> Or else I will discover nought to thee. (v.i.71–85)

The speech has the desired result, as indeed it should, for it is by far and away the best argued statement in the entire play, moving forward in a series of sharply defined logical steps, clearly indicated by the dialectical words and phrases 'What if,' 'Yet,' 'for,' 'Therefore,' 'For that,' 'Therefore,' and 'Or else,' from its hypothetical beginning to its uncompromising end. It is also logical in the larger and more important sense of that word, since it is properly and adequately motivated. Aaron's plea-cum-ultimatum is inspired by his love for the child and his determination to save it, as, for that matter, are all his actions from the moment that the Nurse brings the child to him in IV.ii. In both these respects, the importance of this speech for the development of Shakespeare's art as a poetic dramatist is capital. The pattern of argument established in it is one that he was to go on exploiting in play after play and was never to relinquish. Suitably refined and enriched, it still provides the backbone for such an intense and image-laden piece of writing as Macbeth's great soliloquy at the opening of I.vii, 'If it were done when 'tis done, then 'twere well / It were done quickly.' Aaron here has argued himself into a developing character, as so many of the figures in Shakespeare's subsequent plays were to do. The reality they assume in our minds owes far more, perhaps, than most critics have recognized to their ability – which is, of course, their author's ability – to give such admirably argued and compelling reasons and explanations for their doing the things they want to do and intend to do, or for their not doing the things they have no desire to do and no intention of doing. Aaron dominates the last two acts of *Titus Andronicus* because, unlike the other characters in it and unlike his earlier self, he has such excellent reasons for doing what he does and states those reasons so lucidly and cogently.

Formalization in the Early History Plays

If, as seems likely, the Three Parts of *Henry VI* and *Richard III* were composed soon after the completion of *Titus Andronicus*, these four plays are in themselves clear evidence of how much Shakespeare learned from his dramatization of the pseudo-historical materials that lie behind his 'classical' tragedy. What they show is a steady movement in one direction – towards the imposition of a definite pattern, which grows more pronounced with each play in the series, on his source matter, on the structure of the individual scene, and on the dialogue. The sense of logic, in both the larger and the smaller significance of that word, which is so conspicuous by its absence from much of *Titus Andronicus*, becomes increasingly strong and insistent as the plays follow one another, issuing in a formalization of speech and action that finds its culmination in *Richard III*, the most rhetorically accomplished, stylized, and symmetrical play in the entire canon.

What led Shakespeare to choose the apparently unpromising reign of Henry VI for extended dramatic treatment, in what may well be the first history play of any importance ever to be written in English,* we do not know. The division of the drama into three distinct yet closely related parts suggests that he could have had the example of Marlowe's *Tamburlaine* in mind. So, in a paradoxical kind of way, does the subject matter. Few readers can have reached the end of *2 Tamburlaine* without being left with the lingering question: What happened to the Scythian's conquests after his death? If that same question occurred to Shakespeare,

* See F.P. Wilson *Marlowe and the Early Shakespeare* Oxford 1953.

he may have sought to answer it by looking at what happened to the empire of the English Tamburlaine, Henry v. But, whether this speculation has any validity or not, there can be no doubt whatever about the architectonic powers he brought to bear on the execution of the task he had set himself, selecting and rearranging the materials he found in the works of the chroniclers in the service of a dramatic idea. The most intimidating as well as challenging feature of this material must have been its sheer bulk. The excerpts from the Chronicles printed by Boswell-Stone in his *Shakespeare's Holinshed* and by Geoffrey Bullough in volume III of his *Narrative and Dramatic Sources of Shakespeare*, invaluable though these works are, give no idea of the magnitude of the undertaking. In Holinshed's *Chronicle* alone – and there seems to be no doubt that Shakespeare used the chronicles of Hall and Grafton as well – the account of the period covered in the Three Parts of *Henry VI* runs to about 134,000 words. Moreover, that account moves forward, in true chronicle manner, year by year. Up to 1453, its main concern is with the wars between the English and the French; but the flow of the narrative dealing with these matters is impeded and interrupted time after time by passages devoted to domestic affairs, some of them important, others trivial and ephemeral.

Faced with this largely unorganized mass of material, Shakespeare broke it up into three distinct yet interrelated dramatic units, each having its own specific subject. The main theme of Part I is the loss of the English possessions in France won by Henry v. Part II is about the growth of faction within England itself, leading up to and culminating in the first battle of the Wars of the Roses. Part III dramatizes the continuation of those wars right down to their conclusion in the final Yorkist victory at the battle of Tewkesbury, followed by the killing of the captured Edward Prince of Wales, immediately after that battle, and then by the murder of Henry VI himself in the Tower of London. But, while each of these plays has its own particular theme, they are, nevertheless, drawn together and ultimately woven into a single complex whole by a series of recurrent devices and patterns ranging from the fairly obvious to the more significant and subtle; and, since there is an intimate connection between some of these devices and the kind of dramatic poetry that Shakespeare evolved in the writing of these plays, it is to them that I now turn.

Continuity is assured by the simple, straightforward arrangement of having Part II begin from the point at which Part I ends, and Part III begin from the point at which Part II ends. Less obvious as a unifying factor at the outset, but acquiring a cumulative force as the plays succeed each other, are the repetitive patterns of contrast and parallelism that gradually emerge from them. The clearest and most basic of these patterns, firmly established in the first two scenes of Part I, is that of rise and fall. The play begins with the funeral of Henry v. His death is seen as a national disaster and as the work of adverse stars. Confirmation of this view follows immediately in the form of three Messengers entering one after another to bring news of English defeats in France. The crowning blow is given by the last of them, who tells of the overthrow and capture of Talbot, the greatest of the English generals fighting in France. The second scene presents the obverse of this picture. It opens with the following words from the lips of the Dauphin:

> Mars his true moving, even as in the heavens
> So in the earth, to this day is not known.
> Late did he shine upon the English side;
> Now we are victors, upon us he smiles.

Then comes a temporary setback for the French: their attempt to raise the siege of Orleans is foiled. But at this point Joan la Pucelle makes her entry; identifies the Dauphin; overcomes him in a single combat; and promises him victory. The strength and encouragement she brings to the cause of France make a sharp antithetical contrast to the loss and the discouragement the English have suffered in the defeat and capture of Talbot. This antithesis is endorsed by the events of I.v, in which Joan and Talbot, now released from captivity, fight an inconclusive single combat. In the course of it he recognizes her for a witch and associates her with the devil and the powers of hell.

From this point onwards, the war between England and France is depicted largely in terms of the personal antagonism between Talbot and Joan which is also a struggle between good and evil. In that struggle Joan, in complete defiance of historical fact but to excellent dramatic effect, eventually emerges as the victor. She is present at the battle of Castillon in which Talbot is killed, and speaks a mocking epitaph over his dead body. The English herald has just recited the long list of the hero's various titles, to which Joan retorts:

> Here's a silly-stately style indeed!
> The Turk, that two and fifty kingdoms hath,
> Writes not so tedious a style as this.
> Him that thou magnifi'st with all these titles,
> Stinking and fly-blown lies here at our feet. (IV.vii.72–6)

Her triumph is, however, short-lived. We see her next in v.ii, where, deserted by the fiends that have assisted her hitherto, she is taken prisoner by the Duke of York. In her case, too, the pattern of rise and fall operates. But Shakespeare has not finished yet with the contrast he has so assiduously drawn between her and Talbot. Before she is led away to the stake, in v.iv, Joan is visited by the old Shepherd, her father. He comes to express his love for her, to offer to die with her, and to give her his blessing. But she repels his advances, denies that he is her father, tells him to go away, and, finally, goads him into cursing her. This scene between father and daughter takes the mind back to IV.v, in which Talbot, surrounded by superior French forces and about to make a desperate last stand, is joined by his son John, who is as yet a maiden warrior. Thereupon, the two engage in a friendly contention in honour. The father begs the son to flee, in order that the line of Talbot may be continued, and also to ensure that revenge may, in due course, be taken on the French. But the son will have none of it, arguing that such an action would shame his mother by demonstrating conclusively that he cannot possibly be Talbot's son. Actuated by the same chivalric ideals, the two Talbots, unlike Joan and her father, grow ever closer together in the hour of danger and death, until in the battle that follows the father rescues the son, and then the son rescues the father, before both are killed. In a splendid stage *tableau* old Talbot dies holding the dead body of young Talbot in his arms.

As well as providing a contrast to the behaviour of Joan at her end, the scenes between the two Talbots offer a striking instance of the way in which Shakespeare is now busy knitting speech and action together into a significant whole. The two rescues, one staged and the other reported, have, in a sense, been prepared for, if not anticipated, by the formalized, stichomythic dialogue in which father and son argue with one another:

> TALBOT Shall all thy mother's hopes lie in one tomb?
> JOHN Ay, rather than I'll shame my mother's womb.
> TALBOT Upon my blessing I command thee go.
> JOHN To fight I will, but not to fly the foe.
> TALBOT Part of thy father may be sav'd in thee.
> JOHN No part of him but will be shame in me.
> TALBOT Thou never hadst renown, nor canst not lose it.
> JOHN Yes, your renowned name; shall flight abuse it?
> TALBOT Thy father's charge shall clear thee from that stain.
> JOHN You cannot witness for me, being slain. (IV.v.34–43)

The neat, antithetical balance of statement and counter-statement here is translated into stage action in the double rescue which follows.

It is tempting to speculate that the speech patterns in the dialogue of father and son stimulated Shakespeare's invention, for there is no warrant in the chronicles for the reciprocal rescues. They merely state that young Talbot died 'manfully.' If such were indeed the case, it would be entirely in keeping with Shakespeare's bold and confident handling of his materials throughout the play. In order to create the patterns he needs for purely dramatic purposes, he is quite ruthless in his attitude to and treatment of historical fact. When the battle of Castillon, which brought with it not only the death of Talbot but also the end of the English rule in France, was fought in 1453, Joan had been dead for twenty-two years. Moreover, even the arrangements for a match between Henry VI and Margaret of Anjou, the event with which Part I concludes, were already nine years in the past. Strict chronology has been sacrificed to the needs of the theatre. By playing fast and loose with it Shakespeare has succeeded in compressing the course of the war between England and France into the compass of a single play, while, at the same time, giving a shape and a meaning to the events of that war.

The same pattern of rise and fall makes itself felt through *2* and *3 Henry VI*. The central concern of Part II is with the fall and subsequent murder of Humphrey Duke of Gloucester, engineered by the Bishop of Winchester and the Duke of Suffolk. However, no sooner have Winchester and Suffolk achieved this end than they too are cut off, the Bishop by natural causes acting as the agent of God's justice, and Suffolk by the hand of Walter Whitmore. Their deaths leave the field clear for another rise, that of the sinister figure of Richard Duke of York, who has been waiting expectantly in the background, biding his time until the right occasion for self-assertion occurs. Now he takes up arms against Henry VI, and defeats the Lancastrian forces at the first battle of St Albans. At the opening of Part III, York is at the height of his power. Seated on the throne in the Parliament House, he lays down terms that ensure the succession to him and his heirs, not to Edward Prince of Wales, the son of Henry VI and Margaret. Yet before act I is over, York has been overcome in battle by Margaret's army, taken prisoner by his enemies, and callously done to death. From this point onwards the fortunes of the two sides follow a fluctuating course; but, eventually, at the battle of Tewkesbury, Edward IV triumphs completely, though the audience in the theatre is aware of a foreboding shadow falling across his hopes for the future in the shape of his brother, Richard Duke of Gloucester, who has already made that audience privy to his own designs on the throne.

The prime motivating force behind the entire action is human ambition; and, since ambitious designs are neither respectable nor safe, they usually find their expression through soliloquy. Fittingly, the soliloquies devoted to this topic have a marked Marlovian ring to them, for Marlowe had succeeded, as no English dramatist before him had, in finding a suitable form of utterance for the aspiring man. Shakespeare deliberately alludes to and adopts Marlowe's manner, secure in the knowledge that many in his audience, hearing the familiar strains, would recognize the character speaking the lines as a would-be Tamburlaine.

There is a distinct touch of Marlowe in the words Suffolk utters at the end of Part I, congratulating himself on the success he has enjoyed so far and looking forward to the power he expects his plans to bring him. Left alone on the stage, he says:

> Thus Suffolk hath prevail'd; and thus he goes,
> As did the youthful Paris once to Greece,
> With hope to find the like event in love
> But prosper better than the Troyan did.
> Margaret shall now be Queen, and rule the King;
> But I will rule both her, and King, and realm. (V.V.103–8)

Behind the analogy Suffolk draws lies an evident recollection of the command with which Mycetes sends Theridamas off to capture Tamburlaine:

> Go frowning foorth, but come thou smyling home,
> As did Sir *Paris* with the Grecian Dame. (*1 Tamburlaine* I.i.73–4)

This brief passage is, however, in keeping with the secondary role of the character to whom it is given, merely a subdued overture to the full-throated Marlovian music that makes itself heard in Part II when York, having heard the disastrous terms agreed on between Suffolk and the French for the marriage of Henry VI and Margaret of Anjou, voices his feeling that he is the real loser by the match, and then goes on to proclaim his determination to take over the rule of England:

> Anjou and Maine both given unto the French!
> Cold news to me, for I had hope of France,
> Even as I have of fertile England's soil.
> A day will come when York shall claim his own;
> And therefore I will take the Nevils' parts,
> And make a show of love to proud Duke Humphrey,
> And when I spy advantage, claim the crown,
> For that's the golden mark I seek to hit.
> Nor shall proud Lancaster usurp my right,
> Nor hold the sceptre in his childish fist,
> Nor wear the diadem upon his head,
> Whose church-like humours fits not for a crown.
> Then, York, be still awhile, till time do serve;
> Watch thou and wake, when others be asleep,
> To pry into the secrets of the state;
> Till Henry, surfeiting in joys of love
> With his new bride and England's dear-bought queen,

And Humphrey with the peers be fall'n at jars;
Then will I raise aloft the milk-white rose,
With whose sweet smell the air shall be perfum'd,
And in my standard bear the arms of York,
To grapple with the house of Lancaster;
And force perforce I'll make him yield the crown,
Whose bookish rule hath pull'd fair England down. (I.i.231–54)

Yet Marlovian though this speech is, it is Marlowe with a difference. The rhapsodic manner of Tamburlaine has been toned down and given a more practical bent. Like Aaron extorting an oath from Lucius in v.i of *Titus Andronicus,* York argues his way forward in a series of logical steps from his bitter and disappointed opening to his challenging and decisive conclusion. The rising movement of the speech anticipates and forecasts the rise of York himself which will continue throughout Part II and reach its climax in the first scene of Part III. The pattern of the speech is also the pattern of the action the speech initiates. The integration of words with action that Shakespeare achieves here evidently satisfied him, at least for a time, since he repeats it on an even larger scale and with some variations in Part III. There, at the end of III.ii, the scene in which Edward IV woos Lady Grey and finally capitulates to her terms, Richard of Gloucester is left alone on the stage, just as his father was in I.i of Part II, to voice his frustrations, his ambitions, and the means he intends to resort to in order to realize those ambitions. His soliloquy is both wryer and, by the time it reaches its conclusion, jauntier than York's, for Richard is well on the way to acquiring an idiom of his own, but it progresses in the same logical fashion and offers a kind of preview of much of the remaining action of *3 Henry VI* and of the first half of *Richard III* as well.

As the speech of aspiration is the prologue to rise, so the lament is the epilogue to fall. Opening with an elaborate lament for four voices, *Henry VI* as a whole is punctuated by instance after instance of this well-established dramatic convention which, as Wolfgang Clemen has so ably and thoroughly demonstrated,* had a long history behind it at the time when Shakespeare began his career as a playwright. Most of these laments run true to form, and none more so than the soliloquy in which the Earl of Warwick, severely wounded and left for dead, anticipates his death, looks back on his life, and sums it all up as vanity:

Ah, who is nigh? Come to me, friend or foe,
And tell me who is victor, York or Warwick?

* Wolfgang Clemen *English Tragedy before Shakespeare* London 1961, pp 211–86 and *passim*

Why ask I that? My mangled body shows,
My blood, my want of strength, my sick heart shows,
That I must yield my body to the earth
And, by my fall, the conquest to my foe.
Thus yields the cedar to the axe's edge,
Whose arms gave shelter to the princely eagle,
Under whose shade the ramping lion slept,
Whose top-branch overpeer'd Jove's spreading tree
And kept low shrubs from winter's pow'rful wind.
These eyes that now are dimm'd with death's black veil,
Have been as piercing as the mid-day sun
To search the secret treasons of the world;
The wrinkles in my brows, now fill'd with blood,
Were lik'ned oft to kingly sepulchres;
For who liv'd King, but I could dig his grave?
And who durst smile when Warwick bent his brow?
Lo now my glory smear'd in dust and blood!
My parks, my walks, my manors, that I had,
Even now forsake me; and of all my lands
Is nothing left me but my body's length.
Why, what is pomp, rule, reign, but earth and dust?
And live we how we can, yet die we must. (*3 Henry VI* V.ii.5–28)

The whole structure of this speech, with its long backward look at past glories and its ultimate recognition of the grave as man's last home, together with the elegiac note that pervades it, places it firmly within a long tradition of non-dramatic as well as dramatic poetry. This is the way that great men ended, and had been ending in *de casibus* narrative verse for more than two hundred years, when Shakespeare wrote these lines. The signal to the audience is loud, clear, and familiar; and, to that extent, the speech fulfils its proper function within the total dramatic pattern: it marks the completion of a fall. But the manner of it is narrative rather than dramatic; its length impedes the action; it is general, not specific; and its retrospective nature compels the audience to look back on what has happened at a time when the climax of the play has almost been reached. One expectation is gratified, but another and more important expectation is frustrated. The lament was not without its attendant dangers for the playwright.

The pattern of rise and fall is the most continuous and insistent of all the patterns in the Three Parts of *Henry VI*. But, because it is so common, so well worn, and so stereotpyed a feature of pre-Shakespearian tragedy of both the narrative and the dramatic kind, it calls little attention to itself.

The more original and striking patterns in these plays are of a different nature, and there are two of them. Both, incidentally, are closely connected with meaning; they offer firm indications of the way in which Shakespeare interpreted the historical material he was handling and shaping. The first is a pattern of total opposition and balanced confrontation, which suggests very strongly that far from seeing the Wars of the Roses as a legacy from the deposition and murder of Richard II, as Tillyard and others have argued,* the dramatist, at this stage in his career, looked on them as a necessary and unavoidable consequence of the fact that the claims of York and Lancaster were, as near as makes no difference, equal, so that the only ultimate solution to the quarrel is the union of the two houses.

Skilfully inserted into the structure of *1 Henry VI*, the scene in the Temple Garden, II.iv, is, in terms of its total significance, much the most important scene in the entire play. Within the limits of Part I itself, to which it properly belongs, it goes far towards providing an explanation for the failure of the English forces in France; but, within the framework of the trilogy as a whole, it has the further function of preparing the way for the Wars of the Roses, which will not begin until the last act of Part II, and thus of relating the Three Parts closely to one another and giving them a fundamental unity. It is, therefore, most fitting that it should be sharply marked off in form and style from the rest of the play in which it occurs. Up to the point at which it begins, Shakespeare has been busy in dramatizing the material he has selected from the work of the chroniclers. His play has been a play of action, given over to the staging of battles between the English and the French, of *mêlées* between the supporters of the Duke of Gloucester and the supporters of the Bishop of Winchester in London, and, by way of variation, of the stratagem with which Talbot counters the treacherous scheme of the Countess of Auvergne. The confusion and hurly-burly of war and civil strife have been faithfully rendered through what has been shown and what has been said. The picture presented has been a shifting one, constantly in motion and therefore incapable of formalization. In II.iv, however, Shakespeare abandons the chroniclers for the time being, and relies on his own invention, in order to convey the essence he has distilled from their writings in a manner designed to leave an indelible impression on the minds of an audience in the theatre.

On to the stage come six young men, to continue in the garden a dispute that has become too loud to be longer tolerated within the Temple Hall. The subject of the argument is not clear, nor will it become so until some eighty lines later, but the opposing parties are evidently Richard

* E.M.W. Tillyard *Shakespeare's History Plays* pp 147–9

Plantagenet and the Earl of Somerset. Plantagenet asks Suffolk to judge between him and Somerset, but Suffolk refuses on the grounds that his knowledge of the law is inadequate. Somerset then requests Warwick to pronounce a verdict. The answer he receives is:

> Between two hawks, which flies the higher pitch;
> Between two dogs, which hath the deeper mouth;
> Between two blades, which bears the better temper;
> Between two horses, which doth bear him best;
> Between two girls, which hath the merriest eye –
> I have perhaps some shallow spirit of judgement;
> But in these nice sharp quillets of the law,
> Good faith, I am no wiser than a daw. (11–18)

The precise patterning of line upon line serves a purpose: as well as making it clear why Warwick feels incapable of judging between the two opponents, it also suggests that he views their claims as being of equal validity. At this point, however, Plantagenet and Somerset appeal to the company, setting up another and related pattern as they do so:

> PLANTAGENET Tut, tut, here is a mannerly forbearance:
> The truth appears so naked on my side
> That any purblind eye may find it out.
> SOMERSET And on my side it is so well apparell'd,
> So clear, so shining, and so evident,
> That it will glimmer through a blind man's eye. (19–24)

An absolute refusal to compromise is reflected in the very appearance of the two speeches on the page, and it is fully endorsed by their antithetical contents, where image answers image in calculated reversal. An impasse has been reached. The disputants attempt to break it by acting and appealing for action; but the pattern persists, and with it the deadlock. The scene develops thus:

> PLANTAGENET Since you are tongue-tied and so loath to speak,
> In dumb significants proclaim your thoughts.
> Let him that is a true-born gentleman
> And stands upon the honour of his birth,
> If he suppose that I have pleaded truth,
> From off this brier pluck a white rose with me.
> SOMERSET Let him that is no coward nor no flatterer,
> But dare maintain the party of the truth,
> Pluck a red rose from off this thorn with me.
> WARWICK I love no colours; and without all colour

Of base insinuating flattery,
I pluck this white rose with Plantagenet.
SUFFOLK I pluck this red rose with young Somerset,
And say withal I think he held the right. (25–38)

Patterned action has issued from and become one with patterned speech, to create a *tableau* that is pregnant with meaning. The four young men who came out of the Temple Hall together now stand ranged against each other in two pairs, each holding the emblem of his allegiance in his hand. The spectacle forecasts, embodies, and explains much that is still to happen in Part I, even more of what will happen in Part II, and all that will happen in Part III.

The two main figures in this scene, Plantagenet, soon to become York, and Somerset, also play prominent parts in the two scenes in which Shakespeare develops and exploits yet another formal device, that of exact parallelism. In IV.ii Talbot, with his forces, arrives before the gates of Bordeaux and threatens its citizens with destruction if they do not let him in. He is told that he is in a trap, for the Dauphin's army is close behind him; and at this moment the Dauphin's drum is heard, giving proof that the citizens of Bordeaux have spoken the truth. Thereupon, Talbot decides on a desperate last stand. The two scenes that follow show, in the full meaning of that word, why Talbot is now doomed. At the opening of IV.iii, a Messenger is busy telling York about the French forces that are converging on Bordeaux. But, instead of taking immediate action, York lays the blame for Talbot's predicament on Somerset. At this point Sir William Lucy enters to beg York to 'Spur to the rescue of the noble Talbot.' York's only response is to express the wish that Somerset, 'a traitor and a coward,' were in Talbot's place, and to continue to vent his anger against his rival. Finding no help in York, Lucy, in soliloquy, draws the appropriate moral:

Thus, while the vulture of sedition
Feeds in the bosom of such great commanders,
Sleeping neglection doth betray to loss
The conquest of our scarce-cold conqueror,
That ever-living man of memory,
Henry the Fifth. Whiles they each other cross,
Lives, honours, lands, and all, hurry to loss. (IV.iii.47–53)

The next scene, IV.iv, repeats IV.iii, with minor variations. Somerset enters with his army. He is talking to a Captain sent from Talbot and accusing York of being responsible for Talbot's plight. Once more Sir

William Lucy arrives to ask for help. Somerset's answer is 'York set him on; York should have sent him aid.' Again Lucy draws the moral:

> The fraud of England, not the force of France,
> Hath now entrapp'd the noble-minded Talbot.
> Never to England shall he bear his life,
> But dies betray'd to fortune by your strife. (IV.iv.36–9)

Unlike York, Somerset now relents somewhat, promising to 'dispatch the horsemen straight,' only to be told by Lucy that it is 'Too late.' The deliberate parallelism has made its point.

It is evident that Shakespeare found the two devices examined above effective and satisfactory, for he resorts to both of them again in *3 Henry VI*. This play, when it first appeared in print as a 'bad' octavo in 1595, was described on the title page as 'The true Tragedie of Richard Duke of Yorke, and the death of good King Henrie the Sixt ... ' In one sense this title is misleading, since York is killed in the last scene of act I; but in another it is extremely accurate, for we know from another source that this death-scene must have made a deep impression on those who first saw it. Robert Greene begins his notorious attack on Shakespeare in his *Greenes Groats-worth of Wit* (1592) by referring to the playwright as 'an vpstart Crow, beautified with our feathers, that with his *Tygers hart wrapt in a Players hyde*, supposes he is as well able to bombast out a blanke verse as the best of you ... '* Here the carefully italicized words are a deliberate and pointed misquotation of a line from York's retort to Queen Margaret in which he addresses her as 'O tiger's heart wrapp'd in a woman's hide!' (I.iv.137). Greene obviously assumes that the line is thoroughly familiar to his readers and, in doing so, pays an unconscious and unintentional tribute to the object of his attack, and to the power of the scene from which the line comes.

Clearly modelled on the Temple Garden scene in *1 Henry VI*, I.iv of *3 Henry VI* carries the formalization of violence as far as it can be carried. In the previous scene, I.iii, little Rutland, York's youngest son and a non-combatant, has been cold-bloodedly butchered by Clifford, the most brutal and efficient of the Lancastrian leaders, who then leaves the stage, promising to add the blood of the father to that of the son. No sooner has he gone than York comes on. Weary, alone, and defeated, he soliloquizes for some twenty lines of epic narrative, recounting the events of the battle of Wakefield, which is taking place off stage, for the benefit of the

* Quoted from E.K. Chambers *William Shakespeare: A Study of Facts and Problems* Oxford 1930, vol II, p 188

audience which has not seen them. Then, as the alarum sounds, he explains that the enemy must be near, that he has no hope of escape, and that he knows his end is upon him. On this cue, Queen Margaret, Clifford, Northumberland, and their forces appear. York, unable to resist such odds, nevertheless defies them verbally; and some twenty lines of flyting follow. In these exchanges York gives quite as good as he gets, with the result that Clifford makes to attack him with his sword. But at this point Queen Margaret, hitherto silent, intervenes, not to show York mercy, but to prolong his agony. At her command, he is seized, disarmed, and made to stand upon a convenient molehill. Then, for over a hundred lines, the scene freezes, as it were; no movement takes place on the stage, except for four highly significant and telling gestures.

The confrontation between York and Margaret is much sharper and even more antithetical than that between York and Somerset in the Temple Garden. The rivalry between the two houses remains; but, to add to the completeness of the opposition between them, he is a man, she a woman; he English, she French; he defeated, she victorious. The antithesis already so strongly present in the situation now comes to pervade the dialogue also as Margaret launches into a vindictive speech – forty-three lines of it – made up of taunts and mockery. It begins thus:

> Brave warriors, Clifford and Northumberland,
> Come, make him stand upon this molehill here
> That raught at mountains with outstretched arms,
> Yet parted but the shadow with his hand.
> What, was it you that would be England's king?
> Was't you that revell'd in our parliament
> And made a preachment of your high descent?

Then, having made her statement with one set of rhetorical questions, Margaret moves on to her counter-statement – another set of rhetorical questions:

> Where are your mess of sons to back you now?
> The wanton Edward and the lusty George?
> And where's that valiant crook-back prodigy,
> Dicky your boy, that with his grumbling voice
> Was wont to cheer his dad in mutinies?
> Or, with the rest, where is your darling Rutland?

Finally, out of the statement and the counter-statement, there comes their logical consequence, a telling action, for Margaret continues:

> Look, York: I stain'd this napkin with the blood
> That valiant Clifford with his rapier's point
> Made issue from the bosom of the boy;
> And if thine eyes can water for his death,
> I give thee this to dry thy cheeks withal. (I.iv. 66–83)

The whole thing is most skilfully contrived. Margaret's atrocious taunts lead up to her atrocious gesture which clinches their bitterness. But this is only the first stage. Her speech pauses for a moment before it mounts once more in a calculated gradation of goading imprecations to yet another outrageous action – the setting of a paper crown on York's head, in mockery of his pretensions to the throne. But even this gesture, with its overt reference to the setting of the crown of thorns on the head of Christ, is not the end of the torture. For another ten lines or so Margaret jeeringly compares York as he was to York as he is, makes out the case against him as an oath-breaker, and then gives the order which is the natural and necessary consequence of the indictment she has made: 'Off with the crown and with the crown his head' (107).

It looks as though York's torment is about to end. But it is not. Margaret, the tigress, is merely playing cat-and-mouse with her helpless victim, while Shakespeare, the dramatist, is holding his audience in suspense until he completes the pattern of the action which is one with and inseparable from the rhetorical pattern he is working out. As Clifford steps eagerly forward to finish York off, Margaret restrains him once again, so that she may enjoy the sadistic satisfaction of listening to York's answer, which will show how much she has succeeded in hurting him. He gives it in a speech that is as long as hers was, that takes the same shape as hers did, that makes use of exactly the same antithetical tricks, and that works up to two similar climaxes in which the same two properties, the napkin and the paper crown, are employed. Just as she taunted him with his failure to win kingly power, so he taunts her with her lack of all womanly qualities, including beauty:

> 'Tis beauty that doth oft make women proud;
> But, God he knows, thy share thereof is small.
> 'Tis virtue that doth make them most admir'd;
> The contrary doth make thee wond'red at.
> 'Tis government that makes them seem divine;
> The want thereof makes thee abominable.
> Thou art as opposite to every good
> As the Antipodes are unto us,
> Or as the south to the septentrion.
> O tiger's heart wrapp'd in a woman's hide!

> How couldst thou drain the life-blood of the child,
> To bid the father wipe his eyes withal,
> And yet be seen to bear a woman's face?
> Women are soft, mild, pitiful, and flexible:
> Thou stern, obdurate, flinty, rough, remorseless. (128–42)

The verbal rejoinder is backed up and endorsed by two gestures. York returns the blood-stained napkin to Margaret, saying as he does so: 'go boast of this'; then, removing the paper crown from his head, he tells her: 'There, take the crown, and with the crown my curse.' Thereupon, Clifford and Margaret stab him to death.

The dramatic strength of the scene derives from the tension set up in it between what the eye sees and what the ear hears. The stage picture is formal, even elegant; but the sentiments expressed are violent and barbarous. Yet they, too, have been shaped with studied care. Margaret's long speech of mockery is balanced by York's equally long speech of defiance; on the printed page they look at each other across the narrow bridge provided by a mere two lines of dialogue between Margaret and Clifford. And the shape of the scene is one with its meaning. It imprints indelibly on the mind of a spectator or a reader the implacable nature of the conflict. Moreover, the shape of the scene is also the shape of the play, for it too has an antithetical structure. The battle of Wakefield at the beginning, leading to the murder of little Rutland in I.iii, and of his father York in I.iv, is counterbalanced by the battle of Tewkesbury at the end, leading to the murder of Prince Edward, Margaret's son, in V.v – a murder carried out by Rutland's brothers – and to the murder of his father, Henry VI himself, by Richard of Gloucester in V.vi. With the completion of this pattern, a further layer of meaning has been discovered in events: behind the total opposition of York and Lancaster there lies the operation in the world of divine justice, seeing to it with mathematical precision that every crime receives its fitting punishment.

As well as conveying the political and even the metaphysical implications of the Wars of the Roses, Shakespeare also takes care to show their social consequences, the effect they have on the lives of ordinary men; and for this purpose he reverts to that technique of parallelism which he had already employed in IV.iii and IV.iv of *1 Henry VI*, the scenes in which Sir William Lucy comes first to York and then to Somerset, asking each of them to come to the aid of Talbot. At the opening of II.v of Part III, Henry VI enters to soliloquize on the battle of Towton which is raging about him and on his own position. He draws a nostalgic contrast between himself, called on to fill an office for which he is wholly unsuited, and the shepherd he would like to be. Then, at the conclusion of his speech, there comes, with a splendidly ironical effect, the following stage direction in the Folio text:

> *Alarum. Enter a Sonne that hath kill'd his Father, at one doore: and a Father that hath kill'd his Sonne at another doore.*

Here are two ordinary men whose appearance and experience give the lie to the King's dream about the happy contented life of 'a homely swain.' The Son speaks first, expressing his intention to pillage his victim, and then discovering that the victim is his own father, pressed into service by the Earl of Warwick, while he himself was similarly pressed into service by the forces of the King. All that the King can do is to condole with him, though there is no indication that the Son hears a word the King says. Then the Father speaks. He too intends to spoil his victim, only to realize that the victim is his own son. The King condoles with him also, and again there is no response. An antiphonal lament for three voices follows:

> SON How will my mother for a father's death
> Take on with me, and ne'er be satisfied!
> FATHER How will my wife for slaughter of my son
> Shed seas of tears, and ne'er be satisfied!
> KING HENRY How will the country for these woeful chances
> Misthink the King, and not be satisfied!
> SON Was ever son so rued a father's death?
> FATHER Was ever father so bemoan'd his son?
> KING HENRY Was ever king so griev'd for subjects' woe?
> Much is your sorrow; mine ten times so much.
> SON I'll bear thee hence, where I may weep my fill.
> *Exit with the body.*
> FATHER These arms of mine shall be thy winding-sheet;
> ...
> I'll bear thee hence; and let them fight that will,
> For I have murdered where I should not kill.
> *Exit with the body.*
> KING HENRY Sad-hearted men, much overgone with care,
> Here sits a king more woeful than you are. (103–24)

Realism has been sedulously eschewed; the scene is wholly emblematic. The Son and Father are nameless because they are Everyman; and, in their representative capacities, they speak directly to the audience, as though each of them were entirely alone on the stage. The King addresses them and, through them, the audience. It is proper that he should, for these two figures embody the sufferings of his subjects and the consequences, in concrete terms, of his own incompetence. But they show no awareness either of his presence or of one another's. They cannot, for they are not individuals but an abstract idea – the central horror of civil war – made visible and presented for all to see. What the audience looks at is a kind of triptych, with the King in the central position; what it hears, sounding unmistakably through the repetitive antiphonal pattern of the verse, is the verbal equivalent of that triptych.

This technique of organizing a drama by establishing a close relationship between the rhetorical structure of individual scenes and speeches and the overall structure and significance of the play as a whole, which Shakespeare seems to have evolved in the course of writing *Henry VI*, is carried to its limits in *Richard III*. In a sense, the development of most of the action is already implicit in the first thirty-one lines of the soliloquy Richard utters as he steps on to the stage at the play's opening. It is, of course, essentially a public address directed at the audience, an ample leisurely piece of writing, the right prologue for a play that will be ample and leisurely. In it each statement made is expanded at considerable length through the use of a whole series of parallel images; but these images do take their place in, and are kept subordinate to, the logical argument which provides the backbone of the speech as a whole. Setting the time, the scene, and his own position within, and his attitude to, the circumstances he describes, Richard says:

> Now is the winter of our discontent
> Made glorious summer by this sun of York;
> And all the clouds that lour'd upon our house
> In the deep bosom of the ocean buried.
> Now are our brows bound with victorious wreaths;
> Our bruised arms hung up for monuments;
> Our stern alarums chang'd to merry meetings,
> Our dreadful marches to delightful measures.
> Grim-visag'd war hath smooth'd his wrinkled front,
> And now, instead of mounting barbed steeds 10
> To fright the souls of fearful adversaries,
> He capers nimbly in a lady's chamber
> To the lascivious pleasing of a lute.
> But I – that am not shap'd for sportive tricks,
> Nor made to court an amorous looking-glass –
> I – that am rudely stamp'd, and want love's majesty
> To strut before a wanton ambling nymph –
> I – that am curtail'd of this fair proportion,
> Cheated of feature by dissembling nature,
> Deform'd, unfinish'd, sent before my time 20

Into this breathing world scarce half made up,
And that so lamely and unfashionable
That dogs bark at me as I halt by them –
Why, I, in this weak piping time of peace,
Have no delight to pass away the time,
Unless to spy my shadow in the sun
And descant on mine own deformity.
And therefore, since I cannot prove a lover
To entertain these fair well-spoken days,
I am determined to prove a villain 30
And hate the idle pleasures of these days.

The speech falls into three clearly defined sections, each introduced by a word or words having logical associations. First comes the statement, simple enough in itself but amplified into a full thirteen lines by the antithetical illustrations it receives, that war has now given way to peace. Then, with the sharp turn indicated by the words 'But I,' there follows the counter-statement in which Richard expresses, and does his best to justify, his hostility to the new dispensation, again using a string of picturesque illustrations to give weight and body to his attitude. There are fourteen lines here to balance the first thirteen. And finally, having presented the thesis and the antithesis, Richard proceeds to draw his conclusion from them in the four lines beginning with 'And therefore.' It is the perfect opening for a play that has the formal elegance of a demonstration in logic or mathematics, though the logic which ultimately comes to dominate and control the action is not the perverted ratiocination of Richard but the inexorable even-handed working of divine justice. Acting on the mistaken assumption that, as he tells himself in v.vi of *3 Henry VI*, 'I am myself alone,' Richard challenges God, Nature, society, and his own family, in order to move steadily and irresistibly to the throne, which he ascends in IV.ii. But, at precisely this point, he meets his first check when Buckingham, hitherto his ready second and cat's-paw, proves unwilling to fall in with his expressed desire to see the Princes dead. It is the beginning of the end for Richard, the signal for all the forces he has set himself against to unite in bringing about his overthrow. His fall is as precipitate as his rise was slow and arduous.

But the pattern of rise and fall is not the only pattern to make itself felt within the structure and meaning of *Richard III*, contrast and parallelism also have their place and function. The play has the shape of a great though somewhat lop-sided arch, in which the coronation of Richard in the interval between IV.i and IV.ii is the keystone. I.ii and I.iii have the same place in the rising action as the second and first half of the long scene

IV.iv have in the falling action. The correspondence is exact, highly significant, and heavily emphasized. Richard's attempt to win Queen Elizabeth over to his plan for marrying her daughter, which occupies IV.iv.196–431, is a mirror image of his wooing of Anne Neville in I.ii. In both scenes the circumstances in which the wooing takes place are outrageous and bizarre, and in both it is conducted along the same lines and in the same poetic form – through a 'keen encounter' of wits clashing in stichomythic exchanges. At the end of each verbal duel, Richard, sure that he has won, voices his contempt for his female opponent. When Anne has gone, he says:

> Was ever woman in this humour woo'd?
> Was ever woman in this humour won? (I.ii.227–8)

As Elizabeth leaves the stage, he remarks:

> Relenting fool, and shallow, changing woman! (IV.iv. 431)

In the first case his contempt and confidence are justified, in the second they are not. Elizabeth has not promised him her daughter's hand but merely to find out what that daughter's feelings about the match are. In the very next scene we learn that Elizabeth has espoused her daughter to Richmond. What appeared as a victory to Richard has, in fact, been a defeat. The parallel between the two scenes has ended as a contrast between them.

I.iii and the first half of IV.iv, down to line 125, offer a similar pattern of likeness and contrast. At the opening of I.iii Queen Elizabeth is voicing her fears as to what may happen if her husband Edward IV, now grievously ill, dies. Buckingham then enters to say that the King wishes to make an atonement between Richard and the Queen's kinsmen. He is followed by Richard himself, who proceeds very cleverly to pick a quarrel with the Queen and her kinsmen. As this quarrel grows increasingly bitter Queen Margaret enters unseen from the rear of the stage to overhear all that is going on. For a time she restricts her indignation to sharp and contemptuous asides, but finally she can contain herself no longer, and steps forward to say:

> Hear me, you wrangling pirates, that fall out
> In sharing that which you have pill'd from me. (158–9)

It is a great theatrical moment, and it has its consequences. Confronted by this forgotten representative of the past, all the rest ignore their differences for the time being in order to rebut Margaret's claim that she is the true Queen of England and that they are mere usurpers. In doing so they spur the one-time Queen, now the voice of history, into uttering a long and comprehensive curse on them, which is also an accurate prophecy of what is about to happen in the play. In the course of it Margaret says to Queen Elizabeth:

> Though not by war, by surfeit die your king,
> As ours by murder, to make him a king!
> Edward thy son, that now is Prince of Wales,
> For Edward our son, that was Prince of Wales,
> Die in his youth by like untimely violence!
> Thyself a queen, for me that was a queen,
> Outlive thy glory, like my wretched self!
> Long mayest thou live to wail thy children's death,
> And see another, as I see thee now,
> Deck'd in thy rights, as thou art stall'd in mine! (197–206)

The opening of IV.iv is the same scene in reverse. This time Margaret comes on alone, to announce with gloating satisfaction that all is going as she prophesied it would. Then, seeing Queen Elizabeth and the old Duchess of York approaching, she retires into the background. The newcomers bewail the murder of the little Princes and the other disasters that have flowed from the rivalry of York and Lancaster, while Margaret punctuates their speeches with sardonic asides. Eventually, however, she moves forward, exactly as she did in I.iii, to take her place at the front of the stage with the other two. But this time they do not reject her; they accept her as an ally, because all three of them now recognize Richard as their common enemy. Things have changed; and to underline the nature of that change Margaret repeats the substance of the curse she spoke in I.iii, but with one crucial difference: what was then in the future is now, for the most part, already in the past. The curse has worked. Recalling it all, Margaret says to Queen Elizabeth:

> Thy Edward he is dead, that kill'd my Edward;
> The other Edward dead, to quit my Edward;
> Young York he is but boot, because both they
> Match'd not the high perfection of my loss.
> Thy Clarence he is dead that stabb'd my Edward;
> And the beholders of this frantic play,
> Th' adulterate Hastings, Rivers, Vaughan, Grey,
> Untimely smother'd in their dusky graves. (63–70)

The verbal chain in which name is linked to name is also a causal chain in which punishment is linked to crime; and this chain extends backward beyond the battle of Tewkesbury to the murder of little Rutland and of York himself at the battle of Wakefield. Margaret's first words, after joining the Duchess of York and the Queen, are:

> I had an Edward, till a Richard kill'd him;
> I had a husband, till a Richard kill'd him;
> Thou hadst an Edward, till a Richard kill'd him;
> Thou hadst a Richard, till a Richard kill'd him.

The lines are directed at Queen Elizabeth, but they are taken up and answered by the Duchess of York, who retorts:

> I had a Richard too, and thou didst kill him;
> I had a Rutland too, thou holp'st to kill him. (40–45)

If the play has a 'message' this is it; every crime receives its appropriate punishment. But one is left wondering how much this grim view of historical causation owes to the enticing oportunities for campanological elaboration that the Plantagenets' fondness for the names Richard and Edward held out to a playwright in love with words. The fact that Richard II does not figure in the list at all and that the other Plantagenet name Henry occurs only once, and then in an insignificant manner when the Duchess of York addresses Margaret as 'Harry's wife' (59), is further evidence that when Shakespeare wrote the first tetralogy he did not see the troubles of the fifteenth century as having their origin in the deposition and murder of Richard II.

Character and Individual Idiom

Richard III is a beautifully planned and executed work of art, the culmination of the experiments Shakespeare had been making and of the manner he had been developing in the Three Parts of *Henry VI*. It was also, and has continued to be, a highly successful play in the theatre. Yet, having written it, Shakespeare never wrote another play like it. Why not? At least part of the answer to this rhetorical question is to be found in the passage in his late writing that comes closest to the style of the choric lamentations which are such a feature of *Richard III*. In IV.v. of *Romeo and Juliet* the Nurse discovers Juliet apparently dead, and calls for Capulet and Lady Capulet. Juliet's mother enters, and this dialogue follows:

LADY CAPULET What noise is here?
NURSE O lamentable day!
LADY CAPULET What is the matter?
NURSE Look, look! O heavy day!
LADY CAPULET O me, O me! My child, my only life,
Revive, look up, or I will die with thee! 20
Help, help! Call help.
Enter CAPULET
CAPULET For shame, bring Juliet forth; her lord is come.
NURSE She's dead, deceas'd, she's dead; alack the day!
LADY CAPULET Alack the day, she's dead, she's dead, she's dead!
CAPULET Ha! let me see her. Out, alas! she's cold;
Her blood is settled, and her joints are stiff.
Life and these lips have long been separated.

Death lies on her like an untimely frost
Upon the sweetest flower of all the field.
NURSE O lamentable day!
LADY CAPULET O woeful time! 30
CAPULET Death, that hath ta'en her hence to make me wail,
Ties up my tongue and will not let me speak.
Enter FRIAR LAWRENCE *and* COUNTY PARIS, *with* Musicians.
FRIAR LAWRENCE Come, is the bride ready to go to church?
CAPULET Ready to go, but never to return.
O son, the night before thy wedding day
Hath Death lain with thy wife. There she lies,
Flower as she was, deflowered by him.
Death is my son-in law, Death is my heir;
My daughter he hath wedded; I will die,
And leave him all; life, living, all is Death's. 40
PARIS Have I thought long to see this morning's face,
And doth it give me such a sight as this?
LADY CAPULET Accurs'd, unhappy, wretched, hateful day!
Most miserable hour that e'er time saw
In lasting labour of his pilgrimage!
But one, poor one, one poor and loving child,
But one thing to rejoice and solace in,
And cruel Death hath catch'd it from my sight!
NURSE O woe! O woeful, woeful, woeful day!
Most lamentable day, most woeful day 50
That ever, ever, I did yet behold!
O day! O day! O day! O hateful day!
Never was seen so black a day as this.
O woeful day, O woeful day!

But even now the lament is not over. The patent absurdity of the Nurse's expression of grief does not prevent Paris and Capulet from adding their contributions to the choric threnody. The Friar eventually intervenes to stop it all and put it into the right perspective by saying:

Peace, ho, for shame! Confusion's cure lives not
In these confusions.

The model Shakespeare had in mind when composing this passage was almost certainly, I think, the lamentation that Queen Elizabeth, the old Duchess of York, and the Children of Clarence make after the deaths of Clarence and Edward IV, in II.ii of *Richard III*. Part of it runs thus:

QUEEN ELIZABETH Ah for my husband, for my dear Lord Edward!
CHILDREN Ah for our father, for our dear Lord Clarence!
DUCHESS Alas for both, both mine, Edward and Clarence!
QUEEN ELIZABETH What stay had I but Edward? and he's gone.
CHILDREN What stay had we but Clarence? and he's gone.
DUCHESS What stays had I but they? and they are gone. (71–6)

This lament is obviously meant to be taken seriously, and the lapse into comedy in the last line is unintentional. But the lament in *Romeo and Juliet* is a very different matter. The entire scene in which it occurs, from the Nurse's entry at its opening to the musicians' exit at its close, is high comedy, the last and richest piece of comedy in this very unusual tragedy. From the outset the audience knows that 'Nothing is here for tears, nothing to wail.' On the contrary, there is much to rejoice over: the Friar's plan is working as it was meant to work, and it looks as though Juliet will be reunited with her Romeo. The spectators can, therefore, sit back, fully aware of the factitious nature of what is happening on stage, and assess these formal outpourings of grief for what they are: so many tributes to convention from characters who have already amply demonstrated how little Juliet's happiness really means to them. The empty repetitions of key words in all the speeches, coupled with Capulet's frigidly pretty word play, emphasize the basic insincerity of what is being said. Shakespeare is burlesquing his old manner and, in order that there may be no doubt about it, he has the Nurse, as she rings the changes on three words, speak a parody of the parody the others are uttering. It is evident, I think, that by the time he wrote *Romeo and Juliet* he had come to the conclusion that the formal stylized manner of *Richard III* was not the proper vehicle for the utterance of true feeling.

A further echo of *Richard III* in the same scene suggests that he is now becoming highly critical of another feature of his earlier style, and is making dramatic capital out of his new attitude to it. After the Friar has given the order that Juliet be carried to the church, old Capulet makes yet another attempt to sum up the reversal his hopes have undergone by saying:

All things that we ordained festival
Turn from their office to black funeral:
Our instruments to melancholy bells,
Our wedding cheer to a sad burial feast,
Our solemn hymns to sullen dirges change;
Our bridal flowers serve for a buried corse;
And all things change them to the contrary. (84–90)

Essentially, this passage is the first eight lines of *Richard III* turned back to front, with very interesting results. In the context of *Romeo and Juliet*, and coming from the mouth of Capulet, the lines have lost the expansive energy they had in the mouth of Richard. Their repetitive nature is far more marked; they are altogether too much of a list; they turn in a circle, instead of moving forward. Capulet is taking an unconscionable time to say very little; and that little is blatantly platitudinous. The total effect, like that of the rest of the scene, is comic. Juliet's father, in the last words we hear from him before the final disaster, reveals himself as an unimportant self-important purveyor of commonplaces.

The predilection towards excessive listing that Shakespeare pillories in Capulet's speech was, as his self-critical eye had come to perceive when he wrote *Romeo and Juliet*, one of his major shortcomings as a poetic dramatist in his earliest plays. The lines quoted from York's retort to Margaret at page 67 are a good case in point. Having cited the Queen's lack of the desirable womanly qualities of beauty, virtue, and self-control, York adds them up, rather as though he were doing a sum in arithmetic, to reach the conclusion:

> Thou art as opposite to every good
> As the Antipodes are unto us.

That would seem to be final enough, but it is not enough for York who amplifies it by adding:

> Or as the south to the septentrion.

This is an addition that adds nothing. It merely repeats the previous line in a different and weaker form. Drama cannot afford this kind of excess. The playwright's freedom is more limited than that of other literary artists, because he cannot expect his audience to remain seated, or, in the case of many in Shakespeare's audience, actually standing, for more than two and a half hours or so. He must, therefore, practise strict economy if he is to say anything that matters. He cannot waste his efforts on the diminishing returns that long lists entail. Moreover, the various statements that York makes about women, admirably phrased though they are, are scarcely novel. The speech, once started, tends to develop its own momentum, which is dictated more by the poet's 'invention,' as the Elizabethans would have called it, his readiness to find one illustrative topic after another, than by the demands of character and situation.

A striking example of the kind of excess that reliance on a familiar topic can lead to is provided by Margaret's long speech of encouragement to her troops immediately before the battle of Tewkesbury. Here

Shakespeare seizes on the old metaphor of the ship of state and works it to death by elaborating it in the utmost detail. Margaret says:

> Great lords, wise men ne'er sit and wail their loss,
> But cheerly seek how to redress their harms.
> What though the mast be now blown overboard,
> The cable broke, the holding-anchor lost,
> And half our sailors swallow'd in the flood;
> Yet lives our pilot still. Is't meet that he
> Should leave the helm and, like a fearful lad,
> With tearful eyes add water to the sea
> And give more strength to that which hath too much;
> Whiles, in his moan, the ship splits on the rock, 10
> Which industry and courage might have sav'd?
> Ah, what a shame! ah, what a fault were this!
> Say Warwick was our anchor; what of that?
> And Montague our top-mast; what of him?
> Our slaught'red friends the tackles; what of these?
> Why, is not Oxford here another anchor?
> And Somerset another goodly mast?
> The friends of France our shrouds and tacklings?
> And, though unskilful, why not Ned and I
> For once allow'd the skilful pilot's charge? 20
> We will not from the helm to sit and weep,
> But keep our course, though the rough wind say no,
> From shelves and rocks that threaten us with wreck.
> As good to chide the waves as speak them fair.
> And what is Edward but a ruthless sea?
> What Clarence but a quicksand of deceit?
> And Richard but a ragged fatal rock?
> All these the enemies to our poor bark.
> Say you can swim; alas, 'tis but a while!
> Tread on the sand; why, there you quickly sink. 30
> Bestride the rock; the tide will wash you off,
> Or else you famish – that's a threefold death.
> This speak I, lords, to let you understand,
> If case some one of you would fly from us,
> That there's no hop'd-for mercy with the brothers
> More than with ruthless waves, with sands, and rocks.
> Why, courage then! What cannot be avoided
> 'Twere childish weakness to lament or fear.
>
> (3 *Henry* VI v.iv.1–38)

Dover Wilson, in his note on this speech, calls it 'fine,' and says that it 'gives a measure of Shakespeare's poetic and dramatic power in 1592.'* It seems to me that this comment is radically wrong on both counts. 'Poetically' the oration is laboured and more than a little mechanical. Reading it or listening to it, one cannot but be aware of the conscious and deliberate effort that has gone into establishing a congruence between the various parts of the ship and the various leaders and forces – some of them rather inadequate substitutes for lost leaders and forces – that make up Margaret's army. The ingenuity of it all is unquestionable, but there is something rather dogged about that ingenuity; the determination to produce the perfect match is all too evident. And, before the speech is over, even the ingenuity has broken down. When Margaret says,

> Bestride the rock; the tide will wash you off,
> Or else you famish – that's a threefold death,

her words apply well enough to the idea of a rock as a temporary but dangerous refuge in a high sea, but they are patently absurd when the rock in question is Richard Duke of Gloucester. No one in her army is ever likely to view Richard as a refuge of any kind. Nor is the speech any more defensible on dramatic grounds. Intended to stir up a spirit of defiance and determination to conquer in the men it is addressed to, it says, in effect, through its equating of the three Yorkist brothers with some of the great elemental forces of nature, that all resistance is vain. Moreover, it is ill-timed. The audience is awaiting the clash of the two armies, and is, therefore, likely to feel frustrated when its expectations have to be postponed, instead of being gratified fairly rapidly. It is clear, I think, that Shakespeare has yielded to 'the fascination of what's difficult,' the temptation to take an old image, rework it, elaborate on it, and make it fit a specific situation, to the detriment of his play as a whole. The poet and the rhetorician in him have taken over from, and for the time being submerged, the dramatist in him.

He was not, it must be added, totally unaware of this danger when writing *3 Henry VI*. There is a most interesting moment in the play when he seems to catch himself in the very act, as it were. At the opening of II.v, with the battle of Towton raging around him, Henry VI enters alone, and speaks to the following effect:

> This battle fares like to the morning's war,
> When dying clouds contend with growing light,
> What time the shepherd, blowing of his nails,
> Can neither call it perfect day nor night.

* *3 Henry VI* ed J. Dover Wilson, Cambridge 1952, p 200

> Now sways it this way, like a mighty sea
> Forc'd by the tide to combat with the wind;
> Now sways it that way, like the selfsame sea
> Forc'd to retire by fury of the wind.
> Sometime the flood prevails, and then the wind;
> Now one the better, then another best;
> Both tugging to be victors, breast to breast,
> Yet neither conqueror nor conquered.
> So is the equal poise of this fell war. (II.v.1–13)

The main purpose behind these lines is a utilitarian one: to acquaint the audience with the state of the battle. But there is nothing utilitarian about the way in which that purpose is carried out. The two similes through which the necessary information is conveyed are worked out with loving care; and the tiny cameo of 'the shepherd, blowing of his nails,' in order to warm his hands, brings a wonderful touch of immediacy and specificity to the first of them. In the second, however, where there is almost a simile within the simile when the tide and the wind are depicted as a couple of wrestlers, 'Both tugging to be victors, breast to breast,' the image is developed at length and in such detail that by the time it reaches its conclusion a spectator in the theatre, unable to refer back, as the reader can, to the beginning of it all, may well have forgotten what it is meant to illuminate. Shakespeare seems to have become alive to this difficulty immediately on completing the simile, for he takes the necessary steps to remind us of what it is about by adding at the end of it, almost as though it were an afterthought: 'So is the equal poise of this fell war.'

There was no need for any such explanatory appendix when he used the same image again in *Hamlet*. There, at the opening of act IV, Gertrude asks Claudius to clear the room; and then, responding to her evident agitation, Claudius asks her 'What, Gertrude? How does Hamlet?' She replies:

> Mad as the sea and wind, when both contend
> Which is the mightier.

No further development of the simile follows. It has served its purpose within the structure of a narrative which presses on to the description of action as Gertrude continues thus:

> In his lawless fit,
> Behind the arras hearing something stir,
> Whips out his rapier, cries 'A rat, a rat!'
> And in his brainish apprehension kills
> The unseen good old man. (IV.i.5–12)

Yet brief and strictly functional as Gertrude's simile is, it still sounds and is, I think, meant to sound a little artificial and literary within the context of the play, thus serving as a reminder that at this point in her story the Queen is not telling the whole truth but keeping the promise she made to her son, not to reveal that he is 'mad in craft' (III.iv.188).

Henry VI's lines quoted above also bring out another strongly marked feature of the early manner: its tendency to make two lines, or even one, the basic unit of sense as well as of metre. The first eight lines fall neatly into four distinct couplets sharply separated from one another, with their separateness endorsed by the use of rhyme and of repetition. But such a unit, adequate and suitable though it may be for some purposes, such as the keen encounter of wits between Richard and Anne in the second scene of *Richard III*, has a cramping and confining effect when it provides the staple for a long speech, or, as it does in *3 Henry VI*, for an entire play. It lacks flexibility, and leaves no room for the individual voice to make itself heard. Consequently, the characterization suffers. Figures who express themselves in a basically similar manner tend to make a similar impression on the mind; it is not easy for the reader – the spectator is, or should be, at an advantage in this respect – to keep the secondary characters in the Three Parts of *Henry VI* distinct from one another. The Earl of Warwick, for example, appears in each of those Three Parts, playing a considerable role and exerting a powerful influence on events in Parts Two and Three, yet he leaves little sense of a personality behind him when he dies in act v of Part Three. If one remembers him at all, it is as 'the Kingmaker'; but that is about the sum of it. He has not the stuff of life in him; he says nothing that is really memorable.

Significantly, it is the secondary and even minor characters who speak prose that come to life: Jack Cade and his followers in Part Two of *Henry VI*, and the two murderers of Clarence in *Richard III*. The mere fact that prose is their manner of utterance serves to set them apart from the verse speakers, of course, to make them stand out as different, and therefore to give them a better opportunity of making their mark. But, not only do they speak in prose, they also speak remarkably good prose – good in the sense that it renders, with devastating accuracy, the thought processes, or more often the muddle processes, of the mind from which it comes. Cade's plans for a communist state which will simultaneously be a monarchy with himself as the king of it, together with his followers' enthusiastic reception of this self-contradictory idea, are very much a case in point. He tells the crowd, in a speech which effectively puts an end to the sceptical asides that have punctuated his discourse so far and turns the hitherto critical Dick the Butcher into a fervent supporter of 'reformation':

Be brave, then, for your captain is brave, and vows reformation. There shall be in England seven halfpenny loaves sold for a penny; the three-hoop'd pot shall have ten hoops; and I will make it felony to drink small beer. All the realm shall be in common, and in Cheapside shall my palfrey go to grass. And when I am king – as king I will be –
ALL God save your Majesty!
CADE I thank you, good people – there shall be no money; all shall eat and drink on my score, and I will apparel them all in one livery, that they may agree like brothers, and worship me their lord.
DICK The first thing we do, let's kill all the lawyers.
CADE Nay, that I mean to do. (IV.ii.61–74)

This prose is a far more economical and versatile instrument than the verse which is the staple of *Henry VI* and *Richard III*, because it is capable of so many things at one and the same time. It reveals the absurdity of Cade's proposals – seven halfpenny loaves are to be sold for a penny in a land where the use of money has been abolished – but also the appeal that these proposals have for the mob to whom they are addressed; and, as Cade promptly picks up and appropriates for his own the suggestion of Dick the Butcher, we are made to see his shrewdness as a mob leader and his determination not to relinquish that leadership to any of his followers. The Cade scenes are, in fact, grotesque comedy of a high order. They amuse while they terrify. The rebels are thick-headed fools, but they are also powerful and dangerous, as the wretched Clerk of Chatham discovers when he is hanged for the crime of being literate.

The freedom which the looser element of prose brings with it is particularly evident in the scene in *Richard III*, I.iv, in which the two Murderers of Clarence discuss the issue of conscience while their victim-to-be sleeps. Their concern is with one of the major themes of the play, which they illuminate by approaching it from an essentially practical point of view, asking whether any material advantage can come from heeding the promptings of conscience. When the Second Murderer, having come to the conclusion that it would be a damnable thing to kill the sleeping duke, decides to let him live, the dialogue runs thus:

1 MURDERER I'll back to the Duke of Gloucester and tell him so.
2 MURDERER Nay, I prithee, stay a little. I hope this passionate humour of mine will change; it was wont to hold me but while one tells twenty.
1 MURDERER How dost thou feel thyself now?
2 MURDERER Faith, some certain dregs of conscience are yet within me.

1 MURDERER Remember our reward, when the deed's done.
2 MURDERER Zounds, he dies; I had forgot the reward.
1 MURDERER Where's thy conscience now?
2 MURDERER O, in the Duke of Gloucester's purse!
1 MURDERER When he opens his purse to give us our reward, thy conscience flies out.
2 MURDERER 'Tis no matter; let it go; there's few or none will entertain it.
1 MURDERER What if it come to thee again?
2 MURDERER I'll not meddle with it – it makes a man a coward: a man cannot steal, but it accuseth him; a man cannot swear, but it checks him; a man cannot lie with his neighbour's wife, but it detects him. 'Tis a blushing shamefac'd spirit that mutinies in a man's bosom; it fills a man full of obstacles: it made me once restore a purse of gold that – by chance I found. It beggars any man that keeps it. It is turn'd out of towns and cities for a dangerous thing; and every man that means to live well endeavours to trust to himself and live without it. (I.iv.115–42)

The position the Second Murderer reaches in his final speech there is substantially the same as Richard's, but he has arrived at it in a witty topsy-turvy fashion that is not without its satirical overtones, especially in the meaning it gives to the words 'to live well.' He has 'talked himself alive,' as F.E. Halliday neatly puts it when referring to Hotspur;* and both he and his companion continue to live in our minds as they turn, with the grim humour of professional workmen, to the task in hand:

2 MURDERER Come, shall we fall to work?
1 MURDERER Take him on the costard with the hilts of thy sword, and then chop him in the malmsey-butt in the next room.
2 MURDERER O excellent device! and make a sop of him. (151–4)

At this point, however, Clarence wakes up and, discovering the Murderers' purpose, begins to plead with them for his life. He, of course, speaks blank verse, as befits his rank and the emotional intensity of the situation in which he finds himself; and, to keep up with him, as it were, so do the Murderers. This shift in their style is a clear indication that they have now assumed another role. As the only other characters on the stage with him, they have to put the case for his death to counter his plea for life. But, as they do it, the life drains out of them. To enforce the idea of crime and punishment, which is so central to the play, they combine an intimate

* F.E. Halliday *The Poetry of Shakespeare's Plays* London 1954, p 108

knowledge of England's immediate past that would do credit to a historian with an understanding of the way in which God's justice operates in the world that would not disgrace a theologian. Their wit and humour leave them as they become metamorphosed into the counsel for Clarence's prosecution at the bar of heavenly justice. When he threatens them with divine vengeance if they kill him, they answer thus:

> 2 MURDERER And that same vengeance doth he hurl on thee
> For false forswearing, and for murder too;
> Thou didst receive the sacrament to fight
> In quarrel of the house of Lancaster.
> 1 MURDERER And like a traitor to the name of God
> Didst break that vow; and with thy treacherous blade
> Unripp'dst the bowels of thy sov'reign's son.
> 2 MURDERER Whom thou wast sworn to cherish and defend.
> 1 MURDERER How canst thou urge God's dreadful law to us,
> When thou hast broke it in such dear degree? (197–206)

Both the sentiments and the style in which they are uttered have their place in the overall design of the play; but within the scene where they occur these speeches, and others like them, coming patly, as though parts of a well-rehearsed act, from the lips of the two men we have come to know so well from their earlier exchanges with one another, cannot but seem wildly incongruous and out of character. Shakespeare's growing capacity for giving life to one part of a scene and for endowing minor figures with individuality has come into headlong collision with his perception of the need to keep the main idea which *Richard III* embodies firmly in the minds of his audience.

Did he realize what had happened? It looks as though he did, for there is no more prose in the play. The next group of common folk to make their appearance, the three Citizens who discuss the implications of Edward IV's death, are confined to blank verse and restricted to sentiments of the proverbial variety. Their one scene, II.iii, allows them no chance whatever of escaping from or disrupting the total pattern of the drama. Dighton and Forrest, the murderers of the Princes in the Tower, are also handled with circumspection, since they are not allowed on stage at all. It is just as well, for even the distancing effect that a reported version exerts is not sufficient to disguise the inconsistency between what we are told they are and what we are told they said. Tyrrel, in his soliloquy at the opening of IV.iii, describes them as 'flesh'd villains, bloody dogs,' but then goes on to repeat, for the benefit of the audience, their account of what they saw and what they did:

'O, thus' quoth Dighton 'lay the gentle babes' –
'Thus, thus,' quoth Forrest 'girdling one another
Within their alabaster innocent arms.
Their lips were four red roses on a stalk,
And in their summer beauty kiss'd each other.
A book of prayers on their pillow lay;
Which once,' quoth Forrest 'almost chang'd my mind;
But, O, the devil' – there the villain stopp'd;
When Dighton thus told on: 'We smothered
The most replenished sweet work of nature
That from the prime creation e'er she framed'. (9–19)

These lines, the most lyrical in the entire play, self-consciously contrived and high wrought, have been dictated by other considerations than the need to observe decorum between character and mode of utterance: Shakespeare's end is to move his audience to tears; and, as we listen, it is Shakespeare we are aware of, ventriloquizing through the two dummies.

But, although prose is employed in only one part of one scene in *Richard III*, prose diction has a very important function within the play. Richard speaks two different languages. In his public statements he shows himself the most accomplished rhetorician of all the characters in this rhetorically accomplished drama. Playing one role after another with the verve and the gusto of a virtuoso in the art of acting, he adapts his manner of speech to the part he is taking – kind brother, bold lover, devoted son, indulgent uncle, and so forth. But in his soliloquies and asides he removes the mask, as it were, and speaks to the audience *in propria persona*, using a mocking, blasphemous, slangy manner that we soon come to accept as his authentic voice. The shift from the one mode to the other is, for instance, very clear indeed when he makes his entry into II.ii. The Duchess of York, Queen Elizabeth, and the Son and Daughter of Clarence are busy lamenting the death of Edward IV and Clarence's murder. Richard assumes the attitude appropriate to the situation. Speaking first to Queen Elizabeth, he says:

Sister, have comfort. All of us have cause
To wail the dimming of our shining star;
But none can help our harms by wailing them.

Then, turning to the old Duchess of York, he continues:

Madam, my mother, I do cry you mercy;
I did not see your Grace. Humbly on my knee
I crave your blessing.

He is speaking and behaving exactly as an Elizabethan son was expected to do on coming into the presence of his mother; and the Duchess in response says the ritual words and makes the ritual gesture:

> God bless thee; and put meekness in thy breast,
> Love, charity, obedience, and true duty!

Richard replies with the expected 'Amen!', but then adds in a mocking aside that invites the complicity of the audience:

> And make me die a good old man!
> That is the butt end of a mother's blessing;
> I marvel that her Grace did leave it out. (101–11)

The pieties and proprieties, which are such an essential part of the divine scheme of things that Richard is challenging, have been rendered ridiculous in a way that the original audiences for the play must have found at once shocking and exciting; and much of the damage they have suffered has been done by the slang term 'butt end.' Its occurrence here is cited by the OED as the earliest example of its use in the sense of 'fag-end.'

In fact, Richard has been combining blasphemy with prose diction and lowering commonplace images ever since the first scene. There, after deceiving Clarence completely about his intentions, Richard remarks as his brother leaves the stage:

> Go tread the path that thou shalt ne'er return.
> Simple, plain Clarence, I do love thee so
> That I will shortly send thy soul to heaven,
> If heaven will take the present at our hands. (I.i.117–20)

The outrageous sentiment, which turns the act of murder into a benefit, is capped by the jeering proviso of the last line. And, having discovered the dramatic potential of this kind of writing, Shakespeare exploits it still further in the soliloquy with which Richard ends the scene. As he watches Hastings go, Richard remarks of his brother Edward IV, whose illness they have just been discussing:

> He cannot live, I hope, and must not die
> Till George be pack'd with posthorse up to heaven. (145–6)

Here the reversal of normal expectations that comes with the parenthetical 'I hope' is endorsed and enriched by the ludicrous picture of Clarence as a parcel ready to be sent off by the next celestial post. Later in the same speech, after outlining his plan of action, Richard suddenly pulls himself up by saying:

> But yet I run before my horse to market. (160)

The statement is proverbial, its commoner form being 'I will not run before my mare to market' (Tilley, M649), and it has the effect of both emphasizing Richard's practical nature and also of helping to put him on a special footing with the spectators in the theatre. Since he speaks their language, he must, unlike the other major figures in the play, have much in common with them. Moreover, Richard not only speaks the language of the audience when addressing them directly but he also confides in the audience. His soliloquies and asides supply them with the information they need, advance information, about his plots and plans, so that they are then in a position where they can savour to the full the unconscious irony with which his victims unsuspectingly invite their dooms and go to them. He is so helpful that it is difficult not to feel grateful to him.

Richard has, then, a distinctive idiom of his own, the perfect vehicle for the bizarre humour that he is so addicted to, especially in the first half of the play; and the most marked feature of this idiom is its use of what I have described as prose diction. But, while many of the words he employs are colloquial and belong to the language of everyday life, and while the word order is that of prose, there is nothing colloquial about his rhythms; the regular beat of the blank verse line is impeccably preserved in everything he says. Shakespeare, it would seem, still accepts and adheres to the well-established convention that blank verse which immediately and unremittingly identifies itself as blank verse is the only proper medium for upper-class and royal characters to express themselves through and the only medium consonant with the dignity of tragedy. Moreover, Richard's consistent resort to blank verse has the positive effect of helping to ensure that he, who has so much of the Vice and the Clown in his make-up, never degenerates into an early version of Mr Punch.

Parody and Linguistic Exuberance in the Early Comedies

Comedy, unlike tragedy, sets no store by dignity or by decorum, and thus invites experiment and innovation more readily then tragedy does. In *The Comedy of Errors,* which may well be the earliest of all Shakespeare's comedies, one can see the poetic dramatist gradually at first, and then with increasing rapidity, opening up one new possibility after another. The initial scene, in deliberate contrast to what is to follow it, is near-tragic in the situation it presents, close to the Henry VI plays in its concern with 'mortal and intestine jars' (11), and near-epic in the manner in which it narrates the past. There is an unmistakable echo of Virgil in the lines with which Aegeon begins his tale:

> A heavier task could not have been impos'd
> Than I to speak my griefs unspeakable. (I.i.32–3)

They are a rendering of Aeneas's reply, at the opening of book II of the *Aeneid,* to Dido's request that he tell the story of the fall of Troy:

> *Infandum, regina, jubes renovare dolorem.*

Nor is there any abrupt change in manner when the comedy proper begins with scene ii. The subject is still the 'jars' between Ephesus and Syracuse, the fate of Aegeon, and the risk of sharing that fate which Antipholus of Syracuse will run if he fails to take precautions. The medium continues to be blank verse. Our first assurance that the play is indeed to be a comedy, as its title promises, does not come until line 41, when the wrong Dromio enters, the misunderstandings start, and the comic device of repetition makes its initial appearance. Asked by Antipholus of Syracuse, 'How chance thou art return'd so soon?', Dromio of Ephesus replies:

> Return'd so soon! rather approach'd too late.
> The capon burns, the pig falls from the spit;
> The clock hath strucken twelve upon the bell –
> My mistress made it one upon my cheek;
> She is so hot because the meat is cold,
> The meat is cold because you come not home,
> You come not home because you have no stomach,
> You have no stomach, having broke your fast;
> But we, that know what 'tis to fast and pray,
> Are penitent for your default to-day. (I.ii.43–52)

These lines are not, I think, simply a matter of the servant speaking blank verse because his master does, but rather of fun being made out of the contrast between the rigid verse form and its prosaic content. Furthermore, the rhetorical device – Puttenham calls it '*Clymax*, or the Marching figure'* – that shapes the narrative from line 47 to line 50 is normally met with in contexts that are quite unlike this one. Spenser, who was very fond of it, employs it in an especially memorable fashion in his description of the Bower of Bliss (*The Faerie Queene* II.xii.71), and Kyd works it extremely hard in the passage in which Balthazar, in *The Spanish Tragedy*, lists the various grievances he has against Horatio:

> I think Horatio be my destin'd plague:
> First in his hand he brandished a sword,
> And with that sword he fiercely waged war,
> And in that war he gave me dangerous wounds,
> And by those wounds he forced me to yield,
> And by my yielding I became his slave.
> Now in his mouth he carries pleasing words,
> Which pleasing words do harbour sweet conceits,
> Which sweet conceits are lim'd with sly deceits,
> Which sly deceits smooth Bel-imperia's ears,
> And through her ears dive down into her heart,
> And in her heart set him, where I should stand. (II.i.118–29)

Whether the audience at the earliest performances of *The Comedy of Errors* did or did not associate Dromio's lines with Balthazar's – and the

* George Puttenham *The Arte of English Poesie* (1589), with an introduction by Baxter Hathaway, Kent, Ohio 1970, p 217

popularity of Kyd's play makes it likely that some of them could have done so – they can hardly have been unaware of the element of burlesque that the rhetorical figure brings with it when the speaker is a servant and the subject a dinner that is growing cold. And from this point onwards the tendency towards burlesque gains ground. Any speech that smacks of the passionate or the 'poetical' is suspect. Adriana speaks from the heart, even though it be the heart of a shrew, when, in II.ii, she accuses her husband, as she thinks him to be, of having lost interest in her and of infidelity to her. There is no mistaking the sense of pain and the tone of reproach that inform her utterance when she says, for example:

> How dearly would it touch thee to the quick,
> Shouldst thou but hear I were licentious,
> And that this body, consecrate to thee,
> By ruffian lust should be contaminate!
> Wouldst thou not spit at me and spurn at me,
> And hurl the name of husband in my face,
> And tear the stain'd skin off my harlot-brow,
> And from my false hand cut the wedding-ring,
> And break it with a deep-divorcing vow? (II.ii.129–37)

At the same time, however, there is, even in these nine lines, more than a touch of excess and extravagance; and it becomes still more pronounced in the speech as a whole, which runs to no fewer than thirty-seven lines. If it could be taken straight, the speech would at least verge on the absurd. But within the play it cannot be taken straight. Adriana is addressing not her husband, as she thinks, but his twin brother, who has no idea whatever of what she is talking about. Few things are more ludicrous than the misdirected moral diatribe; and *The Comedy of Errors* is full of such outbursts, especially from Adriana.

The comic potentialities of the misdirected reproof and, along with it, of the misunderstood persuasion to love, are exploited to the full in III.ii. This scene opens with a long speech from Luciana chiding and upbraiding Antipholus of Syracuse, whom she takes for her brother-in-law, for his neglect of his wife, her sister, and for what appears to her as his newly conceived and adulterous passion for herself. Full of moral saws and evocative imagery, this dissuasion from love is fittingly cast in the form of quatrains in alternate rhyme, with a very close coincidence between the verse unit and the sense unit. Appropriately, Antipholus of Syracuse responds in the same form, working the hyperboles of Elizabethan love poetry for all they are worth and piling them up in a crescendo which is at once splendid and absurd. His retort to Luciana's plea that he should treat her sister more kindly is:

Sweet mistress – what your name is else, I know not,
Nor by what wonder you do hit of mine –
Less in your knowledge and your grace you show not
Than our earth's wonder – more than earth, divine.
Teach me, dear creature, how to think and speak;
Lay open to my earthy-gross conceit,
Smoth'red in errors, feeble, shallow, weak,
The folded meaning of your words' deceit.
Against my soul's pure truth why labour you
To make it wander in an unknown field?
Are you a god? Would you create me new?
Transform me, then, and to your pow'r I'll yield.
But if that I am I, then well I know
Your weeping sister is no wife of mine,
Nor to her bed no homage do I owe;
Far more, far more, to you do I decline.
O, train me not, sweet mermaid, with thy note,
To drown me in thy sister's flood of tears.
Sing, siren, for thyself, and I will dote;
Spread o'er the silver waves thy golden hairs,
And as a bed I'll take them, and there lie;
And in that glorious supposition think
He gains by death that hath such means to die.
Let Love, being light, be drowned if she sink. (III.ii.29–52)

This far-fetched outburst of lyricism is clearly designed to create the same reaction in an audience as that with which Berowne responds to Longaville's sonnet in praise of Maria in *Love's Labour's Lost*:

This is the liver-vein, which makes flesh a deity,
A green goose a goddess – pure, pure idolatry. (IV.iii.70–1)

Yet the speech has evidently been written *con amore*. Shakespeare has found a most ingenious and satisfying way, which he will go on developing for some time, of putting his own predilections as a poet to dramatic use. He is giving free rein to that love of image and figure which is already so apparent in *Titus Andronicus*, but he is doing it now in a manner which has nothing of the self-indulgent about it. On the contrary, the speech fulfils the dramatic functions of defining Antipholus's love – love at first sight, doting – and of having a favourable effect on the reluctant Luciana, who will tell her sister, in IV.ii, that Antipholus spoke to her:

With words that in an honest suit might move. (14)

Shakespeare continues to play the same game in the latter part of the scene after Luciana has gone and Dromio of Syracuse has made his entry. Like his master, Dromio has just been 'claimed' by a woman he has never seen before, Nell the kitchen-wench; and, still like his master singing the praise of Luciana, he resorts to far-fetched images in order to describe her. But, whereas Antipholus's images, coloured by the idea of metamorphosis, are glowing and romantic, Dromio's, also coloured by the idea of metamorphosis, are earthy and, eventually, bawdy to boot. His statement that Nell is 'a wondrous fat marriage' provokes the question 'How dost thou mean a fat marriage?' to which he replies:

> Marry, sir, she's the kitchen-wench, and all grease; and I know not what use to put her to but to make a lamp of her and run from her by her own light. I warrant, her rags and the tallow in them will burn a Poland winter. If she lives till doomsday, she'll burn a week longer than the whole world. (III.ii.92–9)

By that associative process, which is so characteristically Shakespearean, the mention of doomsday leads on to a reference to Noah's flood, incapable, according to Dromio, of washing the engrained grime from Nell's face, and thence to his equation of her figure with a globe. It is all, in its own fashion, quite as hyperbolical as Antipholus's glorification of Luciana. The prose of the servant counterpoints the verse of the master; and when Dromio goes on to find geographical analogies to the various parts of the female form he is, in effect, doing exactly what Queen Margaret does in the address to her forces before the battle of Tewkesbury quoted at page 79. On this occasion, however, the different items in the overall analogy are separated from one another by Antipholus's questions which prompt them. Oratory has given way to dialogue; dogged persistence to lively ingenuity.

At the end of his virtuoso performance Dromio relates how he ran from Nell, thinking her a witch, and he concludes by saying:

> And, I think, if my breast had not been made of faith, and my heart of steel,
> She had transform'd me to a curtal dog, and made me turn i' th' wheel. (143–4)

This shambling, tumbling couplet does indeed smack of the 'jigging veins of riming mother wits,' even , perhaps, of the old Plough Monday plays. Nor is this the first occasion on which we have encountered verse of this kind in *The Comedy of Errors*. Writing a play in which slapstick incident and humour have a large part, Shakespeare does not hesitate to let the Dromios in particular talk in the manner and the metres of the interludes.

The comic possibilities inherent in double rhymes seem to have occurred to him during the course of II.i, where, after Dromio of Ephesus has given his account of his meeting with Antipholus of Syracuse in the previous scene, a meeting which resulted in his being beaten, Adriana threatens him with yet another beating if he does not renew his errand. Thereupon Dromio says:

> Am I so round with you, as you with me,
> That like a football you do spurn me thus?
> You spurn me hence, and he will spurn me hither;
> If I last in this service, you must case me in leather. (82–5)

The bouncing rhythms of the last two lines are peculiarly appropriate as a means of expression for one whose lot throughout the play will be to serve as a kind of football for others to kick around as they please. Moreover, there can be no doubt that at one point at least in the play Shakespeare had the old morality plays very much in mind. Having seen Antipholus of Ephesus arrested by an Officer in IV.i, Dromio of Syracuse returns to the house to fetch his 'master's' purse. On his arrival, Adriana asks him: 'Where is thy master, Dromio? Is he well?' The answer she receives is:

> No, he's in Tartar limbo, worse than hell.
> A devil in an everlasting garment hath him;
> One whose hard heart is button'd up with steel;
> A fiend, a fairy, pitiless and rough;
> A wolf, nay worse, a fellow all in buff;
> A back-friend, a shoulder-clapper, one that countermands
> The passages of alleys, creeks, and narrow lands;
> A hound that runs counter, and yet draws dry-foot well;
> One that, before the Judgment, carries poor souls to hell.
> (IV.ii.32–40)

Beginning with a regular blank verse line, this speech modulates briefly into heroic couplets, and thence into couplets of a very different kind as it moves to its climax: the evocation of the morality scene in which the devil carries the soul of sinful man off to hell on his back. It is a scene which goes back at least as far as *The Castle of Perseverance* (1405–25), where it is presented in all seriousness, though not without a touch of humour. By the 1590s, however, it had evidently become comic in its old-fashioned technique, for Shakespeare was not the first playwright to mock it; Robert Greene had done that at some length in scene XV of his *Friar Bacon and Friar Bungay* (c 1590), where Bacon's servant Miles gets rather the better of the devil who has come to take him off by donning spurs as a preliminary to mounting on his back.

Often dismissed as a play that 'depends almost entirely on plot, with little characterisation, and still less poetry,'* – the words are Ifor Evans's, but the view they express continues to be widely held – *The Comedy of Errors* is, if the foregoing analysis of some of its features has any validity, a work in which poetry is used, and very skilfully used in an innovative manner that yet has its roots deep in the past, for purposes that are strictly dramatic. To those who seek for purple passages or listen for Shakespeare's 'native wood-notes wild' it has, it is true, little or nothing to offer. Having carried out a rather reductive critique of it in the introduction to the New Cambridge edition, Quiller-Couch concludes by saying: 'Sundry passages, even in its farcical episodes, show us the born poet, the born romancer, itching to be at his trade.'† The example he cites, like the proverbial drowning man clutching at the proverbial straw, is taken from Antipholus of Syracuse's 'persuasion' of Luciana, quoted at page 92. Shakespeare is indeed 'at his trade' here; but the trade in question is that of the poetic dramatist not that of 'the born romancer.'

It is fairly generally agreed these days that Shakespeare's earliest essays in the field of comedy were *The Comedy of Errors, The Taming of the Shrew*, and *The Two Gentlemen of Verona*, and that this order probably represents the chronology of their composition. A number of critics, following the lead of Peter Alexander,‡ also take the view that all three plays were written before the disastrous plague of 1592–4, which closed the London theatres for the best part of two years. There are others, however, who prefer to think of *The Two Gentlemen* as dating from the time when the theatres reopened, because they see it as a very different kind of play from the other two. My own belief is that Alexander and those who agree with him are in the right. In terms of the development of Shakespeare's dramatic poetry, neither *The Taming of the Shrew* nor *The Two Gentlemen of Verona* shows much advance on *The Comedy of Errors*. In the two later plays Shakespeare seems content to exploit further some, though not all, of the discoveries he had made in his adaptation of Plautus's *Menaechmi*, without introducing much that is radically new in the way of technique. Indeed, if one looks at the three plays with an eye for their structure and their style, the similarities between them are far more marked than their differences. The basic elements are the same in each: two young men, their two servants, and two young women. Moreover, in all three 'poetical' flights carry warning signals with them. In *The Taming of the Shrew* Lucentio's highly conventional exclamations

* Ifor Evans *The Language of Shakespeare's Plays* London 1966, p 18

† *The Comedy of Errors* ed Sir Arthur Quiller-Couch and John Dover Wilson, Cambridge 1922, p xxii

‡ Peter Alexander *Shakespeare's Life and Art* London 1939

of admiration when he sees Bianca for the first time are indicative of certain limitations in him. Having compared her first to Minerva and then to Europa, he goes on to say to his servant:

> Tranio, I saw her coral lips to move,
> And with her breath she did perfume the air;
> Sacred and sweet was all I saw in her. (I.i.169–71)

The modern reader, familiar with Sonnet 130, knows how to respond to this; he remembers:

> My mistress' eyes are nothing like the sun;
> Coral is far more red than her lips' red;
> ...
> And in some perfumes is there more delight
> Than in the breath that from my mistress reeks.
> I love to hear her speak, yet well I know
> That music hath a far more pleasing sound;
> I grant I never saw a goddess go –
> My mistress when she walks treads on the ground.

But an audience in the year 1590, or thereabouts, could hardly be expected to know Sonnet 130, though the close correlation between it and Lucentio's speech suggests that it may well have been written around that time, so, to make the same point that it makes, Shakespeare has Tranio turn to the audience and say to them:

> Nay, then 'tis time to stir him from his trance.

Over against the linguistic debility of Lucentio is set the linguistic vitality of Petruchio. In many ways a comic version of Richard III, Petruchio, like Richard, is a consummate actor-manager. He writes his own scenario, plays his part in it with gusto, dons the appropriate inappropriate costume for his wedding, carries the action 'politicly' through to the conclusion he has in mind for it, and even takes the audience into his confidence. Like Richard, he is a master of the art of rhetoric; and his stichomythic wooing of Katherina comes close to being a parody of Richard's wooing of the Lady Anne. Moreover, just as Richard in his asides and soliloquies often uses a prose diction, so Petruchio draws his images either from the natural world or from common life. When wooing the recalcitrant Katherina he tells her, for example:

> Kate like the hazel-twig
> Is straight and slender, and as brown in hue
> As hazel-nuts, and sweeter than the kernels. (II.i.246–8)

There is a strength and a freshness here that make Lucentio's praise of Bianca appear stale, insipid, and bookish; and the same qualities make themselves felt again in his dispraise of the gown the Tailor has fashioned for Katherina:

> O mercy, God! what masquing stuff is here?
> What's this? A sleeve? 'Tis like a demi-cannon.
> What, up and down, carv'd like an apple-tart?
> Here's snip and nip and cut and slish and slash,
> Like to a censer in a barber's shop. (IV.iii.87–91)

The impression of linguistic vigour and fertility conveyed by these lines is confirmed by a glance at the OED, which cites this passage as the earliest instance of 'snip' in the sense of a small cut made with scissors; appears not to know 'nip,' meaning 'tuck,' at all; cites 'slish' as a nonce-word; and gives no example of 'slash,' for a slit made in a garment, before 1615. It is hardly surprising that a character who can impose his will on the English language in this manner should succeed in imposing it on other characters in the play.

Closely linked with Petruchio's linguistic inventiveness is his skill in the art of picturesque abuse. His rating of the Tailor anticipates the kind of thing that Falstaff and Prince Hal would be saying to each other a few years later:

> O monstrous arrogance! Thou liest, thou thread, thou thimble,
> Thou yard, three-quarters, half-yard, quarter, nail,
> Thou flea, thou winter-cricket thou –
> Brav'd in mine own house with a skein of thread!
> Away, thou rag, thou quantity, thou remnant. ... (IV.iii.106–10)

Shakespeare has discovered a new use for the list, or rather, perhaps, rediscovered an old use of it, since this is the kind of thing that one associates with the work of Skelton, Dunbar, and other proficients in the art of flyting. But, while Petruchio makes poetry out of 'unpoetical' material, his normal medium of expression is, like Richard III's, blank verse. His modulations into prose are few, and they all come in the last two acts. Among them is what is, I think, the most intimate moment between him and Kate in the entire play. In V.ii, after she and Petruchio have witnessed the *dénouement* of the Lucentio-Bianca affair, Kate says to him: 'Husband, let's follow to see the end of this ado.' This dialogue follows:

> PETRUCHIO First kiss me, Kate, and we will.
> KATHERINA What, in the midst of the street?
> PETRUCHIO What, art thou asham'd of me? (128–30)

The shift into prose suggests that for the moment at any rate both of them have dropped the masks they have been wearing hitherto in their dealings with each other.

One other feature of the play looks forward in an interesting manner. Even in Elizabethan drama, where the action usually begins at the beginning, there are often events that have to be reported, because, though germane to the action, they cannot, for various reasons, be staged. The dramatist is then faced with the problem of how to write a narrative that not merely tells what has happened earlier, or what is actually taking place off stage, but tells it in such a fashion that the audience sees it all in its mind's eye and accepts it as part of the action. In the early histories, partly because of the recalcitrant nature of some of the essential matter, this problem had, on occasions, proved almost insoluble. Those accounts, for instance, of the historical roots of the Wars of the Roses, which take up so much space in II.v of *1 Henry VI* and II.ii of *2 Henry VI*, can never have been exactly compulsive listening or compulsive reading. In *The Taming of the Shrew*, however, Shakespeare triumphs over some of the limitations of the stage and makes dramatic capital out of them. The horse on which Petruchio arrives for his wedding could not be shown for two good reasons: horses were not, so far as we know, allowed on the Elizabethan stage; and a horse in the state this is supposed to be in, a victim of every ill that horseflesh is heir to, could not possibly have staggered on to any stage. But, in the wonderful prose aria describing it that Shakespeare gives to Biondello in III.ii, there it is, as large as life and twice as decrepit. As for the wedding itself, it would, if staged, have proved shocking to the religious susceptibilities of the time, and probably have been regarded as blasphemous. But in Gremio's account of it he, badly shaken by what he has seen, acts as a kind of shock-absorber and transmits only the hilarity of the whole thing to the audience:

I'll tell you, Sir Lucentio: when the priest
Should ask if Katherine should be his wife,
'Ay, by gogs-wouns' quoth he, and swore so loud
That, all amaz'd, the priest let fall the book;
And as he stoop'd again to take it up,
This mad-brain'd bridegroom took him such a cuff
That down fell priest and book, and book and priest.
'Now take them up,' quoth he 'if any list.'
TRANIO What said the wench, when he rose again?
GREMIO Trembled and shook, for why he stamp'd and swore
As if the vicar meant to cozen him.
But after many ceremonies done
He calls for wine: 'A health!' quoth he, as if

He had been aboard, carousing to his mates
After a storm; quaff'd off the muscadel,
And threw the sops all in the sexton's face,
Having no other reason
But that his beard grew thin and hungerly
And seem'd to ask him sops as he was drinking.
This done, he took the bride about the neck,
And kiss'd her lips with such a clamorous smack
That at the parting all the church did echo.
And I, seeing this, came thence for very shame;
And after me, I know, the rout is coming.
Such a mad marriage never was before. (III.ii.154–78)

The speech is characterized by its disciplined exuberance. Poetry is being made out of events that follow one another rapidly and compete in outrageousness with one another. Images there are none; but the beard that 'grew thin and hungerly' is vividly present in all its particularity. Moreover, new things are being done with the blank verse line here. The first four lines fall into two blank verse couplets; but the next sense unit runs to three lines, not two, with a marked slide of both sense and rhythm from the end of the second line to the beginning of the third. And this new-found freedom is even more evident in the eight lines that start with the words 'But after many ceremonies done.' Here the heavy stops all occur within the line, not at the end of it, giving a sense of the speaking, as distinct from the declaiming, voice, an effect that is increased and endorsed by the short line 'Having no other reason.' This is a speech that enacts the events it describes.

In *The Two Gentlemen of Verona* verse of this kind, when it does occur, is found in the mouths of the women rather than of the men. Julia, for instance, makes use of it when, disguised as Sebastian, she tells her pathetic tale of playing the part of Ariadne 'trimm'd in Madam Julia's gown,' a part,

Which I so lively acted with my tears
That my poor mistress, moved therewithal,
Wept bitterly; and would I might be dead
If I in thought felt not her very sorrow. (IV.iv.164–8)

In fact, throughout the greater part of the play the two women speak an altogether plainer and simpler language than the two men and, when they do resort to imagery, it is drawn for the most part, like Petruchio's, from the natural world, as in Julia's comparison of her patient self to 'The current that with gentle murmur glides' (II.vii.25–38). Moreover, Silvia in particular does not mince matters. Finding Proteus under her window, she asks him: 'What's your will?', and, on receiving the impudent and ambiguous answer: 'That I may compass yours,' she proceeds to put him in his place in no uncertain terms, saying to him:

> You have your wish; my will is even this,
> That presently you hie you home to bed.
> Thou subtle, perjur'd, false, disloyal man,
> Think'st thou I am so shallow, so conceitless,
> To be seduced by thy flattery
> That hast deceiv'd so many with thy vows?
> Return, return, and make thy love amends.
> For me, by this pale queen of night I swear,
> I am so far from granting thy request
> That I despise thee for thy wrongful suit,
> And by and by intend to chide myself
> Even for this time I spend in talking to thee. (IV.ii.88–100)

In the case of both women there is a close correspondence between word and deed, between the way in which they speak and the way in which they act.

When one turns to consider the men, it soon becomes clear that with them there is no such correspondence. Instead, there is a gross discrepancy between what they say and what they do. Both are much given to lyrical flights of fancy. Valentine, converted to the ranks of lovers, sings the praises of Cupid and then of Silvia in such outrageous terms that even Proteus finds himself compelled to describe his speeches as 'braggardism' (II.iv.160). Yet at the *dénouement* of the play he is quite ready to hand his precious Silvia over to Proteus as though she were a pound of tea. As for Proteus, the most beautiful lines in the comedy come from his lips. Hoist with his own petard at the end of the first act, he remarks:

> O, how this spring of love resembleth
> The uncertain glory of an April day,
> Which now shows all the beauty of the sun,
> And by and by a cloud takes all away! (I.iii.84–7)

These lines are a fitting prelude to his praise of the affective force of poetry later in the play, when he says of it:

> For Orpheus' lute was strung with poets' sinews,
> Whose golden touch could soften steel and stones,
> Make tigers tame, and huge leviathans
> Forsake unsounded deeps to dance on sands. (III.ii.78–81)

Yet these lyrical outpourings do nothing to alter the fact that he is the most unreliable character in the play, fully deserving Launce's description of him as 'a kind of a knave.' He may speak eloquently about poetry, but when Silvia remains unmoved by his 'moving words,' as he calls them, he does not hesitate to resort to rape. Indeed, the very circumstances in which the lines about Orpheus are spoken undermine their validity. They are part of Proteus's advice to the worthless Thurio telling him how to go about the wooing of Silvia, and they are precipitated by the encouraging comment from the decidedly unsympathetic and unromantic Duke of Milan:

> Ay,
> Much is the force of heaven-bred-poesy. (III.ii.71–2)

The context is a wholly cynical one in which poetry is viewed as the most effective instrument of seduction.

It is difficult when reading *The Two Gentlemen of Verona* not to be reminded of those exchanges between Touchstone and Audrey in *As You Like It* that run as follows:

> TOUCHSTONE Truly, I would the gods had made thee poetical.
> AUDREY I do not know what 'poetical' is. Is it honest in deed and word? Is it a true thing?
> TOUCHSTONE No, truly; for the truest poetry is the most feigning, and lovers are given to poetry; and what they swear in poetry may be said as lovers they do feign. (III.iii.12–18)

It is, perhaps, no accident that when Julia, having fainted, makes the speech that brings the truth to light she should do it in prose:

> O good sir, my master charg'd me to deliver a ring to Madam Silvia, which, out of my neglect, was never done. (V.iv.88–90)

The true lovers in this play are the women, who avoid verbal extravagance, and Launce, whose regular medium of expression is prose. Launce refers to Crab as a cur and as 'the sourest-natured dog that lives,' but his devotion to the animal is absolute, leading him, as he explains at the opening of IV.iv, to take on himself the punishment for Crab's various misdemeanours. Alone on the stage with Crab, Launce addresses the audience in a prose aria which, like Gremio's description of Petruchio's wedding, enacts the scene it relates in a simple colloquial diction that draws no attention to itself and thus carries complete conviction with it. Having stated how he saved Crab from being drowned at birth, Launce continues:

> If I had not had more wit than he, to take a fault upon me that he did, I think verily he had been hang'd for't; sure as I live, he had suffer'd for't. You shall judge. He thrusts me himself into the company of three or four gentleman-like dogs under the Duke's table; he had not been there, bless the mark, a pissing while but all the chamber smelt him. 'Out with the dog' says one; 'What cur is that?' says another; 'Whip him out' says the third; 'Hang him up' says the Duke. I, having been acquainted with the smell before, knew it was Crab, and goes me to the fellow that whips the dogs. 'Friend,' quoth I 'you mean to whip the dog.' 'Ay, marry do I' quoth he. 'You do him the more wrong;' quoth I 'twas I did the thing you wot of.' He makes me no more ado, but whips me out of the chamber. How many masters would do this for his servant? (IV.iv.12–27)

Almost entirely monosyllabic and devoid of imagery, this speech is at the other extreme from the 'braggardism' of Valentine in II.iv, where he says of Julia:

> She shall be dignified with this high honour –
> To bear my lady's train, lest the base earth
> Should from her vesture chance to steal a kiss
> And, of so great a favour growing proud,
> Disdain to root the summer-swelling flow'r
> And make rough winter everlastingly. (II.iv.154–9)

Unlike Launce's soliloquy, which tells us what he did for Crab and leaves us in no doubt that he actually did what he said, these lines cause us to wonder whether Valentine understands what he is saying and whether he can possibly mean it; which is, I think, exactly what they are intended to do. But, although hyperbole is almost invariably to be distrusted in these early comedies and brings the sincerity of those who resort to it into question, it is, nevertheless, the hyperbolical passages that stick in the memory, because they are so daring, so rich in imagery, and so splendidly excessive. Using them for purposes that are essentially critical, Shakespeare can afford to give his fancy the rein in cultivating deliberate overstatement. Later in his career, as Maynard Mack has so convincingly demonstrated,* he was to make overstatement the distinctive feature of the utterance of his great tragic heroes. When Valentine speaks his lines, we agree with Proteus that he is indeed guilty of 'braggardism'; but we feel no temptation to use any such word when Cleopatra says of the dead Antony:

* Maynard Mack 'The Jacobean Shakespeare' in *Jacobean Theatre* ed John Russell Brown and Bernard Harris, London 1960, pp 13–15

> His face was as the heav'ns, and therein stuck
> A sun and moon, which kept their course and lighted
> The little O, the earth. (*Antony and Cleopatra* v.ii.79–81)

It looks very much as though the caution, the scepticism, and the evident delight with which overstatement is employed in plays such as *The Two Gentlemen of Verona* were a necessary precondition for the confidence and the 'happy valiancy' with which it is handled in the tragedies that were to come.

Making a Virtue of Virtuosity: *Love's Labour's Lost* and *Richard II*

The three or four years that followed the reopening of the theatres in the summer of 1594, after the plague was over, were, it seems to me, the decisive time in the story of Shakespeare's development as a poetic dramatist. By 7 September 1598, when Francis Meres's *Palladis Tamia* was entered in the *Stationers' Register*, he was, as Meres's list shows, recognized as the author of not only *The Comedy of Errors, The Two Gentlemen of Verona, Titus Andronicus,* and *Richard III,* but also *Love's Labour's Lost, A Midsummer Night's Dream, The Merchant of Venice, King John, Richard II, Romeo and Juliet,* and *Henry IV*. It is not clear whether Meres has both parts of *Henry IV* in mind or simply Part I, nor does it matter much, since it is generally accepted that Part II must have followed hard on the heels of Part I. The writing of eight plays in four years is in itself an impressive achievement, but that achievement becomes even more impressive when one takes into account the sheer diversity of these eight plays. That diversity is only partially revealed by the Folio's division of them into Comedies, Histories, and Tragedies. *Henry IV* is a very different kind of history from *Richard II,* and the dissimilarities between *Love's Labour's Lost* and *The Merchant of Venice* are more apparent than their likenesses. One thing, however, all these plays do have in common: each of them is markedly experimental. They tend to blur the normal dramatic categories, even the categories used by Heming and Condell. Death intrudes on the butterfly world of Navarre and his courtiers; Theseus in *A Midsummer Night's Dream* brings overtones of the history play with him; and Shylock, impelled by the desire for revenge, raises issues that are not usually found in comedy, issues for which *The Merchant of Venice* can provide no satisfactory solution. Both *Richard II* and *King John* are tragical histories; *Romeo and Juliet* leans towards the history play in its concern with a minor War of the Roses, and has obvious affinities with comedies. As for *Henry IV*, it transcends even Polonius's 'tragical-comical-historical-pastoral' kind.

Behind the protean forms these plays assume there lies the artist's urge to give each kind of experience its own unique expression. But, as I have said earlier (p 35), when the artist in question is a poetic dramatist, he may well find difficulty in bringing his impulses as a poet into harmony with the theatre's demand for action and character. The Shakespeare who wrote *Love's Labour's Lost* and *Richard II* was aware of the possible conflict and devised, as I have already suggested, a temporary but also a brilliantly ingenious couple of solutions for it. In each play he puts his own predilection, at the time when it was written, for figurative speech, the pleasures of rhyme, rhetorical virtuosity, and clever word-play to dramatic use, making capital out of what had, hitherto, been something of a liability. The methods he employs to achieve this end are different in the two plays, but the results they bring have this much in common: each play is an almost unqualified artistic success of a rather special and, in the end, limited kind.

The opening of *Love's Labour's Lost*, the dialogue of Navarre and his three courtiers that precedes the arrival of Dull and Costard, is radically different from the opening of any of the plays I have considered in detail so far because it is dominated by rhymed verse. Blank verse accounts for less than a quarter of the verse lines. The other three quarters consist of rhymed couplets and quatrains in alternate rhyme, combining with each other on occasions to give the metre of *Venus and Adonis* and once, in the King's description of Armado, to make a fifteen-line sonnet, concluding with a triplet, instead of the normal couplet. In this respect the opening is a good prelude to what is to follow, for in the comedy as a whole the ratio of rhyme to blank verse is roughly two to one. In the rest of the play it is the quatrains in alternate rhyme and the couplets that take pride of place, together with their offspring the sonnet; but they are joined by heptasyllabic couplets, by snatches of ballad metre, and by the grotesque multisyllabic couplets that Sir Nathaniel devises in order to express his poor opinion of Dull in IV.ii, where he says of the constable, speaking to Holofernes:

> Sir, he hath never fed of the dainties that are bred in a book;
> He hath not eat paper, as it were; he hath not drunk ink; his
> intellect is not replenished; he is only an animal, only sensible
> in the duller parts;

And such barren plants are set before us that we thankful
should be –
Which we of taste and feeling are – for those parts that do fructify
in us more than he.
For as it would ill become me to be vain, indiscreet, or a fool,
So, were there a patch set on learning, to see him in a school.
But, omne bene, say I, being of an old father's mind:
Many can brook the weather that love not the wind. (IV.ii.22–31)

It is hardly surprising that this splendid piece of doggerel, of which it might truly be said 'It is not Poetry, but prose run mad,' has given trouble to compositors and editors ever since it first appeared in print in 1598, for they have to decide whether the bit that Peter Alexander prints as prose ('He hath not eat ... duller parts') is really prose or two lines of unrhymed verse in a very strange metre. Alexander, incidentally, seems to have been in two minds about the matter, since he capitalizes 'He.' Nor does this *tour de force* conclude the tale of the play's metrical variety; there still remain the measures in which the Pageant of the Nine Worthies staggers to its untimely end, including the exquisitely witty choice of alexandrines for the unfinished quatrain in alternate rhyme with which Sir Nathaniel seeks to introduce himself in the role of Alexander the Great.

The metrical virtuosity and inventiveness of *Love's Labour's Lost*, the ease and the grace with which it puts the forms usually associated with narrative and lyrical poetry to dramatic use, suggest that in this comedy we have a Shakespeare who is taking a holiday from the writing of blank verse and enjoying himself enormously in the process; and this impression of a mind engaged in creative play is increased and endorsed by the sheer brilliance of the language. In the mouth of Berowne puns and painted rhetoric become the servants of sparkling paradox. So does logic. Within fifty-six lines of the play's opening Berowne traps the King into offering a definition of the purpose of study – 'that to know which else we should not know' – and, having got the definition, he promptly uses it to 'prove' that the only study proper for the 'little Academe' to undertake is one that will negate every article in the edict which he and his three fellow-students have just sworn to obey. Seeing his drift, the King attempts to preserve his own plan by saying:

These be the stops that hinder study quite,
And train our intellects to vain delight.

But this objection, intended to silence Berowne, has the opposite effect; it triggers off a dazzling display of verbal and dialectical fireworks. Picking up the King's last two words, the clever courtier makes them serve his own ends, retorting:

> Why, all delights are vain; but that most vain
> Which, with pain purchas'd, doth inherit pain,
> As painfully to pore upon a book
> To seek the light of truth; while truth the while
> Doth falsely blind the eyesight of his look.
> Light, seeking light, doth light of light beguile;
> So, ere you find where light in darkness lies,
> Your light grows dark by losing of your eyes.
> Study me how to please the eye indeed,
> By fixing it upon a fairer eye;
> Who dazzling so, that eye shall be his heed,
> And give him light that it was blinded by.
> Study is like the heaven's glorious sun,
> That will not be deep-search'd with saucy looks;
> Small have continual plodders ever won,
> Save base authority from others' books.
> These earthly godfathers of heaven's lights
> That give a name to every fixed star
> Have no more profit of their shining nights
> Than those that walk and wot not what they are.
> Too much to know is to know nought but fame;
> And every godfather can give a name. (I.i.70–93)

It is safe to say that nothing like this had ever been heard before on the English stage. A logical progression of thought, skilfully designed to discredit academic pursuits as pointless and self-defeating, is combined with another process that exploits to the full the various potentialities of individual words, such as 'light' and 'eyes,' and of their opposites 'darkness' and 'blindness,' as well as of the associated words 'truth' and 'falsehood.' The result is tricksy stuff indeed; but what a joy it must have been to write it! In a well-known comment, Dr Johnson says of the line 'Light, seeking light, doth light of light beguile':

> The whole sense of this gingling declamation is only this, that *a man by too close study may read himself blind*, which might have been told with less obscurity in fewer words.*

Johnson should at least have applauded the sentiments to which the

* *Johnson on Shakespeare* ed Walter Raleigh, Oxford (1908) 1949, p 86

speech gives utterance, for they are very much his own. He found fault with Milton for looking at life through the spectacles of books, and in his *Rasselas* he has the sage, Imlac, tell the Abyssinian prince: 'It seems to me, that while you are making the choice of life, you neglect to live.'* But Johnson was put off by the word-play, otherwise he might have recognized that the line he dismisses as tautologous does, in fact, say rather more than he admits, since it includes the idea that a man may read himself metaphorically blind, in the sense that he becomes confused and muddled, as well as literally blind.

In its espousal of the proposition that women's eyes should be the object of study this speech of Berowne's anticipates and prepares the way for his paean to love in IV.iii (quoted at pp 22–3); and in the 'proof' it offers for that proposition it also anticipates his attempt in the same scene to show that black is, at least in so far as Rosaline is concerned, fair, and that no perjury has been committed in the courtiers' breaking of their oaths. In speech after speech the play transmits a sense of the mind revelling in what seem to be the infinite possibilities of language. Especially is this so in the passages of parody with which it is so richly studded. The age's love of 'copie,' of finding as many elegant variations as possible for every word and phrase, is the consistent feature of the speech of Holofernes, who makes his entry into the action with the following words:

> The deer was, as you know, sanguis, in blood; ripe as the pomewater, who now hangeth like a jewel in the ear of caelo, the sky, the welkin, the heaven; and anon falleth like a crab on the face of terra, the soil, the land, the earth. (IV.ii.3–6)

The speech is gloriously ridiculous, a perfect example of what Sir Philip Sidney, in Sonnet 15 of his *Astrophel and Stella*, describes as 'dictionaries' method,' yet it has evidently been written with enthusiasm and with a certain sense of discovery. Shakespeare did not forget that simile of the pomewater that 'hangeth like a jewel in the ear of caelo.' Very soon he was to rework it in a wholly serious context. On first seeing Juliet at the Capulets' ball, Romeo asks her name of a servant. Receiving the answer 'I know not, sir,' he goes on to say:

> O, she doth teach the torches to burn bright!
> It seems she hangs upon the cheek of night
> As a rich jewel in an Ethiop's ear. ... (*Romeo and Juliet* I.v.39–43)

The gap between the absurd and the ecstatic can be a very narrow one;

* *Johnson: Prose and Poetry* selected by Mona Wilson, London 1950, pp 444–5

context may make all the difference; and to make fun of an image is a step towards realizing its potentialities.

The mixture of mockery and love that has gone into the writing of Holofernes's part is even more marked in the special idiom that Shakespeare invents for Armado. Even before the 'fantastical Spaniard' appears, we are carefully instructed as to what we are to look out for. The King offers a character sketch of him in which the emphasis falls heavily on his linguistic eccentricities. We learn from it that Armado is

> A man in all the world's new fashion planted
> That hath a mint of phrases in his brain;

that he is much given to 'high born words'; and, from Berowne, that he is 'A man of fire-new words' (I.i.162–76). Fittingly, we hear Armado, and hear him at some length, before we are allowed to see him. His letter, read out to the courtiers by the King, shows that he shares Holofernes's addiction to lexicographical 'copie,' but along with this there goes also a fondness for constructing sentences in the form of question and answer, and for balanced antitheses. The result is to be seen in such a characteristic piece of the letter as this:

> Then for the place Where? where, I mean, I did encounter that obscene and most prepost'rous event that draweth from my snow-white pen the ebon-coloured ink which here thou viewest, beholdest, surveyest, or seest. (I.i.230–4)

Underlined and, simultaneously, punctured by Costard's monosyllabic interjections,which sum up and, in one case, anticipate all that Armado has to say, the verbosity and circumlocution of the letter are pilloried in no uncertain fashion. Yet there is all the delight that a skilled performer takes in the exercise of his art in the way in which Armado's part is written and sustained, right down to the well-deserved rebuke he addresses to the courtiers when they make fun of his portrayal of Hector in the Pageant of the Nine Worthies. It is not himself but the Trojan hero that Armado defends when he remarks to his tormentors:

> The sweet war-man is dead and rotten; sweet chucks, beat not the bones of the buried; when he breathed, he was a man. But I will forward with my device. [*To the Princess*] Sweet royalty, bestow on me the sense of hearing. (V.ii.652–5)

In giving Armado this generous gesture Shakespeare was, perhaps, making his own apology to a figure that had, it seems obvious, been a joy to dream up and set talking. There was every reason why he should, for the 'man of fire-new words' embodies, in an extreme form, the position of the King and his courtiers in this play, a position which may, in its turn, have something in common with the position of the playwright at the time when he was writing it. *Love's Labour's Lost* is much concerned with the relationship between words and things, and between speech and action. Its judgment on the first issue is concisely stated for us by Costard when he compares the three farthings Armado gave him, under the new and imposing name of 'remuneration,' with the shilling Berowne has just given him, under the older and less imposing name of 'guerdon':

> Gardon, O sweet gardon! better than remuneration;
> a 'leven-pence farthing better; most sweet gardon! ...
> Gardon – remuneration! (III.i.160–3)

As the King of France puts it in *All's Well That Ends Well*, 'The property by what it is should go / Not by the title' (II.iii.128–9). It is the verdict of common sense; but that verdict is neither easily arrived at nor readily accepted by the poet, whose currency is words. The gusto and *élan* with which the parts of Armado and Holofernes are written show Shakespeare's appreciation of the other side of the question.

So does his treatment of the King and his courtiers, which reaches its resolution in V.ii, the last scene of the play. In it the men disguise themselves as Muscovites in order to impress and, they hope, win the Princess of France and her ladies. The women, however, have been forewarned of what is to happen. They therefore exchange masks with each other, so that each of the men woos the wrong woman and undergoes the indignity of being 'dry-beaten with pure scoff,' as Berowne puts it. Nevertheless, the men decide to make the best of a bad job by reappearing in due course as themselves. The only result is that they expose themselves to more jibes, culminating in Rosaline's witty comment on their all too evident discomfiture:

> Why look you pale?
> Sea-sick, I think, coming from Muscovy. (V.ii.392–3)

At last Berowne realizes that the game is up, that he and his fellows have been led a fool's dance, and that the time has come to stop pretending and to acknowledge the truth of experience. He replies:

> Thus pour the stars down plagues for perjury.
> Can any face of brass hold longer out?
> Here stand I, lady – dart thy skill at me,
> Bruise me with scorn, confound me with a flout,
> Thrust thy sharp wit quite through my ignorance,

Cut me to pieces with thy keen conceit;
And I will wish thee never more to dance,
Nor never more in Russian habit wait.
O, never will I trust to speeches penn'd,
Nor to the motion of a school-boy's tongue,
Nor never come in vizard to my friend,
Nor woo in rhyme, like a blind harper's song.
Taffeta phrases, silken terms precise,
Three pil'd hyperboles, spruce affectation,
Figures pedantical – these summer-flies
Have blown me full of maggot ostentation.
I do forswear them; and I here protest,
By this white glove – how white the hand, God knows! –
Henceforth my wooing mind shall be express'd
In russet yeas, and honest kersey noes.
And, to begin, wench – so God help me, law! –
My love to thee is sound, sans crack or flaw.

To which Rosaline cuttingly answers:

Sans 'sans,' I pray you. (v.ii.394–416)

Taking his decision to rely on plain speaking in future – 'russet yeas, and honest kersey noes' – Berowne lingers fondly over the verbal confections he is abjuring, describing them in terms of taffeta, of silk, and of the richest and costliest sort of velvet. He is like a woman, once wealthy but now in much reduced circumstances, visiting a draper's shop; she handles stuff she adores, would dearly like to buy, but can no longer afford; and, in the very moment of turning her back on it, is still unable to resist the temptation of touching yet another bit of the precious material. This farewell to figurative expression by the master of 'painted rhetoric,' the most skilful and brilliant logic-chopper that Shakespeare ever created, is itself full almost to overflowing with dazzling figures, one begetting another. The idea of the battle of the sexes, which matters so much in this play, produces no fewer than five metaphors in the course of three and a half lines when Berowne bids Rosaline:

dart thy skill at me,
Bruise me with scorn, confound me with a flout,
Thrust thy sharp wit quite through my ignorance,
Cut me to pieces with thy keen conceit.

There is a wonderful exuberance about it all, a sense of the imagination delighting in its own creative facility; yet, at the same time, one is also conscious of the presence of the critical intelligence, assessing what is happening, and saying firmly, 'There comes a point at which this kind of thing must stop.'

It seems to me that in this climactic speech Berowne is, in a sense, speaking for his author; for in the last scene of *Love's Labour's Lost* Shakespeare does precisely what Berowne announces he is about to do but does not quite succeed in doing: he alters his style in a radical manner. The Pageant of the Nine Worthies has been played; Armado has challenged Costard to a duel; the fun is at its height; we wonder what further exhibition of affectation and absurdity is to come. What we get is the stage direction '*Enter a Messenger Mounsier Marcade*' (Q1). He is dressed in black; and with his entry a chill falls over the gay animated scene. The dialogue between him and the Princess runs thus:

> MARCADE God save you, madam!
> PRINCESS Welcome, Marcade;
> But that thou interruptest our merriment.
> MARCADE I am sorry, madam; for the news I bring
> Is heavy in my tongue. The King your father –
> PRINCESS Dead, for my life!
> MARCADE Even so; my tale is told. (V.ii.703–8)

Abruptly the movement of the verse has shifted from the major to the minor key as the reality of death intrudes on this shimmering holiday world in which even love has been seen, at any rate by the Princess and her women, 'As bombast and as lining to the time' (V.ii.769) – a diversion, a form of *Zeitvertreib*. And it has all been done by the appearance of a messenger in black and the plainest bit of dialogue in the play. The poetic dramatist has taken over, as it were, from the dramatic poet in order to make his own kind of poetry in which the words take their colouring from the circumstances in which they are spoken. There are forms of experience which cannot be expressed through 'taffeta phrases,' because, as Berowne puts it, 'Honest plain words best pierce the heart of grief' (V.ii.741).

The little scene between the Princess and Marcade is the discovery towards which the play has, from the outset, been moving. What seems to have happened in *Love's Labour's Lost* is that Shakespeare had hit on a theme that was admirably suited to his own stylistic proclivities at this stage in his career, and which, for that very reason, was the perfect vehicle for working out and resolving the conflict between the poet and the playwright in him. The play's assault on artificiality, affectation, and extravagance in speech and manners positively demanded that these things be exhibited in all their fantastic variety. And, since Shakespeare was still more than half in love with the linguistic excesses that he holds up to ridicule, he could treat them with affection as well as with judicious detachment. In the end, victory goes to the Princess and her women, to Costard, and to nature, to things and deeds, as opposed to words and dreams; but, apart from those brief yet pregnant exchanges between the Princess and Marcade, the speeches that linger in the mind after the play is over are those of Berowne, of Armado, and of Holofernes. One comes away from *Love's Labour's Lost* with the conviction that the writing of it must have been a labour of love for its author, as well as a necessary coming to terms with the knowledge he had acquired from his previous work in the theatre.

The shift away from 'Three-pil'd hyperboles' and 'Figures pedantical' was not, however, as Berowne discovered when Rosaline caught him out for using the word 'sans,' so easily made as all that. *Richard II* is, like *Love's Labour's Lost*, very much a transitional play, in the sense that in it, too, the playwright makes his fondness for poetic conceits and lyrical forms of expression serve ends that are wholly dramatic. The most striking and immediately perceptible difference between it and the histories of the first tetralogy is that far less in the form of outward conflict happens in it. To put the matter in its simplest form, *Richard II* is the only one of the histories, apart from the very late *Henry VIII*, in which there is no battle either on stage or off stage. Indeed there is no real struggle for power in it. While Richard is away in Ireland, Bolingbroke lands in England and takes over. By the time Richard returns, an irreversible shift of authority has taken place; and there is, therefore, nothing he can do about it. All this was, of course, a matter of history. Things did happen substantially as the dramatist depicts them. Consequently, the interest of the play centres perforce on something other than outer conflict, even though its main concern is with a deposition. In fact, it falls into two clearly defined parts. The first reveals Richard's fatal error in seizing the lands of the dead Gaunt, an action that calls in question the law of primogeniture by virtue of which he holds the crown, and that almost invites Bolingbroke to retort in kind. The rest of the play is devoted to Richard in defeat. It is of necessity static – Richard is Bolingbroke's prisoner, though it takes him some time to realize it, from the time of his arrival back in England at the opening of III.ii – and this state of affairs results, so far as Richard is concerned, in a different manner of utterance.

The entire play is, of course, extremely eloquent, but the mode of speech in the first part of it is not unlike that of the earlier histories. Challenge still meets challenge, though the parallelism is neither so exact nor so marked, and there is still a strong tendency towards the building up of a speech through units that are essentially couplets in structure, even though they may not rhyme. Bolingbroke's challenge to Mowbray, in the first scene, for example, begins with four lines of free-flowing blank verse, then slips into an unrhymed couplet, and thence into rhymed couplets:

> Now, Thomas Mowbray, do I turn to thee,
> And mark my greeting well; for what I speak
> My body shall make good upon this earth,
> Or my divine soul answer it in heaven –
> Thou art a traitor and a miscreant,
> Too good to be so, and too bad to live,
> Since the more fair and crystal is the sky,
> The uglier seem the clouds that in it fly.
> Once more, the more to aggravate the note,
> With a foul traitor's name stuff I thy throat;
> And wish – so please my sovereign – ere I move,
> What my tongue speaks, my right drawn sword may
> prove. (I.i.35–46)

Now, writing of this sort is the staple of the first part of the play. All the characters, including Richard himself, make use of it; all are equally eloquent, Bolingbroke being no exception. It is not until the second part of the play begins that he becomes the 'silent king' (IV.i.290). But there is, in the first part, one highly significant passage where the style changes. It comes in the prophecy Gaunt makes to York in II.i. This long speech, opening with the words 'Methinks I am a prophet new inspir'd (31), begins with two unrhymed couplets, followed by three separate lines, each of which dispenses the same bit of proverbial wisdom in a different form; wisdom that, for good measure, is then summed up in yet another couplet:

> Light vanity, insatiate cormorant,
> Consuming means, soon preys upon itself. (38–9)

So far, the repetition of the commonplace has been in character, but very little has really been said. Now, however, as Gaunt goes on to speak of 'This royal throne of kings, this scept'red isle,' the manner changes abruptly. The unit of structure is no longer the couplet or the single line, but the paragraph. The speech moves forward in a series of great cumulative waves, as image is piled on image, until the last wave breaks on the rocks of England's present discontents when Gaunt says:

> This land of such dear souls, this dear dear land,
> Dear for her reputation through the world,

> Is now leas'd out – I die pronouncing it –
> Like to a tenement or pelting farm.
> England, bound in with the triumphant sea,
> Whose rocky shore beats back the envious siege
> Of wat'ry Neptune, is now bound in which shame,
> With inky blots and rotten parchment bonds;
> That England, that was wont to conquer others,
> Hath made a shameful conquest of itself.
> Ah, would the scandal vanish with my life,
> How happy then were my ensuing death! (57–68)

That is flexible as well as eloquent writing, but it is also – and this is what matters for my argument – powerfully descriptive both of the state of England and of Gaunt's feelings about it. In this respect it anticipates the style of speech that Richard adopts on his return to England in III.ii, and retains for the rest of the play. On the strength of what he says in the second part of the play, and particularly because he makes such an extensive use there of imagery and figurative language generally, many critics have seen fit to regard Richard as a poet. I think they are wrong; the poetry Richard speaks is Shakespeare's not his. Others, noting his fondness for talking about himself and his position, and his tendency to see himself as one acting a role, have suggested that he is really an actor *manqué*, who might well have done better on the boards than on the throne. This too is, I think, mistaken. Richard is an actor only in the sense that he has to play the part assigned to him by Bolingbroke. It is not at all the part he would like to play or thinks he ought to be playing.

Shakespeare gives the Richard of the second part of the play those flowing lyrical speeches, in which one image sets off another, and that, in its turn, yet another, for a good dramatic reason. The speeches are essentially descriptive; and what they describe is Richard's own consciousness of his situation. It is a fascinatingly paradoxical situation indeed, admitting of no easy definition, since the Richard of the second part of the play is a contradiction in terms: a king who has no kingly power whatever. He is the central figure in the drama, for it is on him that the playwright focuses his, and therefore our, attention. Yet there is no action he can take to alter the course of events. He is, of necessity, a spectator; and the spectacle that absorbs his whole attention is what is happening to himself. He looks at it, he meditates on it, and he tells us what he sees and what he thinks. Lacking the fibre and the tenacity of that other powerless monarch King Lear, Richard does not seek to come to terms with his experience through understanding it. Instead, he descants on it, turning it this way and that, making an occupation for himself out of doing so. He says as much himself in the soliloquy he utters at the opening of v.v, where we find him in prison at Pomfret Castle. It begins thus:

> I have been studying how I may compare
> This prison where I live unto the world;
> And, for because the world is populous
> And here is not a creature but myself,
> I cannot do it. Yet I'll hammer it out.
> My brain I'll prove the female to my soul,
> My soul the father; and these two beget
> A generation of still-breeding thoughts,
> And these same thoughts people this little world,
> In humours like the people of this world,
> For no thought is contented. The better sort,
> As thoughts of things divine, are intermix'd
> With scruples, and do set the word itself
> Against the word,
> As thus: 'Come, little ones'; and then again,
> 'It is as hard to come as for a camel
> To thread the postern of a small needle's eye'.
> Thoughts tending to ambition, they do plot
> Unlikely wonders: how these vain weak nails
> May tear a passage through the flinty ribs
> Of this hard world, my ragged prison walls;
> And, for they cannot, die in their own pride.
> Thoughts tending to content flatter themselves
> That they are not the first of fortune's slaves,
> Nor shall not be the last; like silly beggars
> Who, sitting in the stocks, refuge their shame,
> That many have and others must sit there;
> And in this thought they find a kind of ease,
> Bearing their own misfortunes on the back
> Of such as have before endur'd the like.
> Thus play I in one person many people,
> And none contented. Sometimes am I king;
> Then treasons make me wish myself a beggar,
> And so I am. Then crushing penury
> Persuades me I was better when a king;
> Then am I king'd again; and by and by
> Think that I am unking'd by Bolingbroke,
> And straight am nothing. But whate'er I be,

Nor I, nor any man that but man is,
With nothing shall be pleas'd till he be eas'd
With being nothing. (V.V.1–41)

I have said earlier (p 115) that Richard is not a poet, since he is a king speaking poetry that is Shakespeare's. In one way this passage clinches the point, for it asks to be connected with the actual writing of *Richard II*, and looks very much like an enactment of the creative process that went into its making. 'I have been *studying* how I may *compare* ... ', says Richard. In its total exclusion of prose, in its careful consultation of numerous sources,* and, above all, in its high-wrought artifice, *Richard II* has every appearance of having been studied, and nowhere more so than in the emblem scene, III.iv, which stands at its very centre. Here, making no concessions whatever to realism of speech or manners, Shakespeare 'hammers out' a point by point comparison between the well-tended garden and England as it should be and between the untended garden and England as it is under the rule of Richard. It is appropriate that this particular scene should be hammered out and hammered home, for it embodies the political moral of the play and is primarily a product of the brain or reason, which is seen as the female partner in the creative act.

Within the speech in which it occurs, the statement 'Yet I'll hammer it out' leads one to expect that what follows will be very much excogitated; such is not, however, the impression it produces. On the contrary, it leaves one with a sense of the mind free-wheeling, as it were, musing with no specific end in view. There is a kind of logical structure, of course, as Richard divides the thoughts that come to him into three categories: thoughts of heaven, thoughts of escape, and thoughts of putting up patiently with his present position; but the 'thinking' is done increasingly in the form of images – 'images that yet / Fresh images beget,' as W.B. Yeats puts it in lines that seem to be indebted to this very speech of Richard's – until the 'Thoughts tending to content' issue in that extended picture of the 'silly beggars' that takes up five and a half lines. In other words and to use Shakespeare's own terminology, the soul, meaning the intuitive and imaginative faculty, becomes the dominant partner in the process of composition. And, in keeping with this free movement of the thought, the lines also flow into one another with a liberal use of enjambement.

So far, then, Richard's speech would seem to be a fascinating anticipation of a form of activity that is normally associated with the great Romantic poets: the artist watching himself at work and making poetry

* See *Narrative and Dramatic Sources of Shakespeare* ed Geoffrey Bullough, vol III, London and New York 1960, pp 353–491.

out of the watching. But the speech is not yet complete. Shakespeare, when he wrote *Richard II*, had many years of acting experience behind him; and it is the man of the theatre who now intervenes, with the passage beginning 'Thus play I in one person many people,' in order to bring these musings back to the harsh reality of the prison where they began and to force from Richard the admission that he has been 'unking'd by Bolingbroke' and is, therefore, 'nothing.'

Highly self-conscious and self-critical, Richard's lines at the opening of V.V. are the culmination of something that has been going on since the beginning of III.ii. There, Richard, newly landed from Ireland, is asked by Aumerle:

How brooks your Grace the air,
After your late tossing on the breaking seas? (III.ii.2–3)

Richard answers, 'Needs must I like it well,' and then goes on to address the soil of England, calling on it to take his part against his enemies by producing venomous creatures. As it gathers momentum, this speech, like most of Richard's speeches from this point onwards, becomes increasingly extravagant and fanciful. It ends thus:

Yield stinging nettles to mine enemies;
And when they from thy bosom pluck a flower,
Guard it, I pray thee, with a lurking adder,
Whose double tongue may with a mortal touch
Throw death upon thy sovereign's enemies.
Mock not my senseless conjuration, lords.
This earth shall have a feeling, and these stones
Prove armed soldiers, ere her native King
Shall falter under foul rebellion's arms. (III.ii.18–26)

The line 'Mock not my senseless conjuration, lords' is both a concealed stage direction, demanding that those about Richard make some sort of gesture expressing impatience, and also a sign to the audience to take note of his tendency towards verbal self-indulgence and excess. A similar sign is given in the next scene, when Richard, anticipating the news that Northumberland is about to bring him, pictures the things that may now happen to him in a speech that grows more and more remote from the real matter in hand as it develops, until, seeing that he has moved Aumerle to tears, he suggests that they engage in a weeping-match:

Or shall we play the wanton with our woes
And make some pretty match with shedding tears?
As thus: to drop them still upon one place

> Till they have fretted us a pair of graves
> Within the earth; and, therein laid – there lies
> Two kinsmen digg'd their graves with weeping eyes.
> Would not this ill do well? Well, well, I see
> I talk but idly, and you laugh at me. (III.ii.164–71)

Dramatic poetry of this kind, the dominant mode of *Richard II* after the King's return from Ireland, is, it seems to me, quite brilliant in its adaptation of a manner of writing that appears to have come very easily to Shakespeare at this time – the elaboration of self-consciously beautiful speeches – to a theatrical purpose. The entire speech from which the lines just quoted come is, in its own way, moving and was evidently composed with affection, even, I think, with more than a touch of self-indulgence; yet it also brings out in no uncertain manner, especially in its final sentence, one of Richard's worst failings as a man and still more as a king: his readiness to find a refuge in words, which grow ever more remote from the business in hand, from the harsher and more intractable realities of life. Such behaviour may well conform to the 'popular' notion of the poet as an impractical dilettante, but it has nothing in common with that determination to get things right which led Shakespeare to rewrite Berowne's speech quoted at page 21. Unlike Richard, who has never bothered to learn kingcraft, as he should have done, the true poet works hard and unremittingly at his wordcraft. The reactions of the King's friends and supporters to his displays of impotent grief underline this failing for him and for us. Moreover, these speeches fit the situation as well as the character; for what Richard does here, and will go on doing for the rest of the play, is to exercise the one freedom now left him: his liberty to indulge in verbal extravagance. Shakespeare has it both ways: he writes the poetry he wants to write, and he makes his own critical attitude to that poetry serve also as a criticism of his hero.

'New, Pathetique Tragedie': *Romeo and Juliet*

There can be no doubt that *Romeo and Juliet* was a tremendous popular success. The statement on the title-page of the bad quarto of 1597, to the effect that 'it hath been often (with great applause) plaid publiquely, by the right Honourable the L. of Hunsdon his Seruants,' might in itself be discounted as a publishers' puff, but it is backed by ample testimony from other sources, including John Marston's well-known lines in his *The Scourge of Villanie* (1598), where the satirist asks a devotee of the theatre:

> *Luscus* what's playd to day? faith now I know
> I set thy lips abroach, from whence doth flow
> Naught but pure *Iuliat* and *Romio*. (xi.37–9)*

From what follows on this opening, it would seem that some young men went to see the play in order to pick up honeyed phrases which they would then try out on their girl friends, speaking 'mouingly / From out some new pathetique Tragedie.'

Romeo and Juliet was indeed a 'new pathetique Tragedie' when it was first staged in 1595 or thereabouts. At the time when it was written the theatre knew three kinds of tragedy. Much the most important was the tragedy of ambition and power, usually based on history or on legend that was not clearly differentiated from history: Marlowe's *Dr Faustus* and *Edward II*, Shakespeare's *3 Henry VI*, published in 1595, in a reported version, under the title of *The true Tragedie of Richard Duke of Yorke*, and his *Richard III*. Then there was revenge tragedy: Kyd's *The Spanish*

* *The Poems of John Marston* ed Arnold Davenport, Liverpool 1961, p 168

Tragedy, Marlowe's *The Jew of Malta*, Shakespeare's *Titus Andronicus*; and, finally, domestic tragedy, best represented by the anonymous *Arden of Feversham* (c 1591). *Romeo and Juliet* bears, it is true, traces of all three 'kinds.' Shakespeare may well have thought that the story he was handling was based on fact, and was to that extent historical. He certainly adds to that impression by his treatment of the feud between the Capulets and the Montagues as a kind of miniature civil war. The idea of revenge also finds its place, and an important place it is, within the play, for Romeo's killing of Tybalt, in revenge for the death of Mercutio, is the turning point of the action. And *Romeo and Juliet* is domestic, because its main concern is with love and marriage not power and politics. Nevertheless, the play is quite new in that it is essentially a tragedy of love. In it two young people of no high rank or consequence become arresting and significant through the power, the intensity, and the completeness with which their passion for each other is rendered. Romeo and Juliet are the first of Shakespeare's great ideal figures. By the time he had finished his play, they had already joined those other patterns of love whom Mercutio devalues and mocks as Romeo makes his entry in II.iv.

New in its theme, *Romeo and Juliet* is also new – and, simultaneously, very old indeed – in the tragic intuition for which it finds expression. Critics have argued endlessly and inconclusively about whether it is a tragedy of fate, as the Prologue insists; or a tragedy of character, as the Friar seems to suggest with his frequent warnings about the dangers of haste; or a tragedy of sacrifice, controlled by 'A greater power than we can contradict' (V.iii.153), that works to reconcile the two families; or, as some students of its imagery are prone to think, a kind of *Liebestod*. But, within the play itself, all these interpretations seem like partial and ultimately inadequate rationalizations of something much more elementary, universal, and profound, because what Shakespeare finds expression for is the anguish and incomprehension that men feel when youth, and love, and life vanish suddenly into the dark, or, as Lysander puts it in *A Midsummer Night's Dream*, when 'quick bright things come to confusion' (I.i.149).

A recognition that this is indeed what the dramatist is doing may also go far towards explaining yet another feature of the play that has attracted critical attention: the large comic element in it. A mixture of comedy and tragedy was, as Sir Philip Sidney had reprovingly noticed in his *Apologie for Poetrie*, nothing unusual in Elizabethan drama; but the comedy in *Romeo and Juliet* is not something confined to the Nurse and the other servants, nor does it function as a comment on the main figures and their activities; instead, the hero and heroine have their parts in it. They have to, because this tragedy is quite simply a romantic comedy that goes wrong, that ends by disappointing the expectations it raises, instead of fulfilling them. The first two acts establish a familiar and immediately recognizable pattern, which occurs in comedy after comedy, for what they deal with is the falling in love of two young people and, that commonest of all obstacles to their union, parental opposition. Moreover, there would seem to be every reason why the lovers should eventually attain their happiness, since the feud between their two families is evidently on its last legs when Old Capulet can say to Paris, speaking of himself and Old Montague:

> 'tis not hard, I think,
> For men so old as we to keep the peace. (I.ii.2–3)

Nor, provided one ignores the Prologue, as one must when reading the Folio text from which it is omitted, are the mixed events of acts III and IV any guarantee of a disastrous outcome. It is not until Romeo kills Paris, at V.iii.73, that all hope and possibility of a fortunate conclusion finally disappear, and that the sense of inevitability, so characteristic of tragedy, at last makes itself fully felt.

There are, it seems to me, two very good reasons why the greater part of *Romeo and Juliet* should follow the pattern of romantic comedy. In the first place, if the dramatist is indeed expressing a sense of how quickly 'quick bright things come to confusion,' it is essential that we should be made aware of just how quick and shining his main figures are. Hence, much of the play is devoted to depicting Romeo the clever young man of fashion, friend of Mercutio, and lover of Rosaline, who is suddenly overwhelmed by true love when he meets Juliet. Similarly, we have to see Juliet, the unawakened girl of I.iii, open like a flower into the frank generous woman she becomes on falling in love with Romeo. Growing rapidly in beauty and awareness, as quick things do in response to experience, the lovers acquire a kind of radiance, which persists right into their final moments in the tomb, before 'The jaws of darkness do devour it up.' The tragedy of Romeo and Juliet is, to adapt some words of Berowne's to it, that their loving 'doth not end like an old play,' though it so patently begins like one. The other reason, ultimately inseparable, of course, from that just offered, why Shakespeare chose to write a tragedy in the form of a romantic comedy that ends in disaster was, I take it, because he recognized that this was the sort of tragedy he was best equipped to write round about 1595, and would most enjoy writing.

Experimental in form, *Romeo and Juliet* is also and most appropriately experimental in style, or rather in its wide variety of styles. Resembling *Richard II* and *Love's Labour's Lost* in the way in which it allows the poetic dramatist to put his lyrical impulse to dramatic use, it differs from those two plays in this: that to a far greater degree than in either of them the very exercise of this lyrical impulse calls into being other modes of expression which are not lyrical at all. It is these other non-lyrical modes that point to the future; but the core of the play itself is to be found in the lyrical scenes, and these belong to the lovers.

It has become something of a commonplace of criticism to say that Romeo's love for Rosaline is nothing more than a fashionable affectation, betrayed for what it is by the frigid and conventional conceits of Elizabethan love poetry that the hero has recourse to when describing it to Benvolio (I.i.165–236). There may be an element of truth in this, but Juliet's readiness to employ oxymorons that are quite as strained as any of Romeo's in I.i, when she tries to come to terms with the contradiction presented by Romeo her husband and Romeo the killer of Tybalt, should give one pause. The Romeo of the first scene is 'for the numbers that Petrarch flow'd in' (II.iv.38–9), because he finds himself in the typical situation of the lover in the sonnet tradition – Rosaline, the chaste disdainful lady, pays no heed to his suit. Shakespeare has taken one of the central themes of mediaeval and sixteenth-century love poetry and has transferred it into a dramatic context. And, along with the situation and the language of the sonnet, he also takes over the form. The Prologue to the play is a sonnet, the Chorus at the opening of act II is a sonnet, and, most important of all, the first exchanges between Romeo and Juliet are cast into a sonnet, complete with the usual conventional terms that go with the idea of love as a religion: Juliet is a saint; Romeo a pilgrim worshipping at her shrine. Conventional in this respect, the sonnet of meeting is highly unusual in others. It is a shared sonnet, for which I know of no parallel; and it is shared, because through it love is not only offered but also accepted. Moreover, this sonnet is accompanied by significant action; it begins with Romeo touching Juliet's hand, and as it concludes he kisses her.

The pattern established here continues through the play. The first balcony scene, II.ii, is a dramatized version of the lovers' dialogue by night, as one finds it, for instance, in the Eleventh Song of Sir Philip Sidney's *Astrophel and Stella*, 'Who is it that this dark night / Underneath my window plaineth?' Broken off twice by the Nurse calling from within, it is finally concluded by the coming of the dawn, as such dialogues had been for centuries. Juliet's speech at the opening of III.ii, as she waits for Romeo's arrival, is an epithalamion. Exceptional because it is spoken by the bride, not by a poet or the poet-bridegroom of Spenser's *Epithalamion*, it is, in its impassioned invocation to Night to come quickly, a superb example of the 'kind,' asking to be compared to George Chapman's 'Epithalamion Teratos' in the Fifth Sestiad of *Hero and Leander* (427–80), and to that part of Spenser's poem which begins with the words 'Now welcome night, thou night so long expected' (315).

Unlike the normal epithalamion, Juilet's is, as a consequence of its dramatic setting, shot through with unconscious irony, because the audience knows, as she does not, that Romeo has killed Tybalt and has been banished from Verona by the Prince. Nevertheless, the lovers do have their one night together, and that night is followed by yet another adaptation of a familiar form, the *aubade* this time, to the requirements of the stage, which, with its upper acting area, was so admirably fitted for it, allowing Romeo and Juliet to enter '*aloft*' (Q2) and enabling the audience to watch Romeo making his descent to the main stage as '*He goeth downe*' (Q1). As well as making the parting at dawn visible, Shakespeare also gives it a sharper edge. In the courtly love poem the man goes at dawn because secrecy is part of the code. Romeo has more pressing reasons: his life depends on his leaving the city by daybreak. The situation of the lovers is both harder, because they are actually married, and more desperate than that of the courtly lovers of the traditional *aubade*, and this fact adds a new poignancy to the old discussion about whether the bird that sings is the lark or the nightingale.

Finally, to complete and crown the story of Shakespeare's adaptation of the themes and forms of love poetry to dramatic purposes, the catastrophe of the play is two deaths for love, a motif so common both in the ballad and in the mythological poetry of the late sixteenth century that it might well be regarded as the central concern of love poetry, and so well known that he was, very soon, to make wonderful fun of it and with it when he composed 'Pyramus and Thisby' for the mechanicals to act in *A Midsummer Night's Dream*. 'Pyramus and Thisby' exploits every pitfall that lies in the way of a dramatist attempting to stage such deaths; *Romeo and Juliet* submerges them from view in the lyrical intensity of Romeo's final speech and in the terse directness with which Juliet recognizes what has happened, takes her decision, and acts on it.

I have suggested earlier (pp 24–40) that Shakespeare tended to see life in terms of those contraries which so interested William Blake. They are certainly there in *Romeo and Juliet*. The actions and the poetry of the hero and the heroine embody and make triumphantly vocal one possible attitude to love and marriage, an attitude which had hitherto found its main expression in lyric and narrative; but, in the very process of dramatizing this attitude, Shakespeare seems to have become acutely conscious of other possible attitudes and, consequently, of other possible modes of expression. Romeo and Juliet move in a world which is either hostile to or, at the best, uncomprehending of and unsympathetic to their ideals and aspirations; and this world is represented in three figures in particular: Old Capulet, the Nurse, and Mercutio, each of whom either has from the first, or comes to acquire, a strongly marked and highly individualized personal idiom. Different though they are from each other, however, these three idioms have one thing in common: they are not lyrical. Much closer to the language of everyday intercourse, these modes of speech work as a kind of counterpoint to the poetry of the lovers, and, in doing so, help to give reality and depth to the central experience of the play.

The Nurse and Mercutio are, in a sense, complementary to one another in that they are two aspects of the same break with convention. Mercutio, a kinsman of the Prince, would, in any earlier play of Shakespeare's, have made verse the staple of his speech, while the Nurse would have been largely a creature of prose. In fact, however, the reverse is the case: most of the Nurse's part is in verse; while that of Mercutio, though it runs to almost as much verse as prose, is predominantly prose in its idiom, expressive of an attitude that is practical and down to earth, the counterpart to Romeo's idealism.

It is the Nurse in particular who points the way to the future. How Shakespeare came to invent the extraordinary blank verse he gives her is a mystery. There may well have been an element of the accidental about it. I.iii, the first scene in which she appears, had to be a verse scene because it would be out of keeping for Lady Capulet and Juliet, two upper-class characters, to speak prose, hitherto the medium of the Servants who open the play and of the illiterate Clown of I.ii. And, as Juliet and her mother use blank verse, the Nurse has to follow suit. But Shakespeare knew the Nurse intimately. He had clearly listened to her, or to others like her, and he had been fascinated, as he was to go on being fascinated – witness Mistress Quickly – by her tricks of speech: her love of minute circumstantial detail, her readiness to digress on to any side issue that may arise, her addiction to inset parentheses, her repetitions in her efforts to get back on course, her insistent and irrepressible bawdry, her utter inability to tell a plain tale plainly – in sum, all the characteristic quirks of the born gossip.

The result is a scene the like of which Shakespeare had never written before. Dominated by the Nurse, it is instinct with life, which pours into it from the moment that she opens her mouth. Asked by Lady Capulet, 'Nurse, where's my daughter? Call her forth to me,' the Nurse replies:

> Now, by my maidenhead at twelve year old,
> I bade her come. What lamb! what, ladybird!
> God forbid! Where's this girl? What, Juliet! (I.iii.1–4)

Every word there is expressive of an individual. The oath, 'by my maidenhead,' is carefully qualified in the interests of truth; and the qualification tells us much about the Nurse's past, as well as about her habits of mind. More interesting still, strange things are already beginning to happen to the blank verse structure and rhythm, in order to provide room for this idiom to breathe. There are five separate sentences in the last line and a half; and in the last line the regular beat of the verse is almost completely submerged by the speech rhythm of colloquial prose.

This beginning is, however, a mere foretaste of what is to follow when Lady Capulet and the Nurse move on to discuss the matter of Juliet's age. Asking when Lammas-tide will be, the Nurse is told it will come in 'A fortnight and odd days.' The answer sets her off on what is in many ways the most dramatic speech Shakespeare had yet written, a monologue that reveals a mode of thinking and evokes a way of life, as well as acquainting us with the important fact that Juliet's real relationship so far has been with the woman who suckled her rather than with her mother. It runs thus:

Even or odd, of all days in the year,
Come Lammas Eve at night shall she be fourteen.
Susan and she – God rest all Christian souls! –
Were of an age. Well, Susan is with God; 20
She was too good for me. But, as I said,
On Lammas Eve at night shall she be fourteen;
That shall she, marry; I remember it well.
'Tis since the earthquake now eleven years;
And she was wean'd – I never shall forget it – 25
Of all the days of the year, upon that day;
For I had then laid wormwood to my dug,
Sitting in the sun under the dove-house wall;
My lord and you were then at Mantua.
Nay, I do bear a brain. But, as I said, 30
When it did taste the wormwood on the nipple
Of my dug, and felt it bitter, pretty fool,
To see it tetchy, and fall out with the dug!
Shake, quoth the dove-house. 'Twas no need, I trow,
To bid me trudge. 35
And since that time it is eleven years;
For then she could stand high-lone; nay, by th' rood,
She could have run and waddled all about;
For even the day before, she broke her brow;
And then my husband – God be with his soul! 40
'A was a merry man – took up the child.
'Yea,' quoth he 'dost thou fall upon thy face?
Thou wilt fall backward when thou hast more wit,
Wilt thou not, Jule?' And, by my holidam,
The pretty wretch left crying, and said 'Ay'. 45

To see, now, how a jest shall come about!
I warrant, an I should live a thousand years,
I never should forget it: 'Wilt thou not, Jule?' quoth he;
And, pretty fool, it stinted, and said 'Ay'.

In this astonishing speech blank verse has become an incredibly flexible medium, capable of rendering the meandering movement of chatter. There is no logic here, no antithesis; the whole thing has all the appearance of being completely natural. Blank verse has shed its corsets, as it were; like the Nurse herself it is loose, free, and ample. The style and the woman are one. We know her by the way in which she speaks. Partly, it is a matter of vocabulary. There are words and phrases here – 'Lammas-tide,' 'Lammas Eve,' 'God rest all Christian souls,' 'dove-house,' 'bear a brain,' 'high-lone,' 'waddled,' and 'broke her brow' – which do not occur elsewhere in Shakespeare's writings, and which smack strongly of the idiom of the common people. But quite as important as the vocabulary is the easy relaxed rhythm that pervades the speech. Many of the lines, eg, 18, 22, 23, 25, 28, 31, etc, contain an extra unstressed syllable, and one of them, 48, manages to pack in no fewer than thirteen syllables, leaving one in some doubt as to whether the words 'I never should forget it' are meant to represent two feet, or, as seems more likely, three, making the line an alexandrine. But it really makes no matter, since the total effect created is, in either case, that of the talking, as opposed to the declaiming, voice.

It could be objected to the analysis just offered that the entire speech, down to line 36, comes from the reported First Quarto (1597), which is taken over by the substantive text, the Second Quarto of 1599, for the first thirty-six lines of the scene, and that there is, therefore , no conclusive proof that the lines, as we have them, are, in fact, what Shakespeare wrote. But it is generally agreed that the reporting of Q1 is 'remarkably good in the first two acts';* and the style of the speech from line 37 to the end is precisely the same as that of the previous part of it. Moreover, the Nurse's manner of utterance is consistent and extremely well sustained throughout the play. Nowhere is this more evident than in IV.v, the last scene in which she appears. As it opens, she comes in to stand by the side of Juliet's bed on the morning after Juliet has taken the sleeping potion. The audience, knowing what Juliet has done, waits in suspense for the curtains round the bed to be drawn; and, while it waits, it receives something else and something extra, for through the Nurse's words a marvellous picture is conjured up of Juliet's life as it has been hitherto. It is one of those evocative moments in which Shakespeare adds

* *Romeo and Juliet* ed J. Dover Wilson and G.I. Duthie, Cambridge 1955, p 112

depth and shading to the action he is about to present by creating a past for it. What happens now, or something very like it, has, we are made to feel, happened many a time before in Juliet's life; she is evidently a sound sleeper. But we know, as the Nurse does not, that it will not happen again. And so pathos mingles with comedy as the Nurse attempts to wake her seemingly reluctant charge by saying:

> Mistress! What, mistress! Juliet! Fast, I warrant her, she.
> Why, lamb! Why, lady! Fie, you slug-a-bed!
> Why, love, I say! madam! sweetheart! Why, bride!
> What, not a word? You take your pennyworths now.
> Sleep for a week; for the next night, I warrant,
> The County Paris hath set up his rest
> That you shall rest but little. God forgive me!
> Marry, and amen. How sound is she asleep!
> I needs must wake her. Madam, madam, madam!
> Ay, let the County take you in your bed;
> He'll fright you up, i' faith. Will it not be?
> *Draws the curtains.*
> What, dress'd, and in your clothes, and down again!
> I must needs wake you. Lady! lady! lady!
> Alas, alas! Help, help! my lady's dead!
> O well-a-day that ever I was born!
> Some aqua-vitae, ho! My lord! My lady! (IV.v.1–16)

There is not a single adjective there; there are no figures of speech; the entire address is made up of endearments, including the 'lamb' caught up from the opening of I.iii, of exclamations, and of the small change of everyday intercourse. Yet it is superb dramatic poetry, because it enacts the whole experience, from the blithe unconcern of the beginning to the shocked realization of the end. Moreover, it is entirely in character. No one but the Nurse would take this long to find out what happened. But in her case the slowness is absolutely right and justified as her mind dithers between the job in hand, her affection for Juliet, and the irresistible temptations to bawdy self-indulgence which the thought of the forthcoming marriage suggests to her. And, at the end of it all, one is left with a strong suspicion that she wants the aqua-vitae for herself rather than for Juliet. There is a world of difference between this discovery and Marcus's discovery of Lavinia's true state in *Titus Andronicus*.

The Nurse seems to have sprung out of Shakespeare's imagination much as Pallas was supposed to have sprung from the head of Zeus, fully formed and equipped with her own characteristic idiom from the very outset. Not so Mercutio. On his first appearance, in I.iv, he is, like Romeo and Benvolio, a young man about town, exchanging smart witticisms with his friends, equally at ease with blank verse and rhymed couplets, and capable of the flight of fancy that informs his speech on Queen Mab. He has his bits of bawdy innuendo, but there is nothing exceptional about them. In fact, it is by no means clear, at this stage in the action, what his precise function is to be. In II.i, as he settles into his role of professed enemy of romantic love and of the poetry that goes with it, the bawdy becomes more pronounced; but it is not until II.iv, where he rapidly abandons blank verse in favour of prose, that he finally adopts the manner of speech that one comes to associate with him: a mocking derisive manner that disposes of fashionable duellists and fashionable lovers alike with dexterity and relish. It speaks out in all its devastating directness when he caps Benvolio's exclamation, 'Here comes Romeo, here comes Romeo,' by saying:

> Without his roe, like a dried herring. O flesh, flesh, how art thou fishified! Now is he for the numbers that Petrarch flow'd in; Laura to his lady, was a kitchen-wench – marry, she had a better love to berhyme her; Dido, a dowdy; Cleopatra, a gipsy; Helen and Hero, hildings and harlots; Thisbe, a gray eye or so, but not to the purpose – Signior Romeo, bon jour! (II.iv.37–43)

Mercutio finds his idiom when he finds his role in the play, or rather when Shakespeare finds it for him, and having found it he adheres to it right down to the time of his death. His last words are a mixture of verse and prose; but it is the prose that is dominant, for it seeps into and permeates the verse. His death is a death with a difference. He makes no defiant gesture, utters no heroic lines, casts no lingering look on the past, but voices his bitterness at the absurdity of it all in mocking, punning, self-deprecating understatements that go to the very heart of the matter:

> I am hurt.
> A plague a both your houses! I am sped.
> Is he gone and hath nothing?
> BENVOLIO What, art thou hurt?
> MERCUTIO Ay, ay, a scratch, a scratch; marry, 'tis enough.
> Where is my page? Go, villain, fetch a surgeon.
> *Exit Page.*
> ROMEO Courage, man; the hurt cannot be much.
> MERCUTIO No, 'tis not so deep as a well, nor so wide as a church door, but 'tis enough, 'twill serve. Ask for me to-morrow, and you shall find me a grave man. I am peppered, I warrant, for this world. A plague a both your houses! Zounds, a dog, a rat, a mouse, a cat, to

scratch a man to death! A braggart, a rogue, a villain, that fights by the book of arithmetic! Why the devil came you between us? I was hurt under your arm.
ROMEO I thought all for the best.
MERCUTIO Help me into some house, Benvolio, or I shall faint.
A plague a both your houses!
They have made worms' meat of me.
I have it, and soundly too – Your houses! (III.i.87–105)

Mercutio's main function, within the design of the play as a whole, has been to speak up for the aspect of love, the purely physical, that Romeo is prone to ignore, and, more generally, to insist on the importance of earthy realities. Nowhere does he do so more powerfully and rigorously than he does here, dismissing Romeo's wishful hope that things are not so bad as they seem with calculated scorn, and then simply ignoring his feeble excuse 'I thought all for the best.' Shakespeare's fidelity to the character, as it has grown under his hands, and to the idiom he has forged for that character comes close at this point to endangering the play as a whole by making his hero look singularly ineffectual. Experiment was not without its dangers.

The other character who finds his proper role and its appropriate idiom during the course of the play is Old Capulet. In I.ii, the first scene in which we see much of him, there is little or nothing that is distinctive about his language, or, consequently, about him. His attitude towards the possibility of a match between Paris and Juliet is sensible and considerate, and the rhymed couplets he uses to describe the ladies who will be present at his forthcoming ball –

At my poor house look to behold this night
Earth-treading stars that make dark heaven light –

have the afflatus of Elizabethan love poetry. On his next appearance, however, his manner has undergone a marked change. As he welcomes his guests, in I.v, his speech is jerky, staccato, and, above all, repetitive, creating an impression of age that is particularly evident in such lines as:

Welcome, gentlemen! I have seen the day
That I have worn a visor and could tell
A whispering tale in a fair lady's ear,
Such as would please. 'Tis gone, 'tis gone, 'tis gone! (I.v.19–22)

As he reflects on the past Capulet's tone is mild and mellow, but the same tricks of speech can also be adapted to the expression of anger and impatience, as they are in this same scene when he meets with opposition from Tybalt, and, more effectively still, in III.v, when, learning that Juliet has no intention of marrying Paris, he rounds on her thus:

> How, how, how, how, chopt logic! What is this?
> 'Proud' – and 'I thank you' – and 'I thank you not' –
> And yet 'not proud'? Mistress minion, you,
> Thank me no thankings, nor proud me no prouds,
> But fettle your fine joints 'gainst Thursday next,
> To go with Paris to Saint Peter's Church,
> Or I will drag thee on a hurdle thither.
> Out, you green-sickness carrion! Out, you baggage!
> You tallow-face! (III.v.149–57)

Capulet's role, not clearly envisaged by Shakespeare when he wrote I.ii, but emerging strongly by the time he came to write I.v, is to embody paternal authority and the parental attitude towards love and marriage as they really were in Shakespeare's England, both totally opposed to the romantic love relationship of the hero and heroine. Here, as so often in the play, what Capulet says is at once ridiculous and formidable, which would seem to be the tragedy's verdict on all that he stands for. Unlike Mercutio's idiom, however, Capulet's is not, once found, completely sustained. On his entry in III.v, he is unaware of Juliet's refusal to comply with his wishes and to accept the arrangements he has made to distract her from her grief for, as he thinks, Tybalt's death, and greets her thus:

> How now! a conduit, girl? What, still in tears?
> Evermore show'ring? In one little body
> Thou counterfeit'st a bark, a sea, a wind;
> For still thy eyes, which I may call the sea,
> Do ebb and flow with years. The bark thy body is,
> Sailing in this salt flood; the winds thy sighs,
> Who, raging with thy tears, and they with them,
> Without a sudden calm will overset
> Thy tempest-tossed body. (III.v.129–37)

This well-turned image, with its precise correspondences, belongs to the sonnet tradition and seems to derive ultimately from Petrarch's Sonnet 154, which Wyatt had turned into English in his poem that begins 'My galy charged with forgetfulnes.'* But what is it doing in the mouth of Old Capulet? A possible explanation is that it is quite simply an artistic lapse: that Shakespeare has forgotten for the moment about the idiom he has devised for the old man, and has allowed his interest in the tradition of

* *Collected Poems of Sir Thomas Wyatt* ed Kenneth Muir, London 1949, pp 22–3

love poetry and his fondness for figures to get the better of his sense of dramatic fitness. On the other hand, it might be argued that Capulet's resort to this manner of speech is intended as a signal to the audience indicating that his concern for Juliet, though genuine enough in its way, is essentially shallow. Such an explanation leaves Shakespeare's artistry intact, but assumes that the audience he had in mind was much more sensitive to stylistic changes and far readier to respond to them than most audiences are.

I incline to the first explanation because there are other occasions in the play when the language fails to do what it should be doing. The two most troublesome are, of course, Romeo's playing with the words 'banished' and 'banishment' (III.iii.11–70) and Juliet's punning on the various meanings of 'I' (III.ii.45–51). In each case Shakespeare is attempting to render the state of mind of one who has just received a shocking and most unwelcome piece of news, with the result that he experiences a violent conflict between the rational compulsion to accept the undeniable and the instinctive urge to reject the intolerable by talking it out of existence. He had tried to do it before. Richard III, on waking from his dream in V.iii, is also a man divided in two; the old Richard, who thought himself immune from the emotional consequences of his actions, stares at the new Richard, who recognizes at last what he has done to himself, and seeks to come to terms with him through a kind of logical catechism. The method is in keeping with the logic that pervades the play, but it does not really work, because the two impulses, to accept and to reject, are rather like a couple of gymnasts giving a display that never brings them into contact with each other. Much the same thing happens in *Romeo and Juliet*: the insistent word-play attracts too much attention to itself, so that the purpose behind it is lost to view. Characteristically, Shakespeare did not abandon the effort. He succeeds magnificently in doing what he had failed to do in the two earlier plays when he writes the speech in which Troilus, having witnessed the love-making of Diomed and Cressida, expresses his sense of a self and a universe torn in two: 'This she? No; this is Diomed's Cressida, etc.' (*Troilus and Cressida* V.ii.135–58). In this speech the two impulses fight each other; and the struggle between them is there in the contorted verse and in the processes of thought and feeling, inextricably entangled with each other, which that verse enacts.

From Dialectical Rhetoric to Metaphorical Thinking: *King John*

King John is, it seems to me, the contrary of *Richard II*, dramatizing a very similar political issue from the opposite point of view. *Richard II* deals with a conflict between incompetent right, embodied in Richard, the lawful king who lacks the essential qualities of an able ruler, and competent wrong, embodied in Bolingbroke, the rebel with no legitimate claim to the throne, who has those essential qualities. *King John* is about the converse of this situation: a conflict between an unlawful king, in possession of a throne he has seized, and a lawful claimant to that throne, who has no power of his own to make his claim good, and must, therefore, rely on the support of allies, Wrong, strong in possession, is challenged by right, weak in dependence. In *Richard II*, as its title indicates, the focus is on the victim; in *King John*, as its title indicates, it is on the usurper. The dialectical relationship between these two histories suggests that the writing of the one led to the writing of the other – my own guess is that *King John* came after *Richard II* – and lends strong support to the notion that Shakespeare's profound sense of the interdependence of contraries is one of the most important, if not the most important, of the unifying factors behind the seeming diversity of his work as a whole.

In all other respects, however, *King John* is the odd man out among the histories. Set in the early thirteenth century, not in the period 1398 to 1485, it belongs to no sequence, and it handles political-cum-religious issues of an extremely sensitive kind in England at the time when it was first played. It stands in much the same relationship to the other histories as *Troilus and Cressida* does to the tragedies, among which Heming and Condell, not altogether mistakenly, intended to place it. In fact, the resemblances between *King John* and *Troilus and Cressida* are so numerous and so marked as to suggest that the one play is a first sketch of the other. The most obvious of these resemblances is the satirical attitude towards war, and particularly towards war *communiqués*, which makes itself so strongly felt in act II of the history play, where first the French Herald and then the English Herald appears to claim an overwhelming victory for his side in an off-stage battle which has been completely indecisive. The incident adumbrates the equally indecisive combat between Hector and Ajax, so long and carefully prepared for and such an anticlimax when it eventually takes place, in IV.v of *Troilus and Cressida*. Going deeper still, both plays are ruthless in their exposure of the great gulf between the pretensions expressed by the warring sides and the true motives that inspire their actions. The Bastard's incisive soliloquy on the subject of Commodity, at the end of act II in *King John*, anticipates the mordant verdict that Thersites brings in time after time on the Trojan war: 'All the argument is a whore and a cuckold' (II.iii.68). Behind the warriors stand the wily politicians: the Citizen of Angiers who proposes the match between Blanch and the Dauphin; Pandulph, the papal legate who cynically assesses the likelihood that John will have Arthur murdered and the political profit to be made out of that murder; and the two old dog-foxes, Ulysses and Nestor, who yoke the heroes 'like draught oxen' and make them 'plough up the wars' (*Troilus and Cressida* II.i.102–3). Yet, wily though they are, neither Pandulph nor Ulysses can control the course of events. Pandulph's attempt to end the war between England and France founders because the Dauphin is not the pliable material he expected, just as Ulysses' elaborate scheme for bringing Achilles back into the fighting is thwarted by the hero's love for Polyxena. In the end it is Fortune and the sheer course of events that bring about the desired results; the Dauphin's supply ships are wrecked on the Goodwin Sands; and Hector kills Patroclus.

Underlying all these similarities between the two plays is another and more fundamental likeness. Una Ellis-Fermor has written of *Troilus and Cressida* that in it

> The idea of chaos, of disjunction, of ultimate formlessness and negation, has by a supreme act of artistic mastery been given form. It has not been described in more or less abstract terms; it has been imaged.*

As *King John* moves to its conclusion, with the King himself on his death-bed, Salisbury says something rather like this to the young Prince Henry:

* Una Ellis-Fermor *The Frontiers of Drama* London 1945, p 72

Be of good comfort, Prince; for you are born
To set a form upon that indigest
Which he [John] hath left so shapeless and so rude. (v.vii.25–7)

The 'indigest' is the chaos the play has dramatized. Prince Henry can 'set a form' upon it because, with Arthur dead and John about to die, he is the true, undisputed, legitimate heir to the throne. John, when he seized the throne, was not; and, by his act of usurpation, produced a state of affairs in which, as Pandulph puts it:

All form is formless, order orderless,
Save what is opposite to England's love. (III.i.253–4)

The play is an image of this formless form and orderless order.

The difficulties inherent in creating such an image are, of course, reflected in the actual writing. Like *Richard II*, *King John* contains no prose, it is wholly in verse; but that verse is very different in texture from the verse of *Richard II*. It is not lyrical, or rather, to be more exact, on the rare occasions when a lyrical note is heard it is overdone, indicating affectation or insincerity, and is subjected to a deflating comment. For example, after the Citizen of Angiers has made his suggestion that a match between Blanch and the Dauphin will serve to reconcile France and England, John refers to Blanch as 'this book of beauty,' while France, more simply, tells his son to 'Look in the lady's face.' The Dauphin replies:

I do, my lord, and in her eye I find
A wonder, or a wondrous miracle,
The shadow of myself form'd in her eye;
Which, being but the shadow of your son,
Becomes a sun, and makes your son a shadow.
I do protest I never lov'd myself
Till now infixed I beheld myself
Drawn in the flattering table of her eye.

This is indeed the language of the sonneteers become too clever by half; and, in case the audience has missed the element of deliberate exaggeration in it, Shakespeare gives the Bastard a mocking aside:

Drawn in the flattering table of her eye,
Hang'd in the frowning wrinkle of her brow,
And quarter'd in her heart – he doth espy
Himself love's traitor. This is pity now,
That hang'd and drawn and quarter'd there should be
In such a love so vile a lout as he. (II.i.485–509)

The staple of the play, as of *Troilus and Cressida*, is the rhetoric of argument. Not only is this manner admirably suited to a drama that is made up to a very large extent of claim and counter-claim and of accusation and counter-accusation, but it also serves as the right vehicle for the probing independent attitude that Shakespeare adopts towards the material he finds in his sources. Philip of France is no figure of fun when he puts the case for not breaking the league he has just made with John. He speaks logically as well as colourfully. Nor, I think, is the speech with which Pandulph counters and disposes of that case, subtle and sophistical though it is, meant to be taken as a caricature of the dialectical method. Pandulph succeeds because he produces the better argument.

But there is more to *King John* than exercises in dialectic, serious though these are. Its most dramatic moments are those in which characters make new discoveries either about the nature of the situations in which they find themselves or about their own natures; and at these moments they think in and express themselves through images which not merely beget one another, as Richard II's do, but unite with one another to form a coherent whole and make something hitherto but half apprehended or dimly recognized clear, concrete, and dynamic. Perhaps the most striking and effective instance of this kind of writing is, as Wolfgang Clemen has noticed,* the final speech of the Bastard in act IV. It begins with the simple yet highly dramatic order to Hubert: 'Go, bear him in thine arms.' The 'him' is the dead Arthur, whom Hubert is strongly suspected of having murdered. The command is a test of Hubert's guilt or innocence. As he picks the body up he proves his innocence. The Bastard then continues:

> I am amaz'd, methinks, and lose my way
> Among the thorns and dangers of this world.
> How easy dost thou take all England up!
> From forth this morsel of dead royalty
> The life, the right, and truth of all this realm
> Is fled to heaven; and England now is left
> To tug and scamble, and to part by th' teeth
> The unowed interest of proud-swelling state.
> Now for the bare-pick'd bone of majesty
> Doth dogged war bristle his angry crest
> And snarleth in the gentle eyes of peace;
> Now powers from home and discontents at home
> Meet in one line; and vast confusion waits,
> As doth a raven on a sick-fall'n beast,

* *The Development of Shakespeare's Imagery* London 1951, p 76

> The imminent decay of wrested pomp.
> Now happy he whose cloak and cincture can
> Hold out this tempest. Bear away that child,
> And follow me with speed. I'll to the King;
> A thousand businesses are brief in hand,
> And heaven itself doth frown upon the land. (IV.iii.139–59)

To begin with, the Bastard is bewildered, not knowing what to do, and he voices this bewilderment by taking the verb 'amaze' back to its root, as it were, and seeing himself as one lost in a maze, surrounded by thorns which are dangerous and dangers which are thorny. Shakespeare had used this particular image before. In his long soliloquy in the middle of *3 Henry VI* Richard of Gloucester refers to himself as being

> like one lost in a thorny wood
> That rents the thorns and is rent with the thorns,
> Seeking a way and straying from the way;
> Not knowing how to find the open air,
> But toiling desperately to find it out. (III.ii.174–8)

It is an admirable simile, so much so that it almost asks the reader to pause and admire it. The Bastard's half-concealed metaphor, in which the world is a maze and its dangers are thorns, does no such thing. In it significance is compressed, instead of being exhibited at length. Then, as he watches Hubert holding the dead prince, the Bastard recognizes, with almost blinding clarity, a truth which has not come home to him before: that Arthur should, by right, have been king. The recognition and the shock it brings with it are both there in the paradoxical line 'How easy dost thou take all England up!' Having identified Arthur with England, the Bastard now goes on to work out what the consequences of Arthur's death will be. The Prince's soul has 'fled to heaven,' and so has the soul of the land, 'The life, the right, and truth of all this realm.' As a body politic without a soul, England has now descended to the animal level; and, though there is as yet no explicit mention of dogs, the warring factions into which it must split are clearly envisaged as dogs in the three verbs, 'tug,' 'scamble,' and 'part by th' teeth.' 'The unowed interest of proud-swelling state' is a most pregnant phrase to describe the object for which these dogs fight, conveying as it does the notion that the right to the throne is without an owner, that those who strive for it have done nothing to earn or deserve it, and that they want it merely to satisfy their own pride. In the next three lines, by way of the vivid picture of 'the bare-pick'd bone of majesty' and of the adjective 'dogged,' meaning 'having all the worst qualities of a dog,' the idea of dogs emerges to full view at the same time as it becomes married, so to speak, to the abstract conception of war, to which it brings concreteness, particularity, and motion, causing it to 'bristle his angry crest' and snarl 'in the gentle eyes of peace,' which thus becomes another living thing. But, while the Bastard thinks in images, he also has his mind on the facts. Among those facts is the decision of Salisbury, Pembroke, and Bigot, announced at line 114, to join forces with the Dauphin at Saint Edmundsbury. It is this impending alliance that he refers to when he says:

> Now powers from home and discontents at home
> Meet in one line.

This joining together in a single rank or file – which is what I take 'Meet in one line' to mean – of foreign invaders and native malcontents is, of course, unnatural, and leads straight into the image of 'vast confusion,' 'vast' not only in size but also in appetite, waiting expectantly, as a raven does by a beast that has fallen sick and fallen down because it is sick, for the inevitable end of the unsurped power that is also John himself. Finally, having worked his way through to an understanding of the state of the nation which is simultaneously a moving picture of that state, the Bastard turns to consider what its effect will be on the individual citizen:

> Now happy he whose cloak and cincture can
> Hold out this tempest.

He is still thinking in metaphor; but the cloak that will keep out the rain of disaster is a homely practical thing, preparing the way for the two orders he gives to Hubert and for his own decision as to what to do: 'I'll to the King.' He goes because a thousand matters of urgency are crying out for dispatch, but as he does so the storm of confusion hanging over England fills his mind once more, and he interprets it as a punishment sent from God. 'Heaven' is both the divine power and the sky.

The manner of this speech is that of the great tragedies. Exploiting ambiguities and double meanings, shifting rapidly yet securely from image to image by a process of controlled and directed association, Shakespeare has evolved a way of writing that is also a way of thinking and of comprehending. Contemplating the difficulties he faces and England faces, the Bastard comes to *see* them, as they really are, in his mind's eye. Thought and imagination fuse together to create a pattern of meaning that can be apprehended by an audience as a single complex entity.

In this passage, then, *King John* looks to the future, as it does also, though in a different fashion, in John's temptation of Hubert and of himself at the great turning point of the action in III.iii, a scene I have already analysed (pp 36–8), where the movement of the verse, as it hesitates, breaks off, and then begins afresh, is at one with the thought processes of the King as he vacillates between speaking out and not speaking out. But there is also a great deal in the play that looks back, though with a difference, to the past. Its dominant mode is the declamatory one, employed by all the major characters at one time or another. It is heard most impressively and consistently, however, in the speeches of Constance, who, no matter what readers of the play think of her, always emerges in the theatre as one of the main figures, comparable in interest with John himself and with the Bastard. Old-fashioned though her laments and vituperations may appear by the side of passages such as those I have just examined, they work on the stage because they fit her role, which is almost entirely an impotent one, though it does not begin in impotence. When she first enters, she has allies to back her, and can, therefore, engage in scolding with Elinor, and make telling use of baby talk to express her contempt for the Queen Mother's invitation to Arthur, 'Come to thy grandam, child,' by retorting:

> Do, child, go to it grandam, child;
> Give grandam kingdom, and it grandam will
> Give it a plum, a cherry, and a fig.
> There's a good grandam! (II.i.159–63)

That is positively naturalistic in its neatly calculated spite. But with the conclusion of a peace and of an alliance between England and France there is no longer a place for this kind of speaking. Left powerless by the alliance, Constance is forced into taking up the posture of Niobe; when Salisbury requests her to go with him to the two kings, she replies:

> I will not go with thee;
> I will instruct my sorrows to be proud,
> For grief is proud, and makes his owner stoop.
> To me, and to the state of my great grief,
> Let kings assemble; for my grief's so great
> That no supporter but the huge firm earth
> Can hold it up. [*Seats herself on the ground.*]
> Here I and sorrows sit;
> Here is my throne, bid kings come bow to it. (III.i.66–74)

This too, in its own way, looks forward to the great tragedies both in its resort to overstatement* and in its assertion of the importance of grief. But, unlike the heroes of the tragedies, Constance can take no positive action against her enemies. Deprived first of all hope that Arthur will ever

* See Maynard Mack 'The Jacobean Shakespeare' in *Jacobean Theatre* ed J.R. Brown and B. Harris, London 1960, pp 11–41.

enjoy his rights, and then of Arthur himself, she has nothing to fall back on but words, which she uses not only as an outlet for sorrow but also as a sort of defence against the intolerable demands of facts that she finds unacceptable. Like Richard II, though in a rather different fashion, she can do things with words that she cannot do with men and with events. Instead of allowing and even encouraging one image to beget another, as he does, she prefers to 'set the word itself / Against the word,' as when she tells Salisbury:

> I trust I may not trust thee, for thy word
> Is but the vain breath of a common man:
> Believe me I do not believe thee, man;
> I have a king's oath to the contrary. (III.i.7–10)

Carried to its limit, this method leads to the oxymorons of her invitation to death, 'Thou odoriferous stench! sound rottenness!', where the attraction death has for her is balanced by and united with the natural revulsion she feels from it. Coming from her, the oxymorons are acceptable and effective because her speech in general is so full of rhetorical devices, whereas Juliet's use of the same device (*Romeo and Juliet* III.ii.73–9) jars and seems out of place because her habitual manner of speech is not declamatory.

Yet it would be a mistake to see Constance as wholly or simply a creature of the formal rhetoric she voices so often. The peculiar plangency which distinguishes what she says from the lamentations of Queen Margaret and the other women in the first tetralogy derives largely, I think, from an interplay of the formal with the informal. Time after time she builds up a speech, much as they do, out of repetitive one line units piled one on top of another; but in her case the process does not end with the pile complete but with its falling over under its own weight, as it were, and breaking into fragments. Her invitation to death is very much a case in point:

> Death, death; O amiable lovely death!
> Thou odoriferous stench! sound rottenness!
> Arise from forth the couch of lasting night,
> Thou hate and terror to prosperity,
> And I will kiss thy detestable bones,
> And put my eyeballs in thy vaulty brows,
> And ring these fingers with thy household worms,
> And stop this gap of breath with fulsome dust,
> And be a carrion monster like thyself.
> Come, grin on me, and I will think thou smil'st,

> And buss thee as thy wife. Misery's love,
> O, come to me! (III.iv.25–36)

Something unusual intrudes into the last three lines with the far from elevated verbs 'grin' and 'buss,' but precisely what is going on does not become fully apparent until some ten lines later, when Pandulph's reproof, 'Lady, you utter madness and not sorrow,' leads Constance to say:

> Thou art not holy to belie me so.
> I am not mad: this hair I tear is mine;
> My name is Constance; I was Geffrey's wife;
> Young Arthur is my son, and he is lost.
> I am not mad – I would to heaven I were!
> For then 'tis like I should forget myself. (III.iv.44–9)

These brief, abrupt, factual statements, made up largely of simple monosyllabic words, are the fragments I referred to earlier; and it is Constance's use of them that makes her lamentations so much more moving than those of the women in *Henry VI* and *Richard III*.

What Shakespeare seems to have discovered in writing Constance's part, where rhetoric is pushed to the limit and then beyond it, is the dangers, not of rhetoric – like every other great playwright, he recognized it as an indispensable dramatic instrument, and was to go on employing it for the rest of his career – but of undiluted rhetoric, which can so easily become mechanical and monotonous. To have its greatest effect as a means of heightening and, at the same time, shaping and formalizing feeling, it needs to be set off by something else that at least sounds and looks unrhetorical. To appreciate what this discovery would eventually lead to, it is only necessary to glance at another scene dealing with a character standing, like Constance, on the very verge of madness. In the second scene on the heath, King Lear comes on defying the storm. Counterpointed by the prose and the jingles of the Fool, which Lear disregards, his speech culminates in a kind of vision in which various criminals who have escaped punishment pass before his eyes as he addresses them:

> Let the great gods,
> That keep this dreadful pudder o'er our heads,
> Find out their enemies now. Tremble, thou wretch,
> That hast within thee undivulged crimes
> Unwhipp'd of justice. Hide thee, thou bloody hand;
> Thou perjur'd, and thou simular man of virtue
> That art incestuous; caitiff, to pieces shake,
> That under covert and convenient seeming
> Hast practis'd on man's life. Close pent-up guilts,

Rive your concealing continents, and cry
These dreadful summoners grace. I am a man
More sinn'd against then sinning.

At this point Kent interposes to suggest that Lear enter the hovel, and draws this answer from the King:

My wits begin to turn.
Come on, my boy. How dost, my boy? Art cold?
I am cold myself. Where is this straw, my fellow?
The art of our necessities is strange
That can make vile things precious. Come, your hovel.
Poor fool and knave, I have one part in my heart
That's sorry yet for thee. (*King Lear* III.ii.49–73)

In terms of felt experience the difference between what Lear says and what Constance says is vast; but structurally the two excerpts are remarkably alike. Lear's vision of crime is as rhetorical as her appeal to death in its citing of one instance after another, and it ends in much the same fashion with a return to the more familiar kind of language, which, after an interruption from without, leads the way into the movingly bare simplicity of 'My wits begin to turn' and all that follows it. The crucial difference between Lear's rhetoric and Constance's is not that his is less rhetorical than hers but that it is less obtrusively so. His units are not single lines, but anything from a half line to two lines or more. Moreover, not one of those units starts as the beginning of a line, except for 'Thou perjur'd,' and their construction is varied. 'Hide thee, thou bloody hand' is both like and unlike 'Tremble, thou wretch,' while 'caitiff, to pieces shake' reverses the basic structure of these two commands. Constance's repetition of 'And' and of 'thy' proclaims art; Lear's variations conceal a much subtler art that makes rhetoric sound natural while preserving its power to insist. Nevertheless, the overall structure of the two excerpts remains the same: in each a passage of heightened language is set against a passage of naked simplicity and directness, so that both gain from the juxtaposition.

In suggesting that *King John* points to the future I am not claiming that it is a neglected masterpiece, though I do think it is a better play and a more interesting play than most of its critics allow. It seems to me to be something of a poetic dramatist's workshop, a place in which he reassesses old techniques and tries out new ones. There is much that is tentative about it, and there are occasions when it suffers as a whole because its author cannot resist the promptings of the critical spirit that gives rise to and informs its experimental nature. We approve and applaud when the

Bastard mocks the conventional love poetry of the Dauphin (II.i.504–9), and when he says of the defiance with which the Citizen of Angiers concludes his proposal for a match between Blanch and the Dauphin:

> Here's a stay
> That shakes the rotten carcass of old Death
> Out of his rags! Here's a large mouth, indeed,
> That spits forth death and mountains, rocks and seas;
> Talks as familiarly of roaring lions
> As maids of thirteen do of puppy-dogs! (II.i.445–60)

But how are we to react when the Bastard himself resorts to precisely the same kind of utterance as that which he castigates in the Citizen? Shakespeare the self-critical artist leaves us in no doubt. Informed by Pandulph that the Dauphin absolutely refuses to abandon his invasion of England, the Bastard characteristically voices his approval of the Dauphin's resolution, and then launches into a vaunt that takes up the next thirty lines. Embarrassing enough in itself, this piece of rodomontade, in which the broken John is described as an eagle ready 'To souse annoyance that comes near his nest,' is made even more embarrassing by its being attributed to John, who has, in fact, practically ceased to exercise kingly power and handed over 'the ordering of this present time' to the Bastard because he is quite unable to cope with the situation himself. The speech is, despite its vigorous vocabulary, so patently an unsatisfactory attempt to put a bold face on a disastrous state of affairs as not to require a comment; its hollowness is plain to see. But the comment comes, nevertheless, and from the lips of the Dauphin:

> There end thy brave, and turn thy face in peace;
> We grant thou canst outscold us. (V.ii.159–60)

It is almost as though Shakespeare has gone out of his way to intervene personally in his drama in order to bring his own lapse to the notice of his audience; for, as he evidently realized, the Bastard's vaunt and the Dauphin's fully justified dismissal of it have a most damaging effect on the idea, so carefully built up in the latter part of the play, of the Bastard as the incarnation of the enduring spirit of England and of English resistance. The heroic figure has been allowed to degenerate into a mere 'brabbler.'

Interplay of Verse and Prose: *A Midsummer Night's Dream* and *The Merchant of Venice*

Whereas *King John* is tentative, experimental, and, on occasions, somewhat inconsistent, both in the attitude it adopts towards its subject and in its manner, which seems to be poised rather uneasily and insecurely between that of the first tetralogy of the histories and that of *Troilus and Cressida* and the great tragedies, *A Midsummer Night's Dream* is completely consistent in attitude and assured in manner, the work of a poetic dramatist who is in absolute command of his resources and deploys them with a seemingly effortless ease that tends to mask their range and variety. Here, perhaps for the first time, the inventive and the critical sides of Shakespeare's creativity combine in perfect harmony with each other. Like *Hamlet*, this comedy is both highly original and yet deeply rooted in the past. In part, the tradition out of which it grows is, as C.L. Barber in particular has so well demonstrated,* that of the age-old seasonal festivals, such as May-day, which were still vigorously alive in Shakespeare's England, and which he would, no doubt, have been familiar with from childhood, when he would probably have heard much about fairies also and watched carpenters and the like at their work. But, as well as being firmly embedded in the life of the time, *A Midsummer Night's Dream* is also intimately and critically related to earlier traditions of acting and of dramatic composition.

The link between the play and the dramatic past is, of course, 'Pyramus and Thisby.' Bottom and his fellows are still doing, with no trace of self-consciousness, what their ancestors had done for gener-

* C.L. Barber *Shakespeare's Festive Comedy* Princeton 1959, pp 119–62 and *passim*

ations; but, being men of the sixteenth century, not of the Middle Ages, they draw their material from Ovid, by way of Arthur Golding's translation, instead of from the Bible and the sermon, the sources of the miracle plays and the moralities. Their interlude, like 'The Mousetrap' in *Hamlet*, is not, apart from its obvious dependence on Golding's sublimely bad narrative, a parody of any specific play, but of some of the more delightful absurdities, especially in diction and versification, of the sort of drama that was flourishing when Shakespeare was young. 'A tedious brief scene of young Pyramus / And his love Thisby; very tragical mirth' is a title that smacks irresistibly of that 'lamentable tragedie mixed full of pleasant mirth,' *Cambyses, King of Persia* (c 1561), and which may well allude also to the 'new Tragical Comedy,' *Appius and Virginia* (c 1564) and to Richard Edwards' *Damon and Pithias* (c 1565), described as an 'excellent comedie' on its title page, but twice referred to as a 'tragical comedy' in the Prologue to it (38 and 46).* It was in works such as these that Shakespeare found the models – and the target – for the drumming alliterative invocations to the Fates and the Furies that Pyramus and Thisby utter as a prelude to their self-inflicted deaths. *Damon and Pithias* could provide him with, for example,

> Gripe me you greedy grief,
> And present pangs of death!
> You sisters three with cruel hands,
> With speed now stop my breath! (612–15)

Cambyses, not to be outdone, had such gems to offer as

> But he, when Sisters Three had wrought to shere his vital threed (Prologue, 17),

and an address to Fortune that begins

> O false and fickle frowning dame, that turneth as the winde (449);

and *Appius and Virginia* could contribute 'The furies fell of Limbo lake' (p 23) and two splendid uses of 'imbrue' (pp 36 and 39), including Virginia's cry:

> Bid him imbrue his bloody hands in guiltless blood of me.

The most fascinating thing, however, about 'Pyramus and Thisby' is that its author does not, unless I am mistaken, exempt his own earlier

* My texts for *Cambyses* and *Damon and Pithias* are those printed by Joseph Quincy Adams in his *Chief Pre-Shakespearean Dramas*, Cambridge, Mass. and London 1924. For *Appius and Virginia* I use the text printed by J.S. Farmer in his *Five Anonymous Plays*, London 1908.

self from the fun he makes of others. Having discovered the body of Thisby, Pyramus asks:

> O wherefore, Nature, didst thou lions frame?
> Since lion vile hath here deflower'd my dear. (v.i.283–4)

The first of those lines looks like a transposition into the comic mode of the question Marcus asks, after Lavinia has at last succeeded in revealing that she was raped 'in the ruthless, vast, and gloomy woods':

> O, why should nature build so foul a den,
> Unless the gods delight in tragedies? (*Titus Andronicus* IV.i.60–1)

As for the second, it is hard to read it without catching a distinct echo of Old Capulet's breaking the news of Juliet's 'death' to Paris:

> O son, the night before thy wedding day
> Hath Death lain with thy wife. There she lies,
> Flower as she was, deflowered by him.
> (*Romeo and Juliet* IV.v.35–7)

Nor is the echo in any way surprising or out of place, for 'Pyramus and Thisby' is in its main design, as has often been noted, a parody of *Romeo and Juliet*.

The readiness with which Shakespeare burlesques his own tragedy of love in 'Pyramus and Thisby,' and then virtually stands it on its head by giving it a happy outcome in the story of Lysander and Hermia, is a pointer to the achievement of *A Midsummer Night's Dream* as a whole. Its newness lies not in the exploration of fresh material, fresh attitudes, or, with one possible exception to be made for some of Bottom's speeches, fresh modes of expression, but in the skill and confidence with which it uses new combinations and juxtapositions of situations, themes, and styles, all of which its author had employed before. It is, essentially, a kind of distillation from much that had preceded it. Theseus, for example, dispensing, in act IV, with the oppressive Athenian law, 'Which,' he had once said, 'by no means we may extenuate' (I.i.120), is very like the Duke of Ephesus, in *The Comedy of Errors*, remitting, at the play's end, the sentence he imposed on Aegeon at its opening. He is also the efficient yet beneficent ruler, closely resembling Queen Elizabeth, who, as the ideal against which kings are judged and found wanting, hovers like a shadowy presence in the background of all the histories Shakespeare had written hitherto. Similarly, Egeus, insisting that his daughter marry Demetrius, the man of his choice, recalls Old Capulet in function, in character, and in speech, especially when he cuts short Lysander's account of the events of the night with the words:

> Enough, enough, my Lord; you have enough;
> I beg the law, the law upon his head. (IV.i.151–2)

The fairies, who, at a first glance, may seem like an innovation, develop out of Mercutio's Queen Mab speech (*Romeo and Juliet* I.iv.53–95), for it is there that Shakespeare alters the whole tradition of fairy-lore by making them delicate, airy, diminutive creatures, as distinct from the beings of near-human stature that they had been previously.

Even more striking than the resemblances between some of the characters in *A Midsummer Night's Dream* and some of the characters in the earlier plays are resemblances in situation. Here the obvious precursor, as it is in some respects also the precursor of *Romeo and Juliet*, is *The Two Gentlemen of Verona*, where Proteus eventually returns to his first love, Julia, much as Demetrius eventually returns to his first love, Helena, and where Silvia, once the object of the attentions of Valentine and Proteus, is for a short time rejected by both, just as Hermia, desired at the beginning by both Lysander and Demetrius, finds herself for a time rejected by both in favour of Helena. But in the later play these shifts of affection raise none of the difficulties of motivation and credibility that they do in the earlier, because the responsibility for them rests with Puck, not with the lovers themselves, and because the attitude to love that Puck/Cupid embodies – Puck equates himself with Cupid when he says:

> Cupid is a knavish lad,
> Thus to make poor females mad (III.ii.440–1) –

is one that lays stress on its irrationality and absurdity. Moreover, Shakespeare ensures that his audience remains detached from the lovers in *A Midsummer Night's Dream* by handling their relationship in a style that is different from all the other styles that he has recourse to for other parts of his comedy, for, like *Love's Labour's Lost* with which it has much else in common, it avails itself of an astonishing variety of metrical forms, which it employs to keep different groups of characters distinct from one another.

The major stylistic division is not, however, between different kinds of verse, but between verse and prose, corresponding to the distinction between the rest of the cast and the mechanicals. The mechanicals, except when they are rehearsing or acting their play, use nothing but prose. The other characters, except Theseus and his court when they sit as audience for 'Pyramus and Thisby,' use nothing but verse. This distinction is, of course, the old familiar device for emphasizing differences in rank, but in *A Midsummer Night's Dream* it goes far beyond this function in that it also serves to bring out the contrast between different modes of thought, feeling, and being. The way in which it does this is at its clearest at those points in the play where the prose and the verse come into the closest and most intimate contact with each other: in the scenes between Bottom and Titania. Her first words on hearing his song are: 'What angel wakes me from my flow'ry bed?' (III.i.118). It is an impeccable line of blank verse, and also a wittily allusive one. As they listened to it, many in the original audience of the play would have had, superimposed on the picture the stage offered them of the most ethereal character in the comedy 'translating' the earthiest character in it into an angel complete with an ass's head, a mental picture of Kyd's Hieronymo, aroused by the cries of Bel-imperia, making his entry '*in his shirt, etc.*,' with the famous line: 'What outcries pluck me from my naked bed ... ?' (*The Spanish Tragedy* II.v.1). The allusive wit is visual as well as verbal; so is the comedy of the dialogues between Bottom and Titania, where man transformed into ass voices his asinine appetite as an ass might if it could speak, with no sense whatever of incongruity or awkwardness, to a being who evidently 'looks not with the eyes, but with the mind' and can speak no language but verse.

The dialogues between them are models of courtesy and good manners, for each assumes authority naturally and takes the notion of *noblesse oblige* for granted, Titania as Queen of the Fairies, and Bottom as the acknowledged though uncrowned King of the Mechanicals; and they culminate in the following exchanges:

> TITANIA What, wilt thou hear some music, my sweet love?
> BOTTOM I have a reasonable good ear in music. Let's have the tongs and the bones.
> TITANIA Or say, sweet love, what thou desirest to eat.
> BOTTOM Truly, a peck of provender; I could munch your good dry oats. Methinks I have a great desire to a bottle of hay. Good hay, sweet hay, hath no fellow.
> TITANIA I have a venturous fairy that shall seek
> The squirrel's hoard, and fetch thee new nuts.
> BOTTOM I had rather have a handful or two of dried peas. But, I pray you, let none of your people stir me; I have an exposition of sleep come upon me.
> TITANIA Sleep thou, and I will wind thee in my arms.
> Fairies, be gone, and be all ways away.
> *Exeunt Fairies.*
> So doth the woodbine the sweet honeysuckle
> Gently entwist; the female ivy so
> Enrings the barky fingers of the elm.
> O, how I love thee! how I dote on thee! (IV.i.25–42)

The antithesis is complete: verse rich in similes, a love of music, and an instinctive response to the wealth and beauty of nature, on the one side; prose, no figures of speech, only the most elementary conception of music, and a practical response to the demands of the stomach, on the other. Yet, oddly enough, the most arresting word in the dialogue is Bottom's 'exposition.' Editors and commentators are agreed that it is a malapropism, a mistaken version of 'disposition.' They may be right, but if they are, why does Bottom call it 'an exposition *of*,' not 'an exposition *to*'? The more likely word that he would seem to have in mind is surely 'imposition,' meaning 'the laying on of a burden.' But even that seems a less evocative word than 'exposition'; and so one is driven back to the conjecture that what Bottom really has in mind is some kind of portmanteau word, fusing the sense of 'extreme imposition' into a single verbal unit. Something of the same kind appears to be happening when he responds to Quince's suggestion that they rehearse in the woods by moonlight with the words: 'there we may rehearse most obscenely and courageously' (I.ii.95). Here 'obscenely' would seem to combine the senses of 'obscurely,' meaning 'hidden from public view,' and 'seemly,' or, perhaps, 'unseenly.' In both cases the uncertainty as to precisely what the word means argues that 'exposition' and 'obscenely' are not simple straightforward malapropisms at all, for the essence of a malapropism is the immediate recognition by the hearer of the word intended, but rather the products of what might be termed a creative muddle; and this conclusion is endorsed by Bottom's attempt to describe his experiences of the night when he wakes up from them:

> The eye of man hath not heard, the ear of man hath not seen, man's hand is not able to taste, his tongue to conceive, nor his heart to report, what my dream was. (IV.i.216–20)

The confusion and dislocation of the senses in this passage is both characteristic of the play and very amusing in its own right; but, strangely enough, it is also extremely effective in conveying the mixture of incomprehension, wonder, and gratitude with which Bottom contemplates the 'most rare vision' that has been vouchsafed him. His dream, in which he has played both the lover and the ass, has made a deep impact on his entire being; it has been a synaesthetic experience; and, in an effort to encompass its synaesthetic nature, he has recourse to a prose that makes the kind of leaps and connections that are more usually associated with poetry. Could it be that here we are witnessing the beginning of a process that will ultimately lead to the bold 'mixed' metaphors of the tragedies? We laugh at Bottom's muddles, but we do not laugh when Lady Macbeth asks her husband:

Was the hope drunk
Wherein you dress'd yourself? Hath it slept since,
And wakes it now to look so green and pale
At what it did so freely? (*Macbeth* I.vii.35–8)

Yet the hope that is simultaneously a cloak and a queasy-stomached drunkard on the morning after the night before is inherently as absurd as anything Bottom says. It is the context that makes all the difference to our reaction.

If Bottom's prose opens up new possibilities in the use of language for dramatic ends, as I have suggested, then the verse of the lovers seems deliberately designed to limit our responses to them to those which the playwright regards as appropriate.* When Lysander and Hermia first appear, they speak a blank verse which is not easily distinguishable from that of Theseus, who, in his role of wise and mature governor, very properly retains the same manner throughout the play. But, as soon as they are left alone to face the situation in which they now find themselves, their style alters, becoming both more formal and more lyrical as they proceed to take part in what is, in effect, a duet in blank verse, lamenting the fact that 'The course of true love never did run smooth.' It is a superb piece of writing that condenses much of the experience of *Romeo and Juliet* into a few lines; but its full pathetic potential is carefully held in check by its evident stylization, particularly noticeable in its use of the old device of stichomythia. There follows a brief shift back into more informal blank verse while Lysander explains his plan for their flight from Athens, but then, as Hermia makes her vow to meet him in the woods, heroic couplets take over, and persist for the rest of the scene. The seeming artificiality of the verse form, heavily underlined in the stichomythic exchanges between Hermia and Helena (194–201) and again in Helena's final soliloquy, where the couplets become self-contained and the first line of each is played off against the second, has the effect of making all three lovers look rather like puppets, impelled in all they do by the blind irrational sort of love that Helena rightly defines as 'doting' (230).

It is thus that Shakespeare would have us see all four lovers, and especially the two men after they have fallen victims to Puck's mistakes and mischief; and therefore heroic couplets, varied by the occasional quatrain in alternate rhyme, remain the vehicle for all that they say during the night in the woods, except for a passage of about a hundred and fifty lines in III.ii. Here (195–339) blank verse returns for a time as the

* For this point, and several that follow it, I am indebted to David P. Young *Something of Great Constancy* New Haven and London 1966, pp 63–86.

two girls, whose eyes have not been streaked with the love-juice, temporarily forget about doting in the excitement of the quarrel that arises between them, and suitably lapse into the more naturalistic manner of speech that makes itself heard in, for example, Hermia's heated questions and threats:

> And are you grown so high in his esteem
> Because I am so dwarfish and so low?
> How low am I, thou painted maypole? Speak.
> How low am I? I am not yet so low
> But that my nails can reach unto thine eyes. (III.ii.294–8)

All four abandon rhyme for good when they wake up in their right minds and their right pairs. It has played a considerable part in helping to preserve them as figures of fun, carefully detached from the sympathies of the audience. But now, having ceased to be puppets of Cupid and Puck, they are free to rejoin Theseus and Hippolyta in the comparative liberty of blank verse.

Shakespeare had employed rhyme before as a means of limiting and confining the imaginative response of an audience or reader, especially in that part of *The Taming of the Shrew* that deals with the relationship between Lucentio and Bianca, but never with the same skill and to the same extent as he does in *A Midsummer Night's Dream*. The lovers, however, are only one part of the intricate pattern that makes up the whole; and in the rest of the play it is the other and opposite characteristic of verse, its capacity to stimulate and enlarge the imaginative response, that is very much to the fore. There is every reason why it should be, for in no previous play he had written had the setting, in the fullest possible sense of that word, been such an integral and central part of the dramatic experience. The time of year, the weather, the woodlands, the moonlit night are all active constituent elements of the drama, exerting a powerful natural magic over the mortals who come into contact with them. They must, therefore, be made present in all their potency and plentitude, which means, in effect, that they have to be described, and described in motion. The kind of scene-painting which produces the static verbal equivalent of a backcloth will not suffice. The descriptive passages in *A Midsummer Night's Dream* are as varied as those who voice them, ranging from Titania's forceful evocation of the chaos of the disordered seasons to the delicate fancy of the Fairy whose task is 'To dew her orbs upon the green' and who sees the cowslips as the bodyguard of her mistress, but they all create an impression of multiplicity and movement, right through to Puck's conjuring up of the very spirit of the small hours in the final part of the play:

Now the hungry lion roars,
And the wolf behowls the moon;
Whilst the heavy ploughman snores,
All with weary task fordone.
Now the wasted brands do glow,
Whilst the screech-owl, screeching loud,
Puts the wretch that lies in woe
In remembrance of a shroud.
Now it is the time of night
That the graves, all gaping wide,
Every one lets forth his sprite,
In the church-way paths to glide.
And we fairies, that do run
By the triple Hecate's team
From the presence of the sun,
Following darkness like a dream,
Now are frolic. Not a mouse
Shall disturb this hallowed house.
I am sent with broom before,
To sweep the dust behind the door. (V.i.360–79)

Here, as likewise, though on a much larger scale, in Titania's speech about the seasons (II.i.81–117), the old device of the list is being put to a new use and acquiring a new look in the process. Item still follows item, but the effect produced is one of accumulation, as distinct from mere enumeration, because almost every line contains a verb; the static has been replaced with the dynamic.

The exquisite art with which the descriptive passages and the songs are fitted, both metrically and in terms of imagery and diction, to the nature and function of the characters who speak or sing them is typical of the conduct of the entire play. It is the art of a dedicated craftsman as well as of a great poet, and it extends to minute details. The parts of the tiny fairies – Moth, Peaseblossom, Cobweb, and Mustardseed – are beautifully designed to be played by very young children. Their speeches rarely run to more than a single word, the longest of them being Mustardseed's 'What's your will?' (IV.i.20); often they repeat a formula, one after the other; and, most fascinating of all, the stage directions for such simple actions as they are called on to perform are spoken, in the form of commands, either by Titania or by Bottom:

BOTTOM Where's Peaseblossom?
PEASEBLOSSOM Ready.

> BOTTOM Scratch my head, Peaseblossom. Where's Mounsieur Cobweb?
> COBWEB Ready. (IV.i.5–9)

It is the scrupulous attention to practical minutiae of acting and staging, so evident in passages such as this, that underlies and gives body to the play's concern, in its own lightly tentative yet nonetheless searching and suggestive fashion, with such fundamental matters as the nature of dramatic illusion and the function of the imagination in the process of perception. But these are topics that lie outside the scope of this particular study.

In *The Merchant of Venice* (c 1596) the ratio of prose to verse is somewhat lower than it is in *A Midsummer Night's Dream*, but not substantially or significantly so. The way in which the distinction between the two media operates within the structure of the play is, however, very different. It is true that this distinction does serve, among other things, to separate the characters who are highest in rank – the Prince of Morocco, the Prince of Arragon, and the Duke of Venice, all of whom speak nothing but verse – from the characters who are lowest in rank – Launcelot Gobbo and Old Gobbo, who speak nothing but prose. But this can hardly be its main function, since the social gulf is, in any case, obvious enough, and since none of these figures is of the first importance. Nor does it correspond with the themes and antinomies that many have found in the play. Prose is spoken in Belmont, as well as in Venice; the expression of love is no more confined to verse than the expression of hatred is confined to prose; and the claims of the Old Law, like those of the New, make themselves heard through either medium. This lack of correspondence reinforces the scepticism with which one reacts to these attempts to make the play a matter of direct and rather abstract oppositions, and drives one back to the concrete demonstrable fact that the backbone of its action is one trial after another. Not only are its two great climaxes trials, IV.i a literal trial, and III.ii a test of Bassanio's love of Portia, but also it begins with Bassanio's making a trial of Antonio's love for him in the very first scene, continues, in the second, with a test of Portia's obedience to her father's will, and proceeds in a series of trials, of one sort or another, to reach its conclusion with the business of the rings as a comic test of fidelity.

It is, therefore, fitting that the dominant mode of the play, whether the medium be verse or prose, should be the forensic. The language of *The Merchant of Venice* is the language of argument; the structure of the major speeches in it rhetorical. Its characters argue with themselves, as well as with one another. Morocco finds reasons for his instinctive preference for gold; Arragon for his instinctive preference for silver; and Bassanio for his instinctive preference for lead. Each enlists the aid of logic to justify his choice. But long before any of them makes his choice, which he does in verse, Shakespeare has carefully burlesqued their dialectic in the prose soliloquy of Launcelot Gobbo, at the opening of II.ii, where the conclusion that conscience leads to is deliberately rejected in favour of the conclusion that pleasure and convenience lead to, though conscience has the better of the argument:

> Certainly my conscience will serve me to run from this Jew my master. The fiend is at mine elbow and tempts me, saying to me 'Gobbo, Launcelot Gobbo, good Launcelot' or 'good Gobbo' or 'good Launcelot Gobbo, use your legs, take the start, run away'. My conscience says 'No; take heed, honest Launcelot, take heed, honest Gobbo' or, as aforesaid, 'honest Launcelot Gobbo, do not run; scorn running with thy heels'. Well, the most courageous fiend bids me pack. 'Via!' says the fiend; 'away!' says the fiend. 'For the heavens, rouse up a brave mind' says the fiend 'and run.' Well, my conscience, hanging about the neck of my heart, says very wisely to me 'My honest friend Launcelot, being an honest man's son' or rather 'an honest woman's son'; for indeed my father did something smack, something grow to, he had a kind of taste – well, my conscience says 'Launcelot, budge not'. 'Budge' says the fiend. 'Budge not' says my conscience. 'Conscience,' say I 'you counsel well.' 'Fiend,' say I 'you counsel well.' To be rul'd by my conscience, I should stay with the Jew my master, who – God bless the mark! – is a kind of devil; and, to run away from the Jew, I should be ruled by the fiend, who – saving your reverence! – is the devil himself. Certainly the Jew is the very devil incarnation; and, in my conscience, my conscience is but a kind of hard conscience to offer to counsel me to stay with the Jew. The fiend gives the more friendly counsel. I will run, fiend; my heels are at your commandment; I will run. (II.ii.1–27)

This speech, recalling the central issue of the morality plays and of Marlowe's *Dr Faustus* but also handling that issue in a comic fashion, suggests that there are morality elements in *The Merchant of Venice*, but that these too are being treated comically. It also makes it clear that one of the functions of the prose in the play is to work as a sort of counterpoint to the poetry, for in its evolution it is almost an exaggerated paradigm of the argumentative mode of so many of the verse speeches. Now, of the characters who play a major role, the only one who is not an amphibian, equally at home in verse and prose, is Antonio, who is wholly a creature of verse. His total reliance on it is, in itself, sufficient to set him off from the rest; but his isolation from them is still further endorsed by the fact that only once does he make use of the rhetorical dialectical mode which comes so habitually to them, and then for a most unusual purpose. Early in the trial scene, when Bassanio attempts to argue with Shylock and makes no progress whatever, Antonio eventually interrupts their dialogue to tell his friend:

> I pray you, think you question with the Jew.
> You may as well go stand upon the beach
> And bid the main flood bate his usual height;
> You may as well use question with the wolf,
> Why he hath made the ewe bleat for the lamb;
> You may as well forbid the mountain pines
> To wag their high tops and to make no noise
> When they are fretten with the gusts of heaven;
> You may as well do any thing most hard
> As seek to soften that – than which what's harder? –
> His Jewish heart. Therefore, I do beseech you,
> Make no more offers, use no farther means,
> But with all brief and plain conveniency
> Let me have judgment, and the Jew his will. (IV.i.70–83)

It is a powerful and moving piece of persuasion. Using emphatic repetition and drawing instance after instance from the world of nature, Antonio builds up his plea, culminating in the final sentence introduced by the word 'Therefore,' for the trial to be brought to a speedy end, for the inevitable, as it seems, to be accepted, and for himself to suffer as he must. Whereas the other characters argue for victory, seeking to justify the taking of revenge, the showing of mercy, or the making of a choice, Antonio argues for defeat and self-extinction. But why, one asks, does he have recourse to this manner and for this purpose at this time? And then, looking back over the action, one begins to see a kind of answer. From the outset he has seen himself as the helpless victim of an unintelligible something that he cannot define, the 'it' that he refers to in the speech that opens the play:

> In sooth, I know not why I am so sad.
> It wearies me; you say it wearies you;
> But how I caught it, found it, or came by it,
> What stuff 'tis made of, whereof it is born,
> I am to learn;

> And such a want-wit sadness makes of me
> That I have much ado to know myself. (I.i.1–7)

It is a strange position for the protagonist of a comedy to find himself in. Nor do the events that follow on this opening do anything to improve it; on the contrary, as fortune turns against him, everything conspires to increase his sense of himself as the predestined victim, until, in the trial scene, he actually describes himself as 'a tainted wether of the flock / Meetest for death' (IV.i.114–15). Moreover, he still remains separate and withdrawn even after the trial is over. In the final scene he speaks a mere six and a half lines, one of them being 'I am th' unhappy subject of these quarrels' (V.i.238), as he takes the blame on himself when Portia and Nerissa are wrangling with Bassanio and Gratiano over the matter of the rings.

But Antonio's persuasive plea has yet a further significance. It begins with 'the Jew,' it ends with 'the Jew,' and the summing-up in it that precedes the final deduction concludes with 'His Jewish heart.' His powerful and deep-rooted animosity against Shylock is, in the final analysis, as unintelligible to him as his *taedium vitae.* He may rationalize it as the outcome of their religious differences and of their disagreement over the issue of usury, but at bottom he sees Shylock as a brute fact of nature, one who must act as he does because it is not in him to act otherwise, which also happens to be the way in which Shylock sees him. The Jew's first words, spoken in an aside, after Antonio enters to him and Bassanio in I.iii, are:

> How like a fawning publican he looks!
> I hate him for he is a Christian;
> But more for that in low simplicity
> He lends out money gratis, and brings down
> The rate of usance here with us in Venice.
> If I can catch him once upon the hip,
> I will feed fat the ancient grudge I bear him. (I.iii.36–42)

Curiously yet firmly and convincingly linked together by their loathing of each other, Shylock and Antonio stand apart from all the other characters; and their separation from them is underscored by the fact that each of them has his own particular manner of utterance. In addition to relying entirely on verse, Antonio, a man governed by feelings, expresses what he feels, whether it be his indefinable sense of sadness, his love for Bassanio, or his scorn and hatred of Shylock, in a naked direct fashion which leaves him extremely vulnerable. Shylock, on the other hand, though fundamentally as much driven by feeling as Antonio, has a shrewdness and a capacity for calculation that enable him to conceal what he feels until the time comes for him to satisfy his desires. In his early dealings with Antonio he counters the Merchant's bluntness with the indirections of irony, which can be disavowed. Not limited to one medium of expression, he succeeds in putting his individual stamp on prose and verse alike, so that both become indelibly his. In this respect, he seems to have grown out of Mercutio, as it were, but, unlike Mercutio, he does not have to feel his way towards his idiom; it is there, an inalienable part of himself, from the moment he steps on to the stage. His first exchanges with Bassanio establish some of its characteristic features:

> SHYLOCK Three thousand ducats – well.
> BASSANIO Ay, sir, for three months.
> SHYLOCK For three months – well.
> BASSANIO For the which, as I told you, Antonio shall be bound.
> SHYLOCK Antonio shall become bound – well. (I.iii.1–6)

The habit of itemizing things, so typical of the cautious businessman, together with the fondness for repetition, will remain with Shylock for the rest of the play. Employed in the service of passion, and built into a firm rhetorical structure, they inform the most deeply felt speech that he makes, when, in answer to Salerio's question as to what Antonio's flesh will be good for, he replies:

> To bait fish withal. If it will feed nothing else, it will feed my revenge. He hath disgrac'd me and hind'red me half a million; laugh'd at my losses, mock'd at my gains, scorned my nation, thwarted my bargains, cooled my friends, heated mine enemies. And what's his reason? I am a Jew. Hath not a Jew eyes? Hath not a Jew hands, organs, dimensions, senses, affections, passions, fed with the same food, hurt with the same weapons, subject to the same diseases, healed by the same means, warmed and cooled by the same winter and summer as a Christian is? If you prick us, do we not bleed? If you tickle us, do we not laugh? If you poison us, do we not die? And if you wrong us, shall we not revenge? If we are like you in the rest, we will resemble you in that. If a Jew wrong a Christian, what is his humility? Revenge. If a Christian wrong a Jew, what should his sufferance be by Christian example? Why, revenge. The villainy you teach me I will execute; and it shall go hard but I will better the instruction. (III.i.45–62)

A further feature of Shylock's manner that is already apparent in his dialogue with Bassanio is his distrust of figurative language. Having pointed out that there are 'land-rats and water-rats, water-thieves and land-thieves,' he goes on to add, lest there be any mistake about the matter, 'I mean pirates' (I.iii.21–2). The same prose mind and prose idiom are evident when he speaks in verse, commanding Jessica to 'stop my house's ears – I mean my casements' (II.v.33). In fact, it is the infiltration of prose rhythms and colloquial phrases into his blank verse that serves to hold his prose and verse together, identifying both as his. Blank verse has become completely responsive to a habit of mind, which is also a trick of speech, when Shylock remarks, after Antonio has reminded him that the loan is to be for three months:

> I had forgot – three months; you told me so.
> Well then, your bond; and let me see – but hear you,
> Methoughts you said you neither lend nor borrow
> Upon advantage. (I.iii.62–5)

The same 'let me see' turns up again some thirty lines later when Shylock says:

> Three thousand ducats – 'tis a good round sum.
> Three months from twelve; then let me see, the rate – (I.iii.98–9).

Up to this point Shylock's mannerisms of speech have been mainly a source of amusement, serving to establish his age and his occupation, but now the hesitations and the parenthetical phrases fall away and the repetitions acquire a sarcastically upbraiding force, as he goes on to describe Antonio's treatment of him in the past and to emphasize the gross discrepancy between that past behaviour and the present request for a loan. In a speech that runs to some twenty-four lines (101–24) he uses 'dog' three times, 'cur' twice, 'moneys' four times, and 'money' once. The result is so devastatingly effective that the speech has left its mark on the English language at large. Commenting on Shylock's idiosyncratic use of the form 'moneys,' the OED remarks:

> From Shakespeare onwards, the use of the plural for the singular has been commonly attributed to Jews, whose supposed pronunciation is sometimes ridiculed by the spelling 'monish'.

Within the context of the scene Shylock's sarcasm causes Antonio to reveal his feelings in the naked direct manner I have referred to earlier, and with such violence that Shylock can take advantage of it to utter his deflating line, 'Why, look you, how you storm!' (132); but, as the action develops, the menacing qualities of which his repetition is capable become more and more pronounced. By the time Shylock can say 'Let him look to his bond' three times in the course of six lines (III.i.37–42), and 'I'll have my bond' five times in the course of fourteen lines (III.iii.4–17), repetition is at once the instrument and the mark of a mind obsessed by a single purpose. Combined with the habit of cumulative itemizing, it finds its culmination in the question and answer method that Shylock has recourse to when justifying his determination to have his bond in the trial scene:

> You'll ask me why I rather choose to have
> A weight of carrion flesh than to receive
> Three thousand ducats. I'll not answer that,
> But say it is my humour – is it answer'd?
> What if my house be troubled with a rat,
> And I be pleas'd to give ten thousand ducats
> To have it ban'd? What, are you answer'd yet?
> Some men there are love not a gaping pig;
> Some that are mad if they behold a cat;
> And others, when the bagpipe sings i' th' nose,
> Cannot contain their urine; for affection,
> Mistress of passion, sways it to the mood
> Of what it likes or loathes. Now, for your answer:
> As there is no firm reason to be rend'red
> Why he cannot abide a gaping pig;
> Why he, a harmless necessary cat;
> Why he, a woollen bagpipe, but of force
> Must yield to such inevitable shame
> As to offend himself being offended;
> So can I give no reason, nor I will not,
> More than a lodg'd hate and a certain loathing
> I bear Antonio, that I follow thus
> A losing suit against him. Are you answered? (IV.i.40–62)

Shylock's reduction of his enemy to the animal level supports my earlier contention that he sees Antonio precisely as Antonio sees him; but the most fascinating aspect of the speech is its clear demonstration of how an individual idiom can colour and subdue to its purpose the forensic mode which is so typical of the play as a whole. Admirably sustained through the triumphant crows of delighted satisfaction – 'O wise young judge,' 'O noble judge!', etc – with which Shylock greets Portia's seeming acquiescence in the justice of his plea, his manner ultimately leaves him wide open to the jeers of Gratiano when the case goes against him.

Shylock dominates *The Merchant of Venice*, until he is forcibly ejected, as it were, from its action, because he has the best, meaning the most dramatically effective, lines in it. To a greater degree, I think, than any character Shakespeare had created before him, he is what he says and how he says it. The man is the words he speaks, bearing out Ben Jonson's dictum in his *Discoveries*:

> *Language* most shewes a man: speake that I may see thee. It springs out of the most retired, and inmost parts of us, and is the Image of the Parent of it, the mind. No glasse renders a mans forme, or likenesse, so true as his speech.*

When Shylock leaves the court of justice, defeated and broken, he takes the essential vitality of the play with him. The absence from its last act of the most arresting and unmistakable voice in it, almost, one is tempted to say, a voice crying in a wilderness of monkeys, is something felt, reducing the bickerings over the rings, especially in the stylized exchanges of Bassanio and Portia (v.i.192–208), to mere chatter.

I have said that I miss the sound of Shylock's voice in act v. It is, perhaps, an oversimplification, for the voice cannot be separated from what it says and is so perfectly adapted to saying. It is essentially the voice of protest and also, as that voice so often tends to be, the voice of condemnation, of contempt, and of revenge. It speaks, as does the voice of Antonio, of racial hatred, of religious intolerance, of economic rivalry, and of deep-rooted, instinctive, personal antipathy. And these are issues to which romantic comedy has no answer. They cannot be swept away by ducal decree, still less made non-existent by the donning or the doffing of a disguise. They persist. In a paradoxical kind of way, the Venice of the play is, despite its ridiculous laws and its even more ridiculous administration of them, curiously like the world we live in. At least it is so until Shylock leaves the court to be seen and heard no more. But, while Shylock goes, the serious issues connected with him remain; they have been shelved, not answered or disposed of. Shakespeare tries to restore the atmosphere proper to romantic comedy by moving the action to Belmont once more and falling back on his genius for lyricism. The formalized blank verse duet that Lorenzo and Jessica share at the opening of act v, and Lorenzo's hymn to music that follows it, go some way towards concealing the legerdemain that has so conveniently done the shelving; but Shakespeare does not leave things at this point. Ultimately the great artist's passion for truth gets the better of the need for a happy ending. The long-drawn-out confusions and explanations, shot through with bawdry, are an admission that nothing has really changed, that the world of this play cannot be metamorphosed into the golden world of romance.

* *Ben Jonson* ed C.H. Herford and Percy and Evelyn Simpson, Oxford 1925–52, vol VIII, p 625, lines 2031–5

It is no accident that the last words in the comedy, like the last words addressed to Shylock, come from the lips of Gratiano, a thoroughly dislikable character and, by far and away, the most vulgar figure in it. As he has already gloated over Shylock's downfall, so he now dwells greasily in anticipation on the night he is about to spend with Nerissa. To regard the ending as happy or as a satisfactory solution is to approve of Gratiano, which is, I find, quite impossible.

'Unpoetical' Poetry and Figurative Prose: *Henry IV*

Coleridge said of *Antony and Cleopatra*:

> The highest praise, or rather form of praise, of this play which I can offer in my own mind is the doubt which its perusal always occasions in me, whether it is not in all exhibitions of a giant power in its strength and vigour of maturity, a formidable rival of the *Macbeth*, *Lear*, *Othello* and *Hamlet*. *Feliciter audax* is the motto for its style comparatively with his other works, even as it is the general motto of all his works compared with those of other poets.*

That description applies equally well to *Henry IV* (1596–7), the latest to be composed of the plays mentioned as Shakespeare's by Meres in 1598, for it is precisely the sense of 'a giant power in its strength and vigour of maturity' that its Two Parts convey. In size, in significance, and, above all, in the sheer wealth of invention that has gone into its making, *Henry IV* is among the major achievements. It is also, as I sought to establish, at least in part, at the beginning of this study, one of the most revolutionary of all the plays, a work that profoundly altered the shape and appearance not only of its author's own *œuvre* but also of Elizabethan drama as a whole. In it Shakespeare, fully conscious of the new kind of awareness that he had created and cultivated in his audience and had already exploited so brilliantly in the writing of *A Midsummer Night's Dream*, confidently invites their co-operation and participation in a fresh venture, marked by a 'happy valiancy of style' which is 'the representative and result' of all

* *Coleridge on Shakespeare* ed Terence Hawkes, Harmondsworth 1969, p 269

that he had learned since he first began to write for the theatre. Nor was his confidence in that audience and in their powers of discrimination misplaced; for *Henry IV* was an immediate popular success, and continued to be a popular success right down to the closing of the theatres in 1642, totally unaffected, it would seem, by the decline of the history play in general after 1600.*

Like *A Midsummer Night's Dream* on the one side of it and *Hamlet* on the other, *Henry IV* both affirms its links with the past – Shakespeare's own earlier work as well as the past of English drama in general – and adopts a creatively critical attitude to that past. Its connections with *Richard II*, explicitly spelled out and insisted upon in scene after scene in both parts, are plain for all to see, leading to the widely held though by no means unanimous view that *Richard II*, the Two Parts of *Henry IV*, and *Henry V* were conceived and composed as parts of one grand design, the Second Tetralogy, as it is so often called. It is also evident and generally accepted that both *Henry IV* and *Henry V* owe something to the anonymous *The Famous Victories of Henry V* (c. 1586), though it is difficult to say just how much, because of the mangled and probably much truncated state in which the text of the anonymous play has survived. Pistol's play-scraps, drawn from the ranting drama of the 1580s and early 1590s, testify to Shakespeare's knowledge of and tolerantly critical attitude to that drama; and the long tradition of the Morality Play, and especially of the moral interlude, has left its mark too on *Henry IV*, though the precise nature and significance of that mark is still a matter of dispute.

The play's dependence on the past is, then, clear enough; yet who, in the audience that first saw *1 Henry IV*, could have had the remotest idea of what it was that he was about to enjoy? Assuming that he knew Shakespeare's other plays based on English history, one might reasonably guess that he would enter the theatre expecting a 'tragical history,' for all those earlier plays had been of this kind. He would also, had he given any thought to the matter, have been expecting a play wholly, or almost wholly, in verse, since only one of Shakespeare's previous histories, *2 Henry VI*, had contained a substantial amount of prose, and the two most recent of them, *Richard II* and *King John*, had contained no prose whatsoever. Moreover, all those earlier histories had been historical, in the sense that everything in them had had some basis, however slight, in the chronicles. It is true that Shakespeare had disregarded chronology when it suited him to do so, and that many of his scenes had been largely invented by him; but his inventions can reasonably be viewed as legitimate expan-

* See Harold Child's account of the play's Stage-History in J. Dover Wilson's edition of *1 Henry IV*, Cambridge 1946, pp xxix–xxxi.

sions and explanations of historical facts as he knew them. The brilliant scene of the murder of Clarence, I.iv, in *Richard III*, for example, though mainly a product of the playwright's imagination, has its foundation in fact, or rather in what passed for fact: Holinshed's tantalizing statement, which positively invites dramatic elaboration, to the effect that Clarence was 'priuilie drowned in a butt of malmesie';* and the Temple Garden scene, II.iv, in *1 Henry VI*, while being completely unhistorical, in the sense that no such event took place in real life, does nevertheless point to and provide a dramatically plausible origin for the rivalry between York and Somerset, which was itself real enough, a fact of history.

Henry IV, on the other hand, though it has its tragical scenes and its tragical speeches, is of such a mixed nature that even Polonius's most complex category, the 'tragical-comical-historical-pastoral,' is not large enough to encompass its infinite variety, since it makes no allowance for the play's connections with the moral interlude or for the pronounced vein of parody and burlesque that runs through it. Furthermore, the dominant 'kind,' within the mixture as a whole, is not the tragical but the comical, which is by no means confined to the tavern and Master Justice Shallow's manor in Gloucestershire, but also pervades many of the scenes in which Hotspur appears, makes its way on to the battlefield, and even touches the King himself. As for Prince Hal, he is, of course, deeply and intimately involved in the comedy from the very outset. In keeping with these innovations, the distribution of verse and prose also undergoes a radical change. In the Two Parts taken together there is as much of the one as of the other, for while Part I has rather more verse than prose, Part II has more prose than verse. Nor is this equality between the two media merely a quantitative one; the functions the prose has to perform are as important as those performed by the verse. And, finally, to complete the contrast between *Henry IV* and the histories that had preceded it, about one half of the total action – the scenes in which Falstaff and his associates play a major role – has no basis in the chronicles and bears no relation to the reign of Henry IV. The offspring of a union between Shakespeare's fertility of invention and his powers of observation, these scenes are, in the vivid picture they offer of everyday life in the England that he knew, his own contribution to history, the new kind of history, social history, that was just coming into being at the time when he was writing. William Harrison's *Description of Britain* and *Description of England* were only twenty years old when *1 Henry IV* was first staged, and, since they were published in Holinshed's Chronicle, for which they had been specially written, it seems highly likely that Shakespeare would have read them.

* Quoted from *Richard III* ed J. Dover Wilson, Cambridge 1954, p 184

Novel among the histories in all these respects, *Henry IV* is also novel among them in its structure, though that structure is the outcome of earlier experiments. Some six or seven years before, when he was writing *2 Henry VI*, Shakespeare had devoted the greater part of the Fourth Act in it to a dramatization of Cade's revolt. The scenes in which he does this are, in part, directly related to the main political action, for, as York tells us in soliloquy (III.i.355–83), it was he who seduced Cade into rebelling, in order to find out how much support for the claims of the House of York could be expected from the common people. By the time the revolt actually takes place in the play, however, this aspect of it has been largely forgotten by an audience. What it responds to is the mixture of grotesque comedy and insensate violence which these scenes offer so compellingly, and in doing so that audience may well come to see that the scenes are both a prologue to the Wars of the Roses, which do in fact begin in act V, and also a pointed and telling criticism of the absurdity and senseless butchery of those wars, carried on by the very people who suppress Cade's revolt for the sake of national unity. But, effective though that criticism is, its effectiveness is much reduced from what it might have been because it has not been adequately prepared for and followed up; there is nothing like it in *3 Henry VI*. Similarly in *Richard III* the two murderers of Clarence make their grotesquely comic contribution to the theme of conscience and its workings, but again that contribution is not endorsed and reinforced by other matter of a similar kind. It remains in the end as something rather isolated from the rest of the play, as does the Bastard's great speech on Commodity at the conclusion of act II in *King John*.

In some of the comedies, however, and notably in *Love's Labour's Lost*, Shakespeare had used the device of a character who serves as a comment on the main characters and takes part in an action that serves as a comment on the main action in a much more sustained manner. Armado's pretensions to learning, to love, and to the pursuit of fame are an exaggerated version of the pretensions of the King and his courtiers. Introduced in the first scene of the play through the letter he writes to the King, the fantastical Spaniard takes a parallel course to that followed by the four young men, and, at the end of it, outdoes them all by vowing to hold the plough for the love of Jaquenetta for three years, not the mere year and a day of waiting that they are committed to.

Henry IV, a much more massive and complex structure than *Love's Labour's Lost*, is nevertheless built along very similar lines. In it, as in the earlier comedy, scenes in verse alternate fairly regularly with scenes in prose. But, within this general resemblance, crucial differences are also to be seen. In *Love's Labour's Lost* there is never any doubt as to which part of the action is major and which subsidiary; its centre of interest is that part of the play, the verse part, which deals with the relationship between the King of Navarre and his three courtiers and the Princess of France and her three ladies. But in *Henry IV* this issue is by no means so clear-cut. In Part I, it is true, the scenes in verse, dealing with Hotspur's revolt and involving him, the King, and the Prince, do, at least on a first view, appear to be concerned with more important matters than the prose scenes, where the main interest lies in the relationship between the Prince and Falstaff. Even here, however, there are complications, since the Prince plays a large part in both kinds of scene, since the question of whether he will prove himself the son of his father or the son of Falstaff looms large, and since Falstaff, the Monarch of Wit, is a far bigger and altogether more interesting and sympathetic figure than Henry IV, the King of England. In Part II, with Hotspur dead and Falstaff acquiring an even larger role than he had in Part I, the overtly political side of the play, dealing with the revolts of the Archbishop of York and Lord Bardolph, receives far less attention and excites far less interest than the scenes in which Falstaff is the dominant figure; and, in addition, Falstaff is deeply concerned about and intimately connected with the one political question that is left and that matters most: what kind of king will Prince Hal be?

Closely tied to this difference between the two plays is another. In *Love's Labour's Lost* the prose scenes are essentially parody. The trust which the King and his courtiers place in the power of words to prove and to persuade is exaggerated, to a degree that they find highly amusing without perceiving its relevance to themselves, in the verbal extravagances and eccentricities of Armado, Holofernes, and Sir Nathaniel. But in *Henry IV* the prose scenes, while including parody and burlesque, in plenty, of the verse scenes, have another and wider function: they offer a different view from that provided in the verse scenes, not only of the Prince, but also of the state of the country as a whole and of the nature of the civil war. The connection between the prose and the verse is, at bottom, a dialectical one, giving rise to a series of important questions. Is the King's distrust of the Prince any more justified than Falstaff's trust in the Prince? Is there any essential difference between the behaviour of the great, such as Worcester, who are ready to tear the country apart for their own selfish ends, and the behaviour of Falstaff and his crew, who have no compunction about preying on the commonwealth (Pt I, II.i.78–9) in a more open and direct but also less damaging fashion? What is the truth about war and its effect on those engaged in it? Hotspur speaks up for one aspect of war, the challenge it presents to courage and nobility of spirit, when he tells his men at Shrewsbury:

> O gentlemen, the time of life is short!
> To spend that shortness basely were too long,
> If life did ride upon a dial's point,
> Still ending at the arrival of an hour. (Pt I, V.ii.82–5)

But Falstaff leaves us in no doubt about another aspect of it when, looking at his ragged troop, of whom Hal has just said, 'I did never see such pitiful rascals,' he replies:

> Tut, tut; good enough to toss; food for powder, food for powder; they'll fill a pit as well as better: tush, man, mortal men, mortal men. (Pt I, IV.ii.62–5)

The dialectical process is the core of the play, profoundly affecting its treatment of themes, controlling the concatenation of the scenes, and making the whole question of main plot and sub-plot a pointless and unnecessary one. The way in which Part I handles the idea of honour, presenting two diametrically opposed views of it in the persons, the actions, and the words of Hotspur and Falstaff, with the Prince as the middle term, so to speak, has been much observed and commented on. So has the connection between the play-acting by Falstaff and the Prince, in II.iv of Part I, of Hal's forthcoming interview with his father and the first reconciliation scene, III.ii of Part I, and, looking much further ahead, the ultimate rejection of Falstaff in the final scene of Part II. Less notice has been taken of the skilful placing of the first reconciliation scene itself. Had it followed immediately on II.iv, it would have been adversely affected by the scepticism about the sincerity of Hal's reformation which his practising of an answer engenders. But between the two scenes comes the rebel council of war. It begins in apparent harmony, with Mortimer saying:

> These promises are fair, the parties sure,
> And our induction full of prosperous hope.

But this concord is short-lived. Within fewer than twenty lines it has been broken by Hotspur's forcefully expressed contempt for Glendower's belief in omens and his sense of himself as an 'extraordinary' being. This initial quarrel is followed by a dispute over the division of an England they have not yet conquered, and then by yet another quarrel about poetry. It is all hilariously comic, but it also has its more serious implications. Long before it is over, we have very grave doubts as to whether a rebellion led by men as antipathetic to one another as Hotspur and Glendower are can possibly succeed. The reconciliation scene between the Prince and the King reverses the process. It begins in discord; but, by letting his father talk himself out – something Hotspur never lets anyone do – and then promising reformation, Hal eventually establishes concord between them, a concord that is endorsed by the chime of repetition. The Prince concludes his promise by saying:

> And I will die a hundred thousand deaths
> Ere break the smallest parcel of this vow.

To this the King replies:

> A hundred thousand rebels die in this:
> Thou shalt have charge and sovereign trust herein.
>
> (Pt I, III.ii.158–61)

As the King and his son make their exit together, things are beginning to look black for the rebels. But Shakespeare has more to say on the subject of repentance and reformation. The scene moves to the Boar's Head and opens thus:

> FALSTAFF Bardolph, am I not fall'n away vilely since this last action? Do I not dwindle? Why, my skin hangs about me like an old lady's loose gown; I am withered like an old apple-john. Well, I'll repent, and that suddenly, while I am in some liking; I shall be out of heart shortly, and then I shall have no strength to repent. An I have not forgotten what the inside of a church is made of, I am a peppercorn, a brewer's horse. The inside of a church! Company, villainous company, hath been the spoil of me.
> BARDOLPH Sir John, you are so fretful you cannot live long.
> FALSTAFF Why, there it is; come, sing me a bawdy song, make me merry. (Pt I, III.iii.1–12)

Sic transit contemptus mundi! Repentance and reformation are held up to mockery and ridicule not only here but also throughout the scene, as Falstaff goes on to compare Bardolph's face to hell-fire 'and Dives that lived in purple,' to accuse the innocent Mistress Quickly of having picked his pocket, and then to forgive her in the most sanctimonious manner for an offence she has not committed. Moreover, when the Prince appears on the scene and tells Falstaff about his reconciliation with his father, which will, he says, allow him to 'do anything,' Falstaff's immediate response is 'Rob me the exchequer the first thing thou doest, and do it with unwash'd hands too.' Far from checking this outrageous suggestion, the Prince allows it to stand, and proceeds to tell Falstaff that he has procured him 'a charge of foot.' This act of kindness ensures that Falstaff, like the other major characters, will take the road to Shrewsbury, which is, of course, its primary purpose, but it certainly does not lead an audience to exclaim 'A hundred thousand rebels die in this.' The ambiguities in the Prince's attitude and conduct, that seemed to have been laid to rest in III.ii, have reared their heads once more. The four scenes, working together and commenting on each other, are like a series of shifting planes, corresponding to the way in which reality so often presents itself to us in the actual business of living. In this respect, they are typical of the conduct of the entire play, for Shakespeare uses this same technique throughout its course, right down to the fifth act of Part II, where the death of Henry IV, which is also the accession of Henry V, has double consequences, both of them ironical. It fills the new king's brothers and the Lord Chief Justice with fears that prove to be unjustified, and it fills Falstaff and his followers with hopes that prove to be equally unjustified. The reciprocal relationship of scene to scene is an essential part of the dialectical process which informs the whole drama.

In keeping with the very mixed nature of *Henry IV*, its verse, like its prose, has an extremely wide range. At one end of the scale is the admirable *sermo pedestris* that Shakespeare has now evolved for dealing with ordinary but necessary business – statements of fact, commands, and the like. Unimpeded by imagery and preserving the word order of prose, this vehicle is already in evidence in the last six lines of the King's speech at the opening of Part I; but the economy and directness of which it is capable are seen to best advantage in such passages as the dialogue between the Prince and the Sheriff, with a little contribution from the Carrier, towards the end of the first scene in the Boar's Head, II.iv.

> PRINCE Now, master sheriff, what is your will with me?
> SHERIFF First, pardon me, my lord. A hue and cry
> Hath followed certain men unto this house.
> PRINCE What men?
> SHERIFF One of them is well known, my gracious lord –
> A gross fat man.
> CARRIER As fat as butter.
> PRINCE The man, I do assure you, is not here,
> For I myself at this time have employ'd him.
> And, sheriff, I will engage my word to thee
> That I will, by to-morrow dinner-time,
> Send him to answer thee, or any man,
> For any thing he shall be charg'd withal;
> And so let me entreat you leave the house.
> SHERIFF I will, my lord, There are two gentlemen
> Have in this robbery lost three hundred marks.

PRINCE It may be so; if he have robb'd these men
He shall be answerable; and so, farewell.
SHERIFF Good night, my noble lord.
PRINCE I think it is good morrow, is it not?
SHERIFF Indeed, my lord, I think it be two o'clock.
Exeunt Sheriff and Carrier. (II.iv.488–507)

The only image in the entire passage is the Carrier's 'As fat as butter,' and it, as befits the character, is simply a common proverbial saying (Tilley, B767). Yet verse of this kind is no mean achievement. Its great virtue is that it covers the ground quickly yet unobtrusively while sounding completely natural, so much so, in fact, that in the theatre one is barely conscious that it is verse, which is precisely the effect that Shakespeare is after. The regular rhythm is just sufficiently pronounced, and no more, to set the dialogue off from the prose by which it is surrounded, and to give one a sense of difference; and this sense of difference is needed, for the passage is an interruption of the main business of the scene in which it occurs. The arrival of the Sheriff demands that the Prince assume the official self, which has been in abeyance hitherto, and exercise the authority that official self confers on him. Having done so and got rid of the Sheriff, the Prince reverts to prose and the unofficial self once more. The shift from prose to verse and then back to prose has a dramatic function.

At the other end of the scale *Henry IV* can, in some of its tragical-historical scenes, provide speeches that are indistinguishable in their imagery and manner from some of the great speeches in the mature tragedies. Detached from its context, Northumberland's evocation of chaos, in the first scene of Part II, might well be an extract from *King Lear* or *Macbeth.*

Let heaven kiss earth! Now let not Nature's hand
Keep the wild flood confin'd! Let order die!
And let this world no longer be a stage
To feed contention in a ling'ring act;
But let one spirit of the first-born Cain
Reign in all bosoms, that, each heart being set
On bloody courses, the rude scene may end
And darkness be the burier of the dead! (Pt II, I.i.153–60)

In part the similarity is a matter of ideas and associations. The connections between disorder in the world of man, disorder in nature, darkness, and the action of a violent tragedy are made again in *Macbeth* when Ross tells the Old Man:

Ah, good father,
Thou seest, the heavens, as troubled with man's act,
Threatens his bloody stage (II.iv.4–6),

and then goes on to describe the unnatural darkness that has come over the land. But Northumberland's lines also adumbrate the manner of the great tragedies in their piling-up of image on image. Lear's call for universal destruction, 'Blow, winds, and crack your cheeks ... That makes ingrateful man' (III.ii.1–9), Macbeth's conjuration of the witches, 'I conjure you ... To what I ask you' (IV.i.50–61), and Coriolanus's incredulous sense of the impossible taking place, 'Then let the pebbles on the hungry beach / Fillip the stars' (V.iii.58–9), are all implicit in them. But, in the very act of extending his creative reach, Shakespeare also exercises his critical sense. Northumberland's outburst is greeted by Lord Bardolph with the words: 'This strained passion doth you wrong, my lord.' It has been placed, quite rightly, as a cry of hysteria, for Northumberland, as he has shown already by his failure to support Hotspur and as he will soon show again by fleeing to Scotland, instead of joining with the Archbishop of York, is not of the stuff that goes to the making of a tragic hero. He can speak as the protagonists of the tragedies will, but not act as they will.

The figure who comes closest to being consistently tragic, though he is never completely so because his politic calculating mind is active to the last in weighing practical courses and perceiving advantages to be won, is the King himself. He certainly suffers; but even his suffering is not free from traces of that deviousness which is so much a part of his nature; he is always ready to use it as a lever. He speaks wholly in verse. It goes with his rank, of course, but it is also the right medium for the expression of strong feelings and for attempts to work on the feelings of others, and especially of the Prince. Since it has much to do, Henry IV's verse has a considerable range, and, since it is the verse of the King, it sets something of a norm for the verse of the play as a whole. Its typical qualities are particularly apparent, appropriately enough, in the first scene between father and son, III.ii of Part I. Coming on stage, accompanied by the Prince and sundry lords, the King gets rid of the lords in three lines of what I have called *sermo pedestris*:

Lords, give us leave; the Prince of Wales and I
Must have some private conference; but be near at hand,
For we shall presently have need of you.

Then, left alone with the Prince, the King abruptly changes gear, as it were, by going on to say:

I know not whether God will have it so,
For some displeasing service I have done,
That, in his secret doom, out of my blood
He'll breed revengement and a scourge for me;
But thou dost in thy passages of life
Make me believe that thou art only mark'd
For the hot vengeance and the rod of heaven
To punish my mistreadings. Tell me else,
Could such inordinate and low desires,
Such poor, such bare, such lewd, such mean attempts,
Such barren pleasures, rude society,
As thou art match'd withal and grafted to,
Accompany the greatness of thy blood
And hold their level with thy princely heart?

In this passage the syntax has become complicated because the King is doing several different things at one and the same time. His first four lines, cast in the form of an indirect question, are primarily an appeal for sympathy, coupled with a partial recognition and a partial unwillingness to recognize that he deserves to be punished for what he has done. The arresting phrase, 'some displeasing service,' is both an acknowledgment of guilt and a plea to be excused. But then, when he addresses the Prince directly, in the next three and a half lines, still asking for sympathy but also beginning to scold, the ambiguous 'some displeasing service' becomes the much stronger and more explicit admission of guilt 'my mistreadings,' while the abstract 'revengement' is converted into the more specific 'hot vengeance.' The pace has already quickened. With the direct command 'Tell me else,' it quickens still more as the King builds up his rhetorical accumulation of charges, leaving the verbs that accompany those charges to the very end. Of those verbs the most interesting and significant is 'grafted,' which carries, I think, a half-concealed metaphor with it. Before it can be grafted a scion has to be cut off from its parent tree. The tree in question here is, of course, the King's family tree, which is never mentioned as such yet has its place in the speech, first as 'my blood' and then as 'thy blood.'

The subtle mixture of the metaphorical and the overtly rhetorical in this speech corresponds, more or less, with the combination of genuine feeling and deliberately contrived pressure that lies behind it. Our sense of the King as a complex character derives at least as much from his way of expressing himself as it does from any action that he takes, for, having invented this particular mode of utterance for him, Shakespeare sustains it admirably to the end. It is still present in the long speech that he makes to the Prince after the latter has removed the crown from his pillow. The same somewhat self-dramatizing appeal for sympathy comes through when he says:

> Stay but a little, for my cloud of dignity
> Is held from falling with so weak a wind
> That it will quickly drop; my day is dim. (Pt II, IV.v.99–101)

Cumulative instances followed by metaphor appear as he imagines the state of England after his death:

> Harry the Fifth is crown'd. Up, vanity:
> Down, royal state. All you sage counsellors, hence.
> And to the English court assemble now,
> From every region, apes of idleness.
> Now, neighbour confines, purge you of your scum.
> Have you a ruffian that will swear, drink, dance,
> Revel the night, rob, murder, and commit
> The oldest sins the newest kind of ways?
> Be happy, he will trouble you no more.
> England shall double gild his treble guilt;
> England shall give him office, honour, might;
> For the fifth Harry from curb'd license plucks
> The muzzle of restraint, and the wild dog
> Shall flesh his tooth on every innocent. (120–33)

The summing-up by way of metaphor in the last three lines is arrestingly dramatic, and seems to come from a rather different process of creative thinking from that which lies behind the lines that precede it. The careful gradation evident in 'Revel the night, rob, murder, and commit / The oldest sins the newest kind of ways' and, again, in 'office, honour, might' looks like the working of the conscious mind, citing instance after instance to build up and strengthen the case it is making. But the vivid evocation of license as a wild dog reaches us as something that has grown out of all that has gone before it and has actually presented itself, almost unbidden, to the mind's eye of the King. W.H.Clemen puts the matter well when, with direct reference to this passage, he remarks:

> The fact that we so often only gradually become conscious of what image is meant, indicates that Shakespeare no longer inserts the image 'from outside', but that while writing, he begins to see something in a particular light and then creates an image out of it.

Then, after quoting the three lines in question, he proceeds:

> With regard to *curb*, often employed by Shakespeare in a figurative sense, we are not yet in a position to say that Shakespeare had in

mind the image of a dog. For *curb* means the *curb-chain* and *to curb* signifies *to master, to restrain*. But, taking this as a cue, Shakespeare was led on to the *muzzle* and then to the *dog*.*

The intimate and indissoluble connections between what the King says and what the King does and is, though indubitably there, do not catch the ear and the eye forcefully or immediately. They make themselves felt gradually; and then one has to turn back and look carefully at his speeches in order to see precisely how these connections have been established. One has to do this because the King does not have an idiom of his own, and for a very good reason: there are other characters in the play who, to some degree, resemble him, and, consequently, tend to speak as he does – Worcester, Northumberland, the Archbishop of York, the Lord Chief Justice, and, most significantly, the Prince whenever he is being his official self, and especially when he is with his father. Hotspur, on the other hand, is not at all like anyone else in the play; and his individuality comes through practically everything he says; or, to put this observation the other and, perhaps, the right way round, Shakespeare endows him with such a very distinctive and highly personal idiom that he cannot but be an extremely individualized character. Vigorously and almost aggressively moulding language to his every purpose, Hotspur leaves his imprint on every speech he utters to such an extent that even a few lines from it are at once recognizable as his and no one else's.

The first speech he makes tells us much about him as well as about his actions. Accused by the King of withholding the Scots he took prisoner at the battle of Holmedon, Hotspur replies:

> My liege, I did deny no prisoners.
> But I remember when the fight was done,
> When I was dry with rage and extreme toil,
> Breathless and faint, leaning upon my sword,
> Came there a certain lord, neat, and trimly dress'd,
> Fresh as a bridegroom, and his chin new reap'd
> Show'd like a stubble-land at harvest-home.
> He was perfumed like a milliner,
> And 'twixt his finger and his thumb he held
> A pouncet-box, which ever and anon
> He gave his nose and took't away again;
> Who therewith angry, when it next came there,
> Took it in snuff – and still he smil'd and talk'd –
> And as the soldiers bore dead bodies by,

* *The Development of Shakespeare's Imagery* pp 75–6

He call'd them untaught knaves, unmannerly,
To bring a slovenly unhandsome corse
Betwixt the wind and his nobility.
With many holiday and lady terms
He questioned me: amongst the rest demanded
My prisoners in your Majesty's behalf.
I then, all smarting with my wounds being cold,
To be so pest'red with a popinjay,
Out of my grief and my impatience
Answer'd neglectingly I know not what –
He should, or he should not – for he made me mad
To see him shine so brisk, and smell so sweet,
And talk so like a waiting-gentlewoman
Of guns, and drums, and wounds – God save the mark! –
And telling me the sovereignest thing on earth
Was parmaceti for an inward bruise;
And that it was great pity, so it was,
This villainous saltpetre should be digg'd
Out of the bowels of the harmless earth,
Which many a good tall fellow had destroy'd
So cowardly; and but for these vile guns
He would himself have been a soldier.
This bald unjointed chat of his, my lord,
I answer'd indirectly, as I said;
And I beseech you, let not his report
Come current for an accusation
Betwixt my love and your high Majesty. (Pt I, I.iii.29–69)

It is a superb piece of dramatic narrative, which, like the account of Petruchio's marriage in *The Taming of the Shrew*, virtually adds an extra scene to the play, a scene that takes place in the mind's eye, not on the stage. As one listens to it, one sees the aftermath of battle, so rarely mentioned in heroic poetry, and, in the midst of it all, the two contrasted figures: the brave exhausted soldier and the brisk effeminate courtier, whose affected language the soldier contemptuously mocks as he reports it. So vividly, indeed, is the courtier realized and conjured up that one recognizes in him the chrysalis, so to speak, out of which, a few years later, will emerge the full-blown dragon-fly Osric. Scorn and impatience ring through the entire passage. The images are precise, reductive, and, some of them, admirably designed to bring out the womanish qualities the soldier sees in the courtier. He is a 'popinjay'; 'his chin new reap'd' shows 'like a stubble-land at harvest-home'; he is 'perfumed like a milliner'; and he talks 'like a waiting-gentlewoman,' using 'holiday and lady terms.' But it is not the imagery alone that conveys the scorn and, still less, the impatience. Shakespeare, by his very choice of words and phrases, dictates both the tone and the pace that the actor playing the part of Hotspur must adopt. From the outset the delivery is staccato. 'Breathless and faint, leaning upon my sword' has to be spoken in two rapid bursts with a marked pause between them, thus reproducing the very manner of one who is indeed panting and out of breath. 'To be so pest'red with a popinjay' can only be spat out; and the little bits of parenthesis add to the staccato effect, which is finally endorsed by the incisive and damning summary of the courtier's remarks as 'bald unjointed chat,' meaning 'pointless irrelevant small talk.' And Shakespeare was, it is worth noticing, fully aware that he was controlling the actor's delivery of the lines. In Part II Hotspur's widow, relating the way in which other men modelled their behaviour on that of her husband, tells us explicitly:

> And speaking thick, which nature made his blemish,
> Became the accents of the valiant;
> For those that could speak low and tardily
> Would turn their own perfection to abuse
> To seem like him. (II.iii.24–8)

Instead of speaking quietly and slowly, Hotspur speaks loudly and rapidly, which is what 'thick' surely means in this context, rather than 'in a slurred or badly articulated manner.' His lines are far too good to be thrown away.

Brusque, impetuous, impatient, direct, and courageous, Hotspur makes all this side of his nature evident in his first speech; and it is still further developed and substantiated in much that follows. The opening of II.iii finds him using prose, as he reads and comments on the letter he has just received from a lord who shows no enthusiasm whatever for the plot Hotspur has invited him to take part in. But the prose is as firmly stamped with the personality of the man who speaks it as is the verse, and equally rich in downright railing and reductive imagery. The lord, says Hotspur, is 'my lord fool,' 'a shallow, cowardly hind,' 'a lack-brain,' 'a frosty-spirited rogue,' 'a pagan rascal,' 'an infidel,' and, to cap it all, 'a dish of skim milk'; he could, given the chance, 'brain him with his lady's fan.' Splendidly abusive, this speech, like most things that run to excess, is not without its comic side; and the same mixture of comic excess and virtuoso exuberance carries over into III.i, where it reaches its culmination.

Fanciful, given to the 'poetical,' and filled with a sense of his own importance, Glendower is designed to jar on Hotspur. His description of the omens that accompanied his birth is more than his ally can stomach. It runs thus:

> at my nativity
> The front of heaven was full of fiery shapes,
> Of burning cressets; and at my birth
> The frame and huge foundation of the earth
> Shaked like a coward. (III.i.13–17)

Extravagant in themselves, these lines seem deliberately and cleverly framed to bring out the potential for comedy inherent in English pronounced with a strong Welsh accent; and I very much suspect that Shakespeare hoped some members of his original audience might find the added amusement of catching in them an echo of *The Lamentable Tragedie of Locrine* (c 1591), where the Ghost of Corineus says, in a would-be atmospheric speech preceding the final battle:

> The fire casteth forth sharpe dartes of flames,
> The great foundation of the triple world
> Trembleth and quaketh with a mightie noise,
> Presaging bloodie massacres at hand. (IV.iv.4–7)*

But, no matter whether an audience finds Glendower's speech funny or not, it cannot resist the comedy of Hotspur's answer:

> Why, so it would have done at the same season if your mother's cat had but kitten'd, though yourself had never been born.

The familiar homely prose punctures the inflated verse, and then makes its way into Hotspur's own verse, as he goes on to compare the earthquake, which, according to Glendower, occurred at his birth, to the rumblings of an old woman afflicted with a violent attack of the colic.

The conflict between the two contrasted personalities is a conflict between two styles, for in this scene the styles very emphatically are the men. It is, therefore, an exquisite stroke of art that the quarrel should reach its climax in a hot dispute about the speaking of English and about the value of poetry. Understandably irked by Hotspur's demand that if the Welshman has anything further to say, he should say it in his unintelligible Welsh, Glendower retorts:

> I can speak English, lord, as well as you,
> For I was train'd up in the English court;
> Where, being but young, I framed to the harp

* Text from *The Shakespeare Apocrypha* ed C.F. Tucker Brooke, Oxford 1918

Many an English ditty lovely well,
And gave the tongue a helpful ornament –
A virtue that was never seen in you.

It is a good answer, but the rejoinder it provokes is devastating:

Marry,
And I am glad of it with all my heart!
I had rather be a kitten and cry mew
Than one of these same metre ballad-mongers;
I had rather hear a brazen canstick turn'd,
Or a dry wheel grate on the axle-tree;
And that would set my teeth nothing on edge,
Nothing so much as mincing poetry.
'Tis like the forc'd gait of a shuffling nag. (Pt I, III.i.120–135)

Two different kinds of dramatic poetry have collided with each other. Glendower's speech, with its flowing melodic line, leaves us in no doubt about his love of music; its lyrical cadence is exactly right for its purpose. But so is the tone and the imagery of Hotspur's answer. Dismissive and deliberately provocative in manner, his attack on poetry, couched in that homely idiom, replete with images drawn from everyday life, and especially from life in the country, which we have come to recognize as his ever since he spoke of the courtier, whose 'chin new reap'd / Show'd like a stubble-land at harvest-home,' is itself dramatic poetry of a very high order, and, I think, of a new kind. In response to the demands of character, situation, and structure, Shakespeare is now engaged in making poetry out of what seems to be, at least on the face of it, distinctly 'unpoetical' material.

Not all Hotspur's verse is, however, of this new kind, because there are other qualities in his make-up besides those of which it is so expressive. On his first appearance he resorts to a different manner from that of his initial speech when the King describes Mortimer as 'revolted,' meaning that Mortimer has gone over to the side of the enemy. Filled with generous indignation, Hotspur springs to Mortimer's defence, and replies:

Revolted Mortimer!
He never did fall off, my sovereign liege,
But by the chance of war; to prove that true,
Needs no more but one tongue for all those wounds,
Those mouthed wounds, which valiantly he took
When on the gentle Severn's sedgy bank,
In single opposition hand to hand,
He did confound the best part of an hour

In changing hardiment with great Glendower.
Three times they breath'd, and three times did they drink,
Upon agreement, of swift Severn's flood;
Who then, affrighted with their bloody looks,
Ran fearfully among the trembling reeds
And hid his crisp head in the hollow bank
Bloodstained with these valiant combatants. (I.iii.93–107)

Here, Mortimer's wounds – adumbrating a strong motif in *Coriolanus* – become mouths that attest his integrity; and the river Severn is endowed with human attributes that make it the mythological figure it so often was in the poetry and drama of the late sixteenth and early seventeenth centuries, a masculine equivalent of Milton's Sabrina fair. But why should Hotspur speak in this fashion? The fact that Mortimer is his brother-in-law may have something to do with it, but his own generosity of spirit, an aspect of his character not evident in any of the passages from speeches of his quoted hitherto, matters far more. Moreover, Hotspur is wholly committed to and lives by a firmly held scale of values. For him the military virtues are supreme and the pursuit of honour is the 'ending end,' as Sir Philip Sidney has it, of living. He therefore responds, as a heroic poet would, to the epic single combat of Mortimer and Glendower, reserving the scorn of which his other manner is so capable for the 'bare and rotten policy' which he sees as the enemy of and the antithesis to the heroic code by which he lives. There is, in fact, no contradiction between the 'poetical' Hotspur and the 'anti-poetical' Hotspur; they are necessary and complementary aspects of the same being. Their interdependence is especially clear in the latter part of I.iii, where, like Coriolanus, of whom Menenius says, 'His heart's his mouth; / What his breast forges, that his tongue must vent' (III.i.257–8), Hotspur, equally incapable of suppressing his contempt for the politic King and of resisting the attraction of danger that Worcester dangles before him, allows himself to become a willing and enthusiastic instrument in the hands of his unscrupulous uncle, much as Coriolanus allows himself to be manipulated by the two tribunes.

Hotspur has, in fact, a range of utterance beyond that achieved by any previous character in the plays. He has to have, because he is both comic and tragic. In the first half of Part I it is the comic aspect and the 'unpoetical' verse that goes with it which are uppermost, reaching their climax in the quarrel with Glendower. After that, as he meets with one setback after another and responds to each with a heroic gesture, Hotspur relies increasingly on the other manner, until, maturing rapidly under the stress of adverse experience, the man of whom his widow can say that

by his light
Did all the chivalry of England move
To do brave acts (Pt II, II.ii.19–21)

eventually becomes capable of seeing all human endeavour, including his own, in relation to the great abstract ideas of time and eternity, and voices this vision of things in the moving lines he utters at his end:

O, Harry, thou hast robb'd me of my youth!
I better brook the loss of brittle life
Than those proud titles thou hast won of me:
They wound my thoughts worse than thy sword my flesh;
But thoughts, the slaves of life, and life, time's fool,
And time that takes survey of all the world,
Must have a stop. O, I could prophesy,
But that the earthy and cold hand of death
Lies on my tongue. No, Percy, thou art dust
And food for –
Dies. (Pt I, V.iv.77–86)

These final lines make one realize that Hotspur's two manners are not, in fact, so distinct from one another as I have suggested. The images of the slaves and the fool are still reductive, but, more important than that, Hotspur's addiction to thinking in images persists to the end. It is right that it should, for Shakespeare himself, conscious artist that he was, underlines this tendency in the character at an early stage in the play. Having enticed Hotspur into making his enthusiastic speech about honour, Worcester remarks to Northumberland, and thus to the audience:

He apprehends a world of figures here,
But not the form of what he should attend. (Pt I, I.iii.209–10)

It is fitting that it should be Worcester who makes this observation, for, knowing his nephew's language and the processes of thought that lie behind it, he has, shortly before, used this knowledge to work Hotspur to his purpose. The speech about honour is provoked by Worcester's skilful dangling of a bait, in the form of a challenge to daring couched in Hotspur's own language, in front of his impetuous kinsman, who, of course, finds it quite irresistible. It runs thus:

And now I will unclasp a secret book,
And to your quick-conceiving discontents
I'll read you matter deep and dangerous,
As full of peril and adventurous spirit
As to o'er-walk a current roaring loud
On the unsteadfast footing of a spear. (Pt I, I.iii.188–93)

As well as capturing Hotspur's accent, these lines also capture the essence of the man that Hotspur is. It is not surprising therefore that they should be repeated, in a somewhat altered form, after his death when Morton tells Northumberland:

> You knew he walk'd o'er perils on an edge,
> More likely to fall in than to get o'er. (Pt II, I.i.170–1)

Worcester is not the only character in the play who knows how to manipulate another by using that other's language. Falstaff's excursions into verse are very few indeed; but, when he has difficulty in extracting Pistol's news from him because Pistol will persist in making the occasion an excuse for even more fustian than usual, he adroitly adopts the Ancient's own style to ask:

> O base Assyrian knight, what is thy news?
> Let King Cophetua know the truth thereof. (Pt II, V.iii.100–1)

Here, as on the other occasions when he resorts to verse, Falstaff makes fun of the pretensions of poetry, or rather of the pretentiousness of bad inflated poetry. Yet it is he who defines for us in unforgettable terms the very spirit in which Shakespeare seems to have written the play. Having been rebuked by Prince John for his late arrival in Yorkshire, Falstaff, in soliloquy, attributes the Prince's harshness to his sober-blooded nature and his preference for thin drink, and then proceeds to praise the virtues of sack, saying of it:

> A good sherris-sack hath a twofold operation in it. It ascends me into the brain; dries me there all the foolish and dull and crudy vapours which environ it; makes it apprehensive, quick, forgetive, full of nimble, fiery, and delectable shapes; which delivered o'er to the voice, the tongue, which is the birth, becomes excellent wit. (Pt II, IV.iii.94–9)

The core of this passage is its vivid description of the workings of the creative imagination contained in the words 'apprehensive, quick, forgetive, full of nimble, fiery, and delectable shapes.' The relationship between these words is extraordinarily rich and complex, causing them to enact the process they describe. 'Apprehensive' means not only 'swift to understand' but also 'eager to grasp and seize on an image,' since 'nimble, fiery, and delectable shapes' tend to be elusive; 'quick,' as the later reference to 'the birth' demonstrates, signifies 'pregnant' as well as 'lively,' and through yet another meaning it can have, that of 'briskly burning' when applied to a fire, it leads on to 'forgetive.' This last word is defined by the OED as follows:

> A Shaksperian word of uncertain formation and meaning. Commonly taken as a derivative of FORGE *v.*[1], and hence used by writers of the 19th c. for: Apt at 'forging', inventive, creative.

Scholarly caution is an admirable thing in itself, but in this case it is unnecessary and unjustified. Shakespeare himself defines 'forgetive' for us in the Chorus to act v of *Henry v*, where he says to his audience:

> But now behold
> In the quick forge and working-house of thought,
> How London doth pour out her citizens! (22–4)

Crediting his audience with an imagination like his own, he thinks of that imaginative faculty as a forge that burns brightly and works quickly; and, among the things it forges are nonce-words such as 'forgetive' itself, meaning quite evidently, as some 'writers of the nineteenth century' realized, 'Apt at "forging", inventive, creative.' It is because the 'delectable shapes' are fresh from the forge that they are also 'fiery.'

The language that Shakespeare puts into Falstaff's mouth is certainly the product of such a forging process, and, since much of it goes into the making of lies, it can also be seen as an example of forging in the other sense of that word. Falstaff coins new words, combines existing words to form new compounds, and frequently uses a word in such a way as to alter or extend its significance. From the evidence provided by the OED, the following words and usages in Part I, to go no further, would seem to be original with him: 'peach,' meaning 'to inform against an accomplice' (II.ii.42); 'bacons,' meaning 'rustics, clowns, chaw-bacons' (II.ii.86); 'jure,' meaning 'give you jurors' (II.ii.88); 'shotten herring,' used in a figurative sense (II.iv.122); 'tickle-brain,' meaning 'strong liquor' but, in this case, applied to Mistress Quickly who sells it; 'sneak-cup,' according to the Folio, or 'sneak-up,' meaning 'creeping rogue,' according to the Quarto (III.iii.84); 'soused gurnet,' used as a term of opprobrium (IV.ii.12); 'toasts-and-butter,' meaning 'milksops' (IV.ii.19); 'shot-free,' meaning 'without paying' (V.iii.29); and 'gunpowder,' used as an adjective to describe Hotspur's fiery and explosive temper (V.iv.122). It is also significant that Falstaff is the character who draws most heavily on the writings of Thomas Nashe, that master of slang and neologism. Of the parallels between passages in the play and passages in Nashe, conveniently collected by Dover Wilson in his edition of *1 Henry IV* (pp 191–6), by far the largest number, thirteen, occur in speeches by Falstaff. Hal has the next highest total, seven, all of them in speeches made either to Falstaff or in the milieu to which Falstaff belongs.

Although Falstaff and Hotspur never meet in the play until after

Hotspur's death, the relationship between them is a close one because they are presented in such a manner that each defines the other. In physical appearance, way of life, values, and attitudes they are polar opposites. The contrast they make, seen in its starkest form at the end of Part I, where Hotspur's heroic death is set against Falstaff's brutal and degrading assault on his dead body, is, of course, reflected in their respective styles, which are, however, complementary to each other rather than antithetical. Hotspur's poetry, if I am right about it, acquires a steely kind of resilience, together with immediacy, from the infusion into it of the rhythms and the idioms that one associates with colloquial speech. Falstaff's prose, on the other hand, takes on a richness and suggestiveness far beyond that which one expects of prose, because it is so pervaded by figurative language of the kind that one associates with poetry. His description of the workings of the poetic imagination, for example, is both more vivid and, it seems to me, more convincing than Theseus's description, in verse, of the same phenomenon in *A Midsummer Night's Dream*: 'The poet's eye, in a fine frenzy rolling ... A local habitation and a name' (V.i.12–17), because it gives a much fuller and more concentrated impression of the sheer work and activity involved.

Falstaff's favourite figure is the simile. Our sense, as readers, of his appearance and presence depends in no small measure on the readiness with which he sees himself in terms of the animal world, telling his little page, for example, 'I do here walk before thee like a sow that hath overwhelm'd all her litter but one' (Pt II, I.ii.10–11), or remarking to Hal, ''Sblood, I am as melancholy as a gib cat or a lugg'd bear' (Pt I, I.ii.71–2). But he draws readily and easily on a wide range of familiar things. Seeking sympathy from Bardolph, he says, 'my skin hangs about me like an old lady's loose gown; I am withered like an old apple-john' (Pt I, III.iii.3–4; on the battlefield of Shrewsbury he feels himself 'as hot as molten lead, and as heavy too' (Pt I, V.iii.32–3); and, looking confidently forward to the way in which he expects to entertain the Prince with anecdotes about Master Justice Shallow, he assures us: 'O, you shall see him laugh till his face be like a wet cloak ill laid up!' (Pt II, V.i.81–2), a marvellously precise image, springing directly from close and accurate observation. The same kind of observation, but coupled now with a wild vein of fantasy and exaggeration, goes into the making of his reminiscence of Shallow as a young man:

> I do remember him at Clement's Inn, like a man made after supper of a cheese-paring. When 'a was naked, he was for all the world like a fork'd radish, with a head fantastically carved upon it with a knife. 'A was so forlorn [meagre] that his dimensions to any thick sight

> were invisible. 'A was the very genius of famine; yet lecherous as a monkey, and the whores call'd him mandrake.
> (Pt II, III.ii.298–302)

Here the poetic imagination has developed its own impetus. Lear's vision of unaccommodated man as 'a poor, bare, forked animal' was already within the reach of the dramatist who could give Falstaff these lines. Like the heroes of the tragedies that were to follow, Falstaff, while remaining within the overall framework of comedy, is very much an overstater. The same love of hyperbole as that which informs his picture of Shallow makes itself manifest again in the threat which he holds over the heads of Prince John and the other leaders of the King's forces, when, after requesting that his service in taking Colville prisoner 'be book'd with the rest of this day's deeds,' he goes on to say:

> or, by the Lord, I will have it in a particular ballad else, with mine own picture on the top on't, Colville kissing my foot; to the which course if I be enforc'd, if you do not all show like gilt twopences to me, and I, in the clear sky of fame, o'ershine you as much as the full moon doth the cinders of the element, which show like pins' heads to her, believe not the word of the noble. (Pt II, IV.iii.43–53)

The imagined picture is simultaneously ludicrous – what has Falstaff to do with fame achieved in war? – and impressive in its scope, taking in the great sweep of the night sky through its use of simile within simile and of metaphor, 'the clear sky of fame.' For Falstaff, much given to the simile though he is, is quite ready to resort to metaphor too. In his praise of sack, for instance, he seizes on the well-worn analogy between the human body and the body politic, brings it to life with one active verb after another, and works it out in detail in a manner that prefigures Menenius's treatment of it when he tells the Fable of the Belly in *Coriolanus*. Falstaff's version runs thus:

> The second property of your excellent sherris is the warming of the blood; which before, cold and settled, left the liver white and pale, which is the badge of pusillanimity and cowardice; but the sherris warms it, and makes it course from the inwards to the parts extremes. It illumineth the face, which, as a beacon, give warning to all the rest of this little kingdom, man, to arm; and then the vital commoners and inland petty spirits muster me all to their captain, the heart, who, great and puff'd up with this retinue, doth any deed of courage – and this valour comes of sherris. (Pt II, IV.iii.99–110)

This body, at once human and politic, is as remote from a corpse on the anatomist's dissecting table as it well could be; it has far more in common with England on the eve of the Armada; linguistic virtuosity has resuscitated a moribund commonplace.

Remarkable in its richly figurative nature, Falstaff's prose is also remarkable for the very wide field of reference from which its figures and allusions are drawn. At the centre of that field is everyday life; but the mock sanctimoniousness which Falstaff flaunts so often and so openly, leading Poins to address him as 'Monsieur Remorse' and then, with a pun on 'sackcloth and ashes,' as 'Sir John Sack and Sugar' (Pt I, I.ii.108–9), is reinforced and sustained by numerous references to the Bible. In keeping with his nature, he has the Prodigal Son very much in mind, alluding to him at least twice: first, when he describes the men who make up his ragged company of foot as 'a hundred and fifty tattered Prodigals lately come from swine-keeping, from eating draff and husks' (Pt I, IV.ii.33–4), and then, when he advises the Hostess to replace her tapestries with 'the story of the Prodigal ... in water-work' (Pt II, II.i.140–1). He is familiar with the story of Lazarus (Pt I, IV.ii.24–5); he uses the name Achitophel as a term of opprobrium (Pt II, I.ii.33); and, most felicitously of all, especially when one recalls his chronic impecuniousness and his equally chronic thirst, he mentions Dives no fewer than three times: once under that name (Pt I, III.iii.32), and twice as 'the Glutton' (Pt I, IV.ii.25 and Pt II, I.ii.32). Moreover, when he finds himself so tightly trapped that no evasion seems possible, he extricates himself by enlisting the support of Adam as he says to the Prince:

> Dost thou hear, Hal? Thou knowest in the state of innocency Adam fell; and what should poor Jack Falstaff do in the days of villainy? Thou seest I have more flesh than another man, and therefore more frailty. (Pt I, III.iii.164–7)

Closely allied to Falstaff's readiness with Biblical names and events is his easy command of the language of religion – 'Before I knew thee, Hal, I knew nothing; and now am I, if a man should speak truly, little better than one of the wicked' (Pt I, I.ii.90–3), and the like. But he is also conversant with the theatre, with the moral interludes in which the Vice played such a large part, with plays such as *King Cambyses*, with the style of John Lyly, with romances, which he lays under contribution for such flights of comic extravagance as his naming Bardolph 'the Knight of the Burning Lamp' (Pt I, III.iii.27), and with the street ballads of the time, of which he sings snatches.

The rich verbal mixture produced by this wealth of allusion is in itself sufficient to ensure that whatever Falstaff says is as indelibly stamped with his personality as Hotspur's speeches are with his. But this effect is further endorsed, or so it seems to me, by a trick of speech which is also an index to his most marked and fascinating quality – his dexterity in freeing himself from the tight corners into which his proclivity for lying so often lands him. This particular trick of speech, which might, to adopt Touchstone's phraseology, be labelled 'the Asseveration Conditional,' is heard for the first time within five minutes of his stepping on to the stage, when, deploring, in mockery, Hal's bad influence over him, he says:

> I must give over this life, and I will give it over. By the Lord.
> an I do not I am a villain! (Pt I, I.ii.93–4)

The great virtue of this kind of oath is that it commits him to nothing beyond continuing to be what he is, and can, therefore, be used on any and every occasion, as he conclusively demonstrates some five lines later, when, in response to the Prince's question-cum-test, 'Where shall we take a purse to-morrow, Jack?', he replies, without a moment's hesitation:

> Zounds, where thou wilt, lad: I'll make one. An I do not, call me villain and baffle me.

Established here, in Falstaff's first scene, the device, while undergoing a multitude of ingenious variations, persists as a constant element in his speech right down to IV.iii of Part II. The bigger the lies he tells, the harder it is worked, occurring time after time in his account of his battle with the 'rogues in buckram,' where, at one point, it is actually doubled as he says, after the Prince has asked incredulously, 'What, fought you with them all?':

> All! I know not what you call all, but if I fought not with fifty of them, I am a bunch of radish. If there were not two or three and fifty upon poor old Jack, then am I no two-legg'd creature.
> (Pt I, II.iv.177–81)

Its disappearance from Falstaff's speeches after IV.iii of Part II, where he employs it in his attempt to make Prince John give him full credit for taking Colville prisoner is not, I think, accidental. Convinced that he can manipulate Shallow exactly as he wishes – he says of him, 'I have him temp'ring between my finger and my thumb, and shortly will I seal with him' (Pt II, IV.iii.126–7) – he does not require its assistance in his dealings with the Justice; and its absence from his speeches in the rejection scene tellingly underscores how complete and how badly misplaced his confidence in the new king is. For once, he speaks the truth. It is a fatal mistake.

Of the major characters in the play, Hotspur and Falstaff are the two who are given highly distinctive idioms of their own. But Shakespeare's fertility in devising ways of speaking which are so expressive of character that they are inseparable from character is now so rich and exuberant that he generously extends it to many of the less important figures as well, and especially to Mistress Quickly and Master Justice Shallow, whose modes of utterance, different though they are in other respects, have this much in common, that each would seem to be a fine distillation from much careful observation of how people do, in fact, talk. One can watch the Hostess grow under the dramatist's hand. On her first appearance, in II.iv of Part I, she has eight speeches in all, most of them amounting to no more than a line each. Yet even within this brief space something of the essential Quickly already begins to come through. Five of the speeches are exclamations, and of these five no fewer than four are prefaced by the words 'O Jesu,' which serve equally well to introduce the flutter created in her by an unexpected arrival and the pleasure she takes in Falstaff's acting. We see her next in III.iii, and by this time, in keeping with the larger role she now has, her manner has taken on some further characteristics. Asked by Falstaff, 'Have you inquir'd who pick'd my pocket?', she replies:

> Why, Sir John, what do you think, Sir John? Do you think I keep thieves in my house? I have search'd, I have inquired, so has my husband, man by man, boy by boy, servant by servant. The tithe of a hair was never lost in my house before. (53–7)

And, in addition to the repetitive itemizing which makes this speech sound so authentic, Mistress Quickly is now having trouble in understanding some of Falstaff's innuendoes, with the result that she unwittingly makes damaging comments on herself, such as 'I am no thing to thank God on, I would thou shouldst know it' (118–19), and the like.

In Part II Mistress Quickly really comes into her own. The typical quirks of speech established in Part I remain with her and develop, though she now uses 'O Jesu' far more sparingly. The cumulative itemizing reappears as she tells Fang and Snare of Falstaff's indebtedness to her:

> A hundred mark is a long one [ie, score] for a poor lone woman to bear; and I have borne, and borne, and borne; and have been fubb'd off, and fubb'd off, and fubb'd off, from this day to that day, that it is a shame to be thought on. (II.i.30–4)

Her difficulties with the English language, already evident in some of her misunderstandings, have now flowered into full-blown malapropisms as she does violence to the unfamiliar words 'homicidal' and 'homicide' in exclaiming thus on Falstaff:

> Ah, thou honeysuckle villain! wilt thou kill God's officers and the King's? Ah, thou honey-seed rogue! thou art a honey-seed; a man-queller and a woman-queller. (II.i.48–51)

But, in addition to the established tricks, a new one, indicative of a whole habit of mind and way of life, now makes its appearance: her memory for and fondness for dwelling on minute circumstantial detail, as exemplified in her immortal answer to Falstaff's query, 'What is the gross sum that I owe thee?': 'Marry, if thou wert an honest man ... Deny it, if thou canst' (II.i.82–99), and, more briefly, in her refusal to admit Pistol:

> Tilly-fally, Sir John, ne'er tell me; and your ancient swagg'rer comes not in my doors. I was before Master Tisick, the debuty, t' other day; and, as he said to me – 'twas no longer ago than Wednesday last, i' good faith! – 'Neighbour Quickly,' says he – Master Dumbe, our minister, was by then – 'Neighbour Quickly,' says he 'receive those that are civil, for' said he 'you are in an ill name.' Now 'a said so, I can tell whereupon. 'For' says he 'you are an honest woman and well thought on, therefore take heed what guests you receive. 'Receive' says he 'no swaggering companions.' There comes none here. You would bless you to hear what he said. No, I'll no swagg'rers. (II.iv.79–91)

As we listen to that, we not only know Mistress Quickly as she is but also recognize in her the Platonic idea, as it were, of the inveterate gossip. The heavy incidence of 'says he,' the doubling back on the track in search of greater precision that turns 't'other day' into 'no longer ago than Wednesday last,' and the invocation of Master Dumbe as a proof of veracity, all these quirks of speech ring absolutely true.

Shallow, like the Nurse in *Romeo and Juliet*, is substantially complete in the first speech he utters, as he greets his kinsman Silence:

> Come on, come on, come on; give me your hand, sir; give me your hand, sir. An early stirrer, by the rood! And how doth my good cousin Silence? (Pt II, III.ii.1–3)

Never blessed with much in the way of brains, he has become addle-pated with age, and uses repetition as a kind of stopgap while he searches around for something else to say. When he is called on to take some action, no matter how simple, he goes into a flap; and his state of dither is faithfully reproduced in his answer to Falstaff's request to see the men Shallow is providing for the army:

> Where's the roll? Where's the roll? Where's the roll? Let me see, let me see, let me see. So, so, so, so, so – so, so – yea, marry, sir. Rafe

Mouldy! Let them appear as I call; let them do so, let them do so.
Let me see; where is Mouldy? (Ibid 96–100)

Living partly in the present and partly on the memories of the wild youth that he has fabricated for himself, he allows his mind to swing from one to the other, rather like a pendulum, in a manner that can be at once comic yet not without its touches of pathos. Reminiscing over the past, he says: 'Jesu, Jesu, the mad days that I have spent! and to see how many of my old acquaintance are dead!' The following dialogue ensues:

SILENCE We shall all follow, cousin.
SHALLOW Certain, 'tis certain; very sure, very sure. Death, as the Psalmist saith, is certain to all; all shall die. How a good yoke of bullocks at Stamford fair?
SILENCE By my troth, I was not there.
SHALLOW Death is certain. Is old Double of your town living yet?
SILENCE Dead, sir.
SHALLOW Jesu, Jesu, dead! 'A shot a fine shoot. John a Gaunt loved him well, and betted much money on his head. Dead! 'A would have clapp'd i' the clout at twelve score, and carried you a forehand shaft a fourteen and fourteen and a half, that it would have done a man's heart good to see. How a score of ewes now?
SILENCE Therafter as they be – a score of good ewes may be worth ten pounds.
SHALLOW And is old Double dead? (Ibid 32–51)

It is, I think, a fascinating example of the dramatist discovering something as he creates. The idiom Shakespeare has devised for defining Shallow and breathing the breath of life into him is intended primarily to convey his age and the folly that goes with it, as it manifests itself in his utter inability to concentrate. But here Shakespeare seems suddenly to have perceived and then developed another potentiality latent in that idiom: it is so right, so true, in terms of character, that it can become the vehicle for conveying a larger truth about human experience in general. As the two old men talk, they make us aware of the way in which the immediate and the practical – in this case the price of cattle – so often compete for our attention with the less immediate but ultimately far more important – in this case the inevitability of death. This dialogue might not unfittingly be regarded as a familiar comic version, and none the less affecting for that, of the Virgilian *lacrimae rerum*.

The Hostess and Shallow are not the only figures in the Falstaffian milieu who, to use F.E. Halliday's pregnant phrase once more, succeed in talking themselves alive. Ancient Pistol does it with his ranting fustian, which, in its empty posturing, is emblematic of the man who utters it; Francis does it with his parrotted 'Anon, anon, sir' and his addiction to 'O, Lord, sir'; and, best of all the minor characters, Doll does it with her easy transitions from professional sweetness and sentimentality to her equally professional command of violent abuse. At one moment she tells Falstaff, 'Come, I'll be friends with thee, Jack. Thou art going to the wars; and whether I shall ever see thee again or no, there is nobody cares' (Pt II, II.iv.62–4); at the next she voices her contempt for Pistol in a spendid mixture of the aggressive and the picturesquely dismissive, saying to him:

> Away, you cut-purse rascal! you filthy bung, away! By this wine, I'll thrust my knife in your mouldy chaps, an you play the saucy cuttle with me. Away, you bottle-ale rascal! you basket-hilt stale juggler, you! Since when, I pray you, sir? God's light, with two points on your shoulder? Much! (Ibid 120–5)

Even the two carriers who appear for a few wholly convincing minutes at the opening of II.i in Part I are clearly differentiated from one another, though both speak the timeless language of those who work with horses. The following exchange between them rings as true today as it did when it was written:

> SECOND CARRIER Peas and beans are as dank here as a dog, and that is the next [ie, quickest] way to give poor jades the bots; this house is turned upside down since Robin Ostler died.
> FIRST CARRIER Poor fellow never joyed since the price of oats rose; it was the death of him. (8–12)

But, while they both speak the same language, the Second is the more graphic speaker of the two, because, as his reference to 'Peas and beans' that 'are as dank here as a dog' shows, he lards his speech with homely similes. Moreover, from the evidence provided by two of these similes, the one concerning a tench and the other a loach, he would appear, as Dover Wilson notes,* to be something of a fisherman in his spare time. It is a most interesting example of the way in which a poet's use of figures that beget one another by a process of association can give an identity, which the poet himself in all probability never thought of, to a fictional character.

In a play so crowded with figures of whom one may truly say, 'by their words and accents ye shall know them,' where does the Prince stand, has he an authentic voice of his own? The answer would seem to be no, because linguistically considered the Prince is a chameleon, taking his

* Ed cit p 134

verbal colouring from his surroundings, as he himself acknowledges when, telling Poins of his encounter with Francis and the other tapsters at the Boar's Head, he says:

> To conclude, I am so good a proficient in one quarter of an hour that I can drink with any tinker in his own language during my life.
> (Pt I, II.iv.17–19)

A man for all companies, he suits his language and style to the manner of those he finds himself dealing with or associating with. When he is with Falstaff, he tends to speak like Falstaff, competing with him in the concoction of 'unsavoury similes' (Pt I, I.ii.72–7) and seeking to outdo him in the art of being abusive, as he does when, playing the role of the King to Falstaff's rendering of the Prince, he asks the latter:

> Why dost thou converse with that trunk of humours, that bolting-hutch of beastliness, that swoll'n parcel of dropsies, that huge bombard of sack, that stuff'd cloak-bag of guts, that roasted Manningtree ox with the pudding in his belly, that reverend vice, that grey iniquity, that father ruffian, that vanity in years?
> (Pt I. II.iv.433–8)

When he is with the King, the Prince speaks as his father does and, more than that, wins that father's commendation for doing so. After listening to Hal's far from accurate account of how he addressed the crown after taking it from his father's pillow, the King says:

> O my son
> God put it in thy mind to take it hence,
> That thou mightst win the more thy father's love,
> Pleading so wisely in excuse of it! (Pt II, IV.v.178–81)

In nothing else are the King, the Prince, and Prince John more akin than in their worship of an extremely pragmatic deity who smiles on success.

The Prince can also adopt the manner of Hotspur. His first attempt at it takes the form of a rough though effective parody, as he tells Poins:

> I am not yet of Percy's mind, the Hotspur of the north; he that kills me some six or seven dozens of Scots at a breakfast, washes his hands, and says to his wife 'Fie upon this quiet life! I want work'. 'O my sweet Harry,' says she 'how many hast thou kill'd to-day?' 'Give my roan horse a drench' says he; and answers 'Some fourteen,' an hour after, 'a trifle, a trifle'. (Pt I, II.iv.98–104)

Later the Prince strikes a note that comes much closer to Hotspur's own when he offers to challenge Hotspur to single combat (Pt I, V.i.83–100); but the spirit of competition, which underlies so much that the Prince says as well as does, makes itself clearly felt in the promise of reformation that he gives to his father in III.ii of Part I, where, after praising his great rival, he goes on to say:

> For the time will come
> That I shall make this northern youth exchange
> His glorious deeds for my indignities.
> Percy is but my factor, good my lord,
> To engross up glorious deeds on my behalf;
> And I will call him to so strict account
> That he shall render every glory up,
> Yea, even to the slightest worship of his time,
> Or I will tear the reckoning from his heart. (144–52)

The unremittingly commercial imagery tells one much. The Prince uses others for his own practical ends, treating them as mere agents to be discharged when they have served their purpose. He picks up and employs their characteristic modes of utterance in much the same fashion. He has no voice of his own because he has no inner life of his own. His whole existence, including its holiday side, is confined to the realization of his very definite but also very limited aims. To have a distinctive idiom is to be vulnerable to parody. No one parodies the Prince. His having no voice of his own is a source of strength to him in his role of king to be, but it is also indicative of his incompleteness as a man.

By the time that Shakespeare had finished *Henry IV*, early in 1598 in all probability, what I have called the making of his dramatic poetry was over. The instrument had been forged; it asked to be used; and he proceeded to use it. The three years, or thereabouts, that elapsed between the completion of *Henry IV* and the composition of *Hamlet* were a time of wonderfully copious, confident, and varied activity, giving birth to four comedies, yet another history play, and the first of the Roman tragedies; but, in so far as the dramatic poetry is concerned, they were a time of exploitation and consolidation rather than of further development. For that one has to wait until the appearance of *Hamlet* itself.

Index

This book

was designed by

ANTJE LINGNER

and was printed by

University of

Toronto

Press